The Body as Material C

MW00639928

Bodies intrigue us. They promise windows into the past that other archaeological finds cannot by bringing us literally face to face with history. Yet 'the body' is also highly contested. Archaeological bodies are studied through two contrasting perspectives that sit on different sides of a disciplinary divide. On one hand lie science-based osteoarchaeological approaches. On the other lie understandings derived from recent developments in social theory that increasingly view the body as a social construction. Through a close examination of disciplinary practice, Joanna Sofaer highlights the tensions and possibilities offered by one particular kind of archaeological body, the human skeleton, with particular regard to the study of gender and age. Using a range of examples, she argues for reassessment of the role of the skeletal body in archaeological practice, and develops a theoretical framework for bioarchaeology based on the materiality and historicity of human remains.

JOANNA R. SOFAER is Senior Lecturer in Archaeology at the University of Southampton. As an osteoarchaeologist and prehistorian, she has published widely on human bioarchaeology and European prehistory. Her previous publications include *Children and Material Culture* (editor; 2000).

Topics in Contemporary Archaeology

Series Editor
Richard Bradley, University of Reading

This series is addressed to students, professional archaeologists and academics in related disciplines in the social sciences. Concerned with questions of interpretation rather than the exhaustive documentation of archaeological data, the studies in the series take several different forms: a review of the literature in an important field, an outline of a new area of research or an extended case study. The series is not aligned with any particular school of archaeology. While there is no set format for the books, all books in the series are broadly based, well written and up to date.

The Body as Material Culture

A Theoretical Osteoarchaeology

Joanna R. Sofaer

Archaeology, University of Southampton

CAMBRIDGE
UNIVERSITY PRESS

CAMBRIDGE UNIVERSITY PRESS
Cambridge, New York, Melbourne, Madrid, Cape Town, Singapore, São Paulo

Cambridge University Press
The Edinburgh Building, Cambridge CB2 2RU, UK

Published in the United States of America by Cambridge University Press, New York

www.cambridge.org
Information on this title: www.cambridge.org/9780521521468

© Joanna R. Sofaer 2006

First published 2006

Printed in the United Kingdom at the University Press, Cambridge

A catalogue record for this book is available from the British Library

ISBN-13 978-0-521-81822-3 hardback
ISBN-10 0-521-81822-2 hardback

ISBN-13 978-0-521-52146-8 paperback
ISBN-10 0-521-52146-7 paperback

This book is for Jaco and Noah

Contents

Illustrations

Tables

Preface

Human remains are compelling in their materiality. The tangibility and physicality of human remains first attracted me to study them, and inspired this book. Yet it is more than just the bodies themselves that I find engaging. It is the ways that bodies change over a lifetime and, in doing so, express the histories and lives of people. In other words, how the bodies of people come to be how they are, and how they are understood.

The human body is material and historical. Together, these two aspects lend it to archaeological investigation. Yet within the discipline, with regard to the study of human remains, these two aspects rarely seem to meet. Archaeological bodies are studied through two contrasting approaches that sit on different sides of a disciplinary divide. On one side lie science-based osteological approaches that focus on the skeleton as the material remains of the body. While these approaches recognise variation between individual bodies, osteological conceptualisations are necessarily fixed, universal and transhistorical in order that the body may be subject to scientific analysis and comparisons between bodies made. On the other side lie approaches to the body situated in recent developments in social theory. These increasingly view the body as a social construction that is contextually and historically produced, but hardly touch on the human remains themselves.

These two contrasting understandings of the body are often seen as incompatible. However, as an osteoarchaeologist who is also interested in social theory, I have felt for some time that it would be both useful and interesting to bring them together. My first attempt to do this was in the mid-1990s when I wrote my PhD on the tensions between method and theory in the archaeology of gender. In it I used three distinct case studies to suggest different ways of approaching a single theoretical problem, identifying tensions as being differently located in archaeological approaches to bodies, objects and contexts. But at that time I felt confined by disciplinary conventions and so not only did I maintain the distinction between bodies, objects and contexts in my thesis, but in accordance with convention, published my case studies in a series of articles divided between journals dealing with human osteology, and those dealing with more traditional forms of material culture. There was a degree of dissatisfaction in seeing my work broken up in this way, but there appeared to be few, if any, venues for expressing the theoretical linkages that had informed it. More generally, archaeology was missing a theoretical framework within which bioarchaeological insights into social relations could be described.

This book takes on the materiality and historicity of the body by developing a relationship between the study of the human skeleton and archaeological approaches that rely on the investigation of objects. I want to explore theoretical and practical strategies for linking them, by addressing some of the tensions and possibilities offered by the study of archaeological bodies and their particular qualities, grounded specifically within archaeological practice. The perspective of this volume is practice based. I want to examine the ways that archaeological bodies can be reconceptualised in terms of a methodological framework that joins osteoarchaeology and object-based archaeology, and to explore the implications of that framework for archaeological understandings of the body. In seeking to do this, the bodies that form the focus of this volume are skeletons rather than iconographic representations. More specifically, they are the skeletons of anatomically modern humans (*Homo sapiens*), skeletal remains being common forms of archaeological bodies.

I begin my analysis in Chapter 1 by exploring the disciplinary divide between osteoarchaeology and material-culture-based archaeology. My description of this divide is largely situated in the British and American archaeological experience as these represent two different and contrasting models of disciplinary construction. In Britain the dichotomy between osteoarchaeology and interpretative archaeology may be particularly strong compared to other national settings such as the United States where the Boasian fourfold perspective lends it a slightly different complexion. Nonetheless, this split may be considered a general feature of both models, and of a range of different national practices in general.

Following on from this, Chapter 2 outlines the way that the body has been appropriated as an archaeological resource and the subsequent fractures that have emerged within the modern discipline. Current archaeological practice with regard to the body is based on a series of deep-rooted underlying binary oppositions that have had a profound influence in defining conventional divisions in the archaeological allocation of the study of the body.

Chapter 3 unpicks these oppositions to yield a number of conceptual, theoretical and methodological tensions. Many of these tensions revolve around traditional archaeological distinctions between bodies and objects. They can also be related to a distinction between the biological and the material. In Chapter 4 I argue, however, that the skeletal body is fundamentally material possessing its own material qualities. These qualities are related to the biological processes that form and renew the matter of which it is made. The materiality of specific bodies emerges from material qualities which permit or constrain their development. The materiality of the body forms a common axis between the body and objects, placing the body within the sphere of archaeological investigation. While archaeologists are familiar with the idea that objects are created by bodies and that ideas and attitudes, rather than occupying a separated domain from the material, may be inscribed in objects (Knappett 2005; Tilley 1999a), they are perhaps less routinely aware that the body is itself created in relation to a material world that includes objects as well as other people. Throughout the life course the human skeleton may be modified through intentional or unintentional human action. During the human 'career' (Goffman 1959, 1968) bodies are literally created through social practices. The body can be regarded as a form of material culture.

The implications of the body as material culture are explored in Chapters 5 and 6 through discussions of gender and age, two areas in which the body takes a central and contested role in archaeology. For gender and age, the tensions between osteoarchaeology and traditional material-culture-based interpretative archaeology are particularly acute, arising from the practice of associating artefacts with osteologically sexed and aged individuals. As a result, reconceptualising the methodological relationship between the two may be particularly productive. These chapters are not conventional case studies in the sense of taking a single body of material and working through it. Rather they act as conceptual figures that aim to stimulate considerations of the potentials, as well as limitations, of working with the body as material culture. They aim to offer new ways of thinking about gender and age in archaeological practice, situated in terms of notions of material expression and process, and the hybridity of the body.

I have deliberately chosen not to deal with taphonomic processes although there are strong arguments that can be made to view post-mortem processes in terms of material culture (Parker Pearson 1999a). Nor have I dealt with the ways in which dead bodies can be manipulated as material statements or deliberately made into objects (e.g. Baby 1961; Solís *et al.* 2002). Equally, this is not a book that deals with detailed osteological methods. For this readers should look elsewhere (e.g. Bass 1995; Brickley and McKinley 2004; Buikstra and Ubelaker 1994). My focus is on a theoretical framework for understanding the living body from the skeleton with regard to specific difficulties that sit within current archaeological method and practice, and suggesting a theoretical location for bioarchaeology within the discipline. The illustrative examples that I use are necessarily selective.

Throughout this book I use the term 'interpretative archaeology' following historical convention to designate a particular archaeological tradition based on the study of objects (cf. Hodder 1991; Hodder *et al.* 1995), although I do not believe that this form of archaeology is inherently more interpretative. The term 'osteoarchaeology', while in use elsewhere in relation to both human and animal remains, is employed here to refer to the study of human bones alone and should be taken to include biological and physical anthropology.

This book has seen many iterations and changes since it was first conceived in the late 1990s although central themes and theoretical axes have remained constant. While writing it many new publications have appeared and literature on the body has exploded exponentially. I am aware that some of what I say may prove controversial. Perhaps that is inevitable in a book that is transdisciplinary and that deals with a topic about which people have taken up positions. What is here is necessarily a personal view of the body, though it is one with which I hope some readers will sympathise. At least it may provoke some thought not just about how we talk about the body, but about how we *do* archaeology.

JOANNA SOFAER

Acknowledgements

Writing this book has been an enjoyable experience, not least because I have had the pleasure of talking to many friends and colleagues about 'the body' while it was in progress. They include Joanna Brück, Chris Evans, Clive Gamble, Andy Jones, Yvonne Marshall, Marie Louise Stig Sørensen and Jaco Weinstock. Richard Bradley, Martin Jones and Marie Louise Stig Sørensen encouraged me to write it before I had even started, and Richard Bradley, Clive Gamble, Matthew Johnson, Andy Jones, Marie Louise Stig Sørensen and Sonia Zakrzewski were kind enough to read all, or part, of the manuscript once I had finished. I am particularly grateful for their very useful comments.

1   Bodies and boundaries

> They have cut the Gordian knot with a well-honed sword. The shaft is broken: on the left, they have put knowledge of things; on the right, power and human politics.
>
> Latour 1993: 3

This is a book about bodies as material and historical phenomena. Bodies intrigue us because they promise windows into the past that other archaeological finds cannot. They are literally the past personified. As the mortal remains of the very people who created and lived in the past, they bring us face to face with history. Above all, it is the *physicality* of the body that draws our interest. We instinctively recognise their bodies as we recognise our own; they are essentially *us*.

Attendant to this intuitive concern with identifying with the physical body runs an increasing public interest in what can be learnt from a body after its discovery, as illustrated by the success of the recent British television series *Meet the Ancestors*. Spindler's (1994) popular book *The Man in the Ice* proudly proclaims the account as 'a classic of scientific discovery, [which] shows us the fullest picture yet of Neolithic man, our ancestor'. A clear message emerges from these examples: bodies provide solid scientific information about the past. They are not simply morbid sensations or curiosities, but have real scientific value. The archaeologist is no longer either a romantic Indiana Jones figure or a boffin in an ivory tower, but a scientist in a white lab coat. The impression given of the archaeological study of the body is of an uncontroversial, objective, scientific enterprise.

Yet within archaeological circles, though the body is a defined space of discussion and analysis (Meskell 1998a), it is highly contested. The archaeological study of the body sits uneasily between two apparently conflicting, and continually developing, traditions within the discipline. On one hand lie the publicly visible science-based osteological approaches to studying the human body, grounded in an empirical tradition, with their concerns of sexing, ageing, diet, palaeopathology, genetic distance and metric studies of normal variation. On the other lie academically influential understandings of the body derived from social theory, in particular sociology and anthropology, which increasingly view the body as a social construction. Osteological studies recognise and study variation between individual bodies but osteological conceptualisations of the body itself are necessarily fixed, universal and transhistorical in order that the body may be subject to scientific analysis and comparisons between bodies made. By contrast, those who identify the body as a social construction perceive it as fluid and culturally specific. At its most extreme, for them bodies are historically bound individuals whose very subjectivity precludes even the prospect of science as an appropriate methodology for study.

Debates and discussions on the relationship between biology and culture within social anthropology (e.g. Ingold 1990; Hinde 1991; Goldschmidt 1993; Toren 1993; Robertson 1996) have, so far, had little impact within archaeology. Despite recent attempts to describe human life-ways through the skeleton (e.g. Larsen 1997; Robb *et al.* 2001; Peterson 2002; Roberts and Cox 2003), in archaeology there often seems to be little relationship between the biological study of the human skeleton and socio-theoretical understandings of the body. While osteological determinations, particularly of age and sex, are regularly used as the basis for archaeological interpretation through the association between people and artefacts in mortuary contexts, there is no explicit framework for integrating osteoarchaeology within archaeological thought. Once sex or age has been determined, the body no longer seems of interest to the archaeologist. The physiological aspects of the body which form the foundation of osteological assessments are often silent in the process of interpretation as, in the search for social meaning, the emphasis shifts from the body to objects surrounding it. Archaeological practice tends to focus on artefacts surrounding bodies rather than on bodies themselves.

The skeletal body is employed as a means of underpinning interpretations rather than as a source for generating them. Even approaches which emphasise phenomenology and embodied experience, thereby involving the body as a locus for understanding, neglect to incorporate osteoarchaeological insights. Despite the physicality of the body, which naturally lends itself as a potential material resource, the skeletal body is rarely used explicitly for interpretation. Osteological research often remains distinct from more traditional material-culture-based interpretative approaches, notwithstanding the wide range of data that can be gained from the study of human remains that could potentially contribute to understanding social life and identity. This situation is somewhat inconsistent with the aims of archaeology given the potential of human remains for shedding light on past lives and the fact that those remains are the very people whose material expression archaeologists study. Archaeological attitudes to the body create tension: archaeology relies on the skeletal body to create understandings, but archaeological interpretations seem to float free of it. Despite some concern that it has been difficult to locate and identify 'real people' and relate them to the archaeological record (Johnson 1989; Tringham 1991; Meskell 1998b), skeletons are such 'real people'. Indeed, identifying them as people and identifying with the past through them is perhaps the attraction of osteoarchaeology. There is nothing more real and concrete than human remains and by forming an integral part of the archaeological record they remind us in a very real way about our own mortality.

The allocation of the body

A key problem in archaeological approaches to the body is that, while we need to recognise the body as a material entity in order to do archaeology, within the discipline archaeology has constructed divisive, seemingly impermeable boundaries that allocate and predetermine interpretative responsibility. Tension between osteoarchaeology and material-culture-based archaeology is not an inevitable product of the material on which different kinds of archaeologists base their analyses, in this case human bones or cultural artefacts. It represents a deep rift within the discipline which can be characterised in terms of historically constructed boundaries between science on one hand and humanism on the other. The division of study according to perceived expertise and method of study is an important feature of academic discourse (Polanyi 1958) that forms part of a wider demarcation of social groups and knowledge, the importance of which has been frequently recognised by sociologists, anthropologists and philosophers of science (Douglas 1973; Kuhn 1977; Bourdieu 1984). The specific ways in which boundaries are established and maintained through historical conventions have important implications for archaeological practice.

In order to explore the implications of the disjunction between the study of human skeletal remains and material-culture-based archaeology, I want to examine the ways that conventions surrounding practice originate and operate, leading to the institutionalisation of that divide. A critical awareness of the way that fields within the discipline are historically defined and socially maintained is important in order to situate archaeological practice and understand the broader relationship between osteoarchaeology and other forms of archaeological endeavour before returning to a discussion of the implications for bodies themselves.

The origins and establishment of the disciplinary divide

The historical framework that forms the socio-political backdrop to the development of the separate study of past human beings, and of archaeology as an element of that study, has deep and complex roots. The elevation of humankind is the product of a long Judeo-Christian tradition that emphasises the uniqueness of humans within the world (Gans 1985). The nature and form of the distinctive qualities of people have long been a subject of debate (Fudge *et al.* 1999) but classical notions are based on the uniqueness of human culture and language (Ingold 1988). Recent contributions have re-explored these issues to suggest that the particularity of humanness lies in self-consciousness, a perception of the self in relation to others that allows social relations to exist and to be elaborated in and through the material world (Ingold 1986). Conversely, they have questioned the separation of people from animals, suggesting that the irreducible animality of humans may be their only instinct capable of saving them from the excesses of their 'humanity' (Ham and Senior 1997).

The principle of human uniqueness, however, remains key to claims for archaeology as a discipline with its focus on human history. Indeed, the investigation of that uniqueness could be seen as its raison d'être. The rich variety of human lives has challenged fixed ideas of what a human should be. As Clark (1988: 25–6) points out, 'once we realise that human variety is not an error . . . and that we must expect our species always to be variegated, we can begin to think about constructing social orders that will provide a place for all'. The unity of humanity as famously declared in the 1950 and 1951 UNESCO statements is therefore a moral and political statement (Haraway 1988), but it is also one that takes biologism as its starting point, ascribing humanness to members of the species *Homo sapiens*. Creatures that do not belong to this taxon are not human though they might resemble us very closely. The unity of humankind therefore lies in being a breeding population such that 'my ancestors and my descendants alike may be yours as well' (Clark 1988: 25). Human beings are designated and defined through the biological criteria upon which social, intellectual or spiritual characteristics are overlaid. The identification of the body as human allows the study of people as a unit across time and space.

The interpretation of human variation is the challenge that archaeology seeks to meet, but the history of this interpretation has been somewhat chequered. The unity of humankind has not always been seen as self-evident. The biological and the social have been drawn together and enrolled in contests over the relationship between physical characteristics and social or moral behaviour (Twine 2002). The articulation of race, for example, saw the labelling of particular phenotypes in terms of symbols of cultural characteristics that were deployed in political agendas (Proctor 1988; Gilman 1991). Because phenotypic expression is a level of biology, these differences were presented as neutral 'natural-technical' objects of knowledge, whereas when deconstructed they are temporal, historically situated interpretations of surface variations in appearance in organisms that may be ascribed no determinative impact on patterns of culture or intellectual abilities (Ingold 1986; Banton 1987; Wade 1993; Twine 2002). Similarly, the naturalisation of gender roles represents an interpretation of body differences in which biology is held to determine behaviour in a manner that has been demonstrated to be culturally constructed and historically constituted (Strathern 1980; Haraway 1989; Wade 1993).

Disciplinary structures

In seeking to explore human history, different models of disciplinary structure have emerged largely along national lines with differing approaches to the relationship between the biological and the social. In the English-speaking world, the fourfold approach in the United States incorporating anthropology, archaeology, biological (physical) anthropology and linguistics emerged in the early twentieth century as a direct response to the prevailing articulation of race. While not uncontroversial at the time (Stocking 1968; Barkan 1988; Marks 1995), Franz Boas pioneered an approach that sought to disrupt problematic and undesirable interpretations (Stocking 1968). He advocated a focus on cultural traditions rather than on racial descent (Boas 1911). His ground-breaking and influential work on the relationship between environmental and hereditary effects on body size demonstrated that the human body was not a fixed entity but subject to environmental influence (Boas 1912).

Today, following Boas's philosophy, in academic institutions in the United States the fields of social anthropology, archaeology, biological anthropology and linguistics often co-exist under one umbrella department, although the relationships between them are stronger in some directions than in others, particularly where direct links can be made between past peoples and their living descendants. Nonetheless, there are still boundaries between the fields, particularly when it comes to the study of the human body and the study of objects. Haraway (1988: 210) points out that the disjunction between race and culture in Boasian anthropology, and its overwhelming emphasis on the latter, 'left Boasian physical anthropology at best ambiguously authorized to speak about the biological dimensions of "man"'. It did, however, claim the study of the physical body as its focus through scientific means. Thus, the study of past human bodies has conventionally been the province of biological anthropology with its interest in human evolution, as well as the study of variation in anatomically modern human groups (Haraway 1988). The post-World War II period saw an emphasis on the importance of behaviour and adaptation in an evolutionary perspective with population-level investigations of health, disease and environmental stress (Spencer 1981; Haraway 1988; Johnson and Mann 1997). Developments from the 1990s on have seen an extension of this perspective with the emergence of a more focused bioarchaeology that tends to stress the interaction between biology and behaviour with concentration on the life-ways of more recent populations recovered from archaeological sites (see Powell *et al.* 1991; Grauer 1995; Larsen 1997). In spirit, these interests mirror Boas's original programme yet also reconfigure it by placing the emphasis on biology as well as human action. With increasing focus on the biological impact of behaviour, this has led on one hand to increasing closeness in questions that are posed by osteoarchaeologists and traditional material-culture archaeologists. On the other hand, it has paradoxically led to a methodological distancing of the study of the physiological body from that of social life.

In Britain, approaches to the relationship between the biological body and social life took another path with an altogether different social and institutional framework to the bringing together of disciplines that characterised the American experience. In Britain, in a pre-war climate of colonialism, the Boasian critique of race did not play a major role and evolutionary anthropology and ideas about the classification of races and ethnic groups remained influential (Barkan 1988, 1992). Furthermore, the emphasis placed on population movement in Europe meant that poor links between past groups and their living counterparts often precluded the development of strong relationships between fields. Institutional distinctions between them were thus largely maintained. Historically, the study of the human body was the province of scholars with medical backgrounds some of whom became interested in the past. This arrangement reinforced the divide between the study of physiology and sociality. Despite a growing interest in human palaeontology, the ethnographic and archaeological study of objects formed distinct areas of study, separated from each other and from the study of the physiological body.

In the wake of World War II, British academia underwent radical changes linked to major shifts in socio-political life and national identity that promoted the rejection of scientific racism and eugenics (Barkan 1992; Spencer 1997). New synthetic theories of evolution led to a flowering of adaptation-based approaches in the study of the bio-history of humanity. The study of modern humans, however, remained divided with a clear distinction between the examination of objects (archaeology) and bodies (human biology). Given the established, though largely informal, personal and sometimes sporadic links between archaeologists and medical practitioners in Britain, it is perhaps not surprising that a more systematic osteoarchaeology grew largely from the archaeological involvement of scholars with medical backgrounds (Roberts and Manchester 1995; Mays 1997), one of the best-known figures being Calvin Wells. In the theoretical climate of 1960s' Britain, this led to emphasis on diagnosis-orientated case studies analogous to the case histories of living patients and palaeopathology (Mays 1997).

The past decade has seen a rapid rise in the number of human osteoarchaeology courses offered in archaeology departments in British universities and concomitant changes in the backgrounds of workers within the field who no longer exclusively hold science degrees. This reflects the constant state of flux inherent in the wider development of modern archaeology's disciplinary identity. However, the establishment of osteological research has taken place as a distinct epistemological category rather than as a fully integrated sub-field. An important ramification of the external origins of osteoarchaeology has been the persistence of established communication boundaries between osteoarchaeology and interpretative archaeology that act to maintain the 'outsider' status of osteoarchaeology in relation to the discipline as a whole (Sofaer Derevenski 2001). This may be in part because of the historically troublesome dialectic and tension between the biological and the social. In Britain (in contrast to the American Boasian solution), a clear separation between the two is perceived as a way to disentangle and remove the discipline from undesirable connotations that previous linkages created. However, there have been calls for British workers to move towards a more population-based approach characteristic of the United States and to orientate their research towards mainstream archaeological issues (Mays 1997). This might lead to a reconsideration of the relationship between biology and society explored through the human body.

Variation between national traditions of enquiry such as that described between the United States and Britain, is a feature of the development of hybrid fields centred on interdisciplinary co-operation (Lindholm-Romantschuk 1998: 29). Key founding figures set influential and long-lasting research agendas, and their sets of contacts as part of their own personal histories led to the construction of field- and country-specific research networks (Lindholm-Romantschuk 1998: 29). Nonetheless, on both sides of the Atlantic the different disciplinary models have similar outcomes in terms of a divide between the study of the human skeleton and objects. There is an increasing trend towards the sub-disciplinary specialisation of practitioners, with the division of study falling along essentially typological lines, and skill specialisation according to material differences in the data generating division between different aspects of the study of human history. Hence the widely accepted reliance on ceramic, flint, metal or other specialists in the analysis of objects. When it comes to the study of bones, such specialisation becomes even narrower as not all bones are studied together as a group (Sofaer Derevenski 2001). The elevated status of humans as the focus of study means that human bones are distinguished from those of animals. The study of the human skeleton forms a distinct field with researchers usually being trained and specialising in their analysis alone.

Specialisation and disciplinary boundaries

The study of the physical remains of the human body is thus designated as a specialist activity with a consequent emphasis on skills production as units of academic endeavour (cf. Whitley 1984). Although many osteoarchaeologists are unhappy with perceptions of what they do as a set of techniques rather than a general approach or paradigm (cf. Coles 1995), site reports – the traditional backbone of archaeological publication and a main outlet for the publication of osteoarchaeology – reinforce this perception and render individual elements of investigation highly impermeable to other workers. While those studying the human skeleton feed their results to other archaeologists (often the excavators of a given site) who synthesise a wide range of data presented to them and who are consequently considered to be the arbiters of interpretation, typically the human bone report – like that of other materials such as faunal remains, plants or soils – is published separately at the back of a volume or attached in the form of an appendix. This traditional presentational format reinforces the classification of research outcomes as specialist and promotes a message that such reports are inaccessible or uninteresting to others from outside that specialism (Sofaer Derevenski 2001; Jones 2002a). Indeed, the very idea of 'specialist' suggests a highly defined knowledge base, and the better defined a field is in terms of a shared knowledge base, the more impervious are its external boundaries (Becher 1989). In turn, this results in the separation of osteoarchaeology from other facets of the discipline, leading to feelings of marginalisation (Albarella 2001; Sofaer Derevenski 2001). In common with other specialists in archaeology, osteoarchaeologists are viewed as service providers to those higher up the disciplinary hierarchy who carry out the overall synthesis and thus the 'real' interpretation of the data.

Nonetheless, because others base interpretations on their conclusions, the denotation of particular individuals as specialists lends them a certain authority. The authority invested in specialists and their reports perpetuates the divide between the study of the physical body and interpretative archaeology in as much as the accumulation of authority lends the specialist value and social power. The authority of the archaeological specialist derives both from their perceived personal experience with a body of material accumulated over time, and from the authority given to science as both paradigm and produced outcome of the investigation of that data (Macdonald 1998). Those who study the physical body form part of a wider scientific community in a way that material-culture-based archaeologists do not. One measure of this is the way that osteoarchaeology receives funding for major projects from sources that have interests in other areas of science research. Indeed, the investigation of the human skeleton forms part of the growing sub-discipline of archaeological science, which takes its cue from the hard sciences of physics, chemistry and biology.

Scientific modes of enquiry are often regarded as distinctive and incompatible with humanistic approaches (Jones 2002a). They use different forms of discourse with different terminologies that are reflected in contrasting styles of writing (Joyce 2002a). The construction of disciplinary boundaries along the lines of science and humanism is also visible in outlets for the dissemination of ideas. Other than site reports, edited volumes are often a primary vehicle for formal communication between osteoarchaeology and material-culture-based archaeology. There are comparatively few specifically archaeological journal-based opportunities for direct communication between the fields. Furthermore, although the very emergence of osteoarchaeology indicates that disciplinary boundaries may be permeable, in academic departments osteoarchaeologists rarely contribute to teaching related subjects (cf. Coles 1995). Despite the impact of contextual archaeology, studies of the physical body are rarely integrated with interpretative archaeology in an explicit manner. This is something of a paradox given that the power and value of the body to the investigation of human history is precisely *because* it is the nexus between biology and culture. It appears that disciplinary boundaries present greater barriers in some directions than in others.

The classification of particular activities as science leads to the naturalisation of differences that are socially and culturally constructed. Among philosophers and historians there is scepticism regarding an understanding of science as something special and distinct from other forms of cultural and social activity (Woolgar 1988; Longino 1990) and awareness that science entails cultural assumptions and social relationships

(Macdonald 1998; Fox Keller and Longino 1996). The knowledge production process is created and supported by a social network of scientists (Latour 1987). Views of science as an orderly cumulative enterprise have been challenged (Kuhn 1962) and rhetorical strategies used in the composition of scientific papers analysed (Latour and Woolgar 1979). Academic enquiry is engaged in a continuous struggle for the intellectual legitimacy of ideas and publications (Bourdieu 1969) and is in a constant state of 'essential tension' between innovation and pre-existing knowledge (Kuhn 1977).

The production of knowledge within archaeology, as in any discipline, can be identified as part of a larger organisational system that is both socially and intellectually determined (Merton 1973; Latour 1987), rather than a reflection of some inherent means of categorising knowledge (Lindholm-Romantschuk 1998). Academic disciplines are social constructs (Storer 1972; Lindholm-Romantschuk 1998) and understandings of disciplinarity – in this case the relationship between the study of the physical body (osteoarchaeology) and objects (interpretative archaeology) – may therefore have social and political implications with regard to the perception of particular approaches within the discipline.

Particular bodies

The body in archaeology is caught between the two poles of science and humanism. On one hand there is a tendency to concede the skeletal body to biological science through osteoarchaeology. On the other, there has been an explosion of theorising about the body much of which, while focusing on lived aspects of bodily experience, fails to incorporate the archaeological evidence in terms of the physical body or human remains found in the archaeological record.

There is therefore a need for an archaeologically grounded approach to the body that while recognising and incorporating influences from other disciplines, does so taking cognisance of their value to archaeology and with due regard for the specific archaeological substance of the body. Being unfleshed, archaeological bodies are particular in that they are devoid of those external features that are involved in the primary recognition of the body and which have been a key feature of much theorising about the body and understandings of corporeality in other disciplines. Nor do they have body fluids such as blood or semen which have been key to analysing the body in anthropological works (e.g. Douglas 1966). The dead archaeological body, while a person, by definition lacks the qualities required for action and sociality and can therefore be considered qualitatively different from living bodies. Yet we cannot take an empiricist view and assume that osteological data speak for themselves. Archaeological bodies are not well captured either by biology or by social constructionism as the body is simultaneously biological, representational and material. How to get to social action and sociality by translating and transforming bodies thus becomes a key question.

I do not believe that there is any 'real' authoritative body in an essential sense or that there is only one kind of body. Rather, I want to suggest that there is a theoretical and methodological space in which many kinds of bodies can be drawn together and that the physicality of the archaeological body forms the locus for this incorporation. Such an approach sits in contrast to many current discussions of the body in archaeology which implicitly seem to explode, divide and allocate the body leading to its fragmentation. The breaking up of the body arises partly out of its central role in the development of key elements of archaeological thought, including the more recent emergence of the body as a discrete context for archaeological investigation. This has seen competing claims for the body in archaeology which are both stimulating and contradictory. It is to these that I now wish to turn.

2   The body as an archaeological resource

> we continually walk a fine line between constructivism and the claim to
> authenticity made by bodily phenomena.   Benthien 2002: 12

The body is a major class of archaeological evidence and a vital archaeological resource. From the moment of its discovery, the body forms
a focus for analysis as it is excavated, photographed, drawn, described,
lifted and finally removed, often to a laboratory for osteological examination. Bodies may be recorded separately from other finds on individual skeleton recording sheets (Museum of London Archaeology Service
1994; Parker Pearson 1999a), emphasising their privileged interpretative position. The single body is often taken as the basic unit of analysis
in the mortuary domain (Chapman 2000: 174). Indeed, one measure
of the importance of the body is that mortuary contexts are lent their
classifications and denotation as 'mortuary' through the presence of a
body.

Bodies have been studied in terms of their placement and arrangement, often by reference to orientation and position, with differences
between bodies interpreted in terms of the categorisation of past individuals or social groups (e.g. Pader 1982; Lucy 2000). The treatment of
the dead body and choice of means of its disposal, whether through cre-
mation, inhumation, or its disarticulation and disaggregation, has been
identified as a strong social statement and as a metaphor for social organisation (Parker Pearson 1999a). More recently, the deliberate fragmentation of bodies has been seen in terms of the enchainment of people
and artefacts with a series of scales in the relationship between linked
body parts of a single individual, groups of related whole bodies and
sets of artefacts (Chapman 1999, 2000). Irrespective of the final interpretation of a body, right from the start of the 'archaeological process'
(Hodder 1999) the remains of the human body are treated as special
and may be regarded in ways that distinguish them from other archaeological finds. The body thus has a unique status in archaeological
practice.

The body in archaeological thought

The body has also played a key role in the development of archaeological thought. This is not only in terms of interpreting the physical remains of the body, but also in understanding the spaces through which bodies move and the ways that the body may be represented and depicted. Despite cries for an archaeology of the body and perceptions that archaeology once again lags behind its sister disciplines in its awareness of key issues (Turner 2003), the recent upsurge of explicit interest in the body in archaeology (e.g. Meskell 1996, 1998a, 2000a; Rautman 2000; Hamilakis *et al.* 2002a; Fisher and DiPaolo Loren 2003; Meskell and Joyce 2003) follows in a disciplinary tradition that has been interested in bodies for some time, albeit perhaps in a less overt manner. Rather than rectifying a straightforward failure to address body issues, current archaeological engagement with the body reflects a particular awareness of specific concerns following on from those identified within sociology and anthropology (e.g. Foucault 1978; Turner 1984; Butler 1990, 1993; Laqueur 1990; Shilling 1993), particularly following the development of a range of feminist theories and critiques (Morgan and Scott 1993).

Described bodies

From the start of systematic excavation the body has been a focus for investigation by those interested in human history. For example, in *The Ancient History of Wiltshire* (1810–21), Colt Hoare offered descriptions of bodies from the excavation of several hundred prehistoric barrows with the aim of lending antiquarianism empirical strengths within an intellectual matrix that included discourses on human anatomy (Turnbull 2001: 18–19). Detailed drawings of bodies illustrating their position and skeletal elements such as Ramsauer's recording of the Hallstatt graves (see Hodson 1990), alongside the emphasis given to human remains in written communications to scholarly societies and journals (e.g. Oxley 1820), are striking features of archaeological endeavour throughout the nineteenth century. Bodies spurred antiquarian investigation, with an intellectual premium placed on the investigation of mortuary contexts (Turnbull 2001: 20).

    In the nineteenth and early twentieth centuries, observations and comparisons between 'primitive' bodies and European bodies were closely tied to notions of cultural evolution with understandings of national characteristics rooted in biological disparities (Stocking 1968; Trigger 1989; Fausto-Sterling 1995). While a growing emphasis on ethnicity and diffusionism challenged this evolutionism (Trigger 1989), the body remained key to archaeological arguments. The skeletal body provided a key source of evidence for culture history through the osteological categorisation of people according to racial type. The spread of material culture was linked to the differential distribution of different types of bodies understood in terms of migration and movement. The most infamous advocate of this approach was Kossinna (1911) who directly equated ethnic variations with racial differences and stages of cultural development over time. While other culture historians such as Childe rejected Kossinna's overtly racist agenda, focusing on identifying contemporary groups of peoples in terms of mosaics of ways of life and interactions (Trigger 1989) and technological differences as explanations for cultural variation (Sofaer Derevenski and Sørensen 2005), the body remained an important source of evidence for the spread of cultural complexes by human movement through, for example, the use of cranial indices (Brodie 1994).

Behaving bodies

The theoretical revolution of New Archaeology and processualism in the 1960s and 1970s was a key turning point in the study of the body in archaeology. While histories of the discipline often describe this period in terms of a move towards a more scientific, quantified and systematic archaeology (Trigger 1989), and its proponents may not have specifically identified 'the body' as a focus of investigation, the New Archaeology marked a significant shift in the principles and practice of archaeology that involved the deployment of the body in a new way as a unit of archaeological analysis. The agenda of New Archaeology as described by both Clarke and Binford moved the focus away from regional studies of artefacts separated and independent from bodies – what Clarke (1973: 13) called 'a discipline in which artifacts, assemblages, sites and their contents are identified and related as relics of communities in accordance with the rules formulated in terms of artifact taxonomies – the traditional Montelian paradigm' – towards a wider understanding of artefacts seen as linked to the actions of people in the form of the material correlates of human behaviour (Binford 1972). In getting to grips with the relationship between human behaviour and the material record, one of the key features of the New Archaeology was its reliance on ethnographic observation. This was vital to the development of middle-range theory in providing the basis from which to establish relationships between archaeological observations and archaeologically unobservable human behaviour. The New Archaeology relied heavily on ethnography because its emphasis on behaviour, or 'Archaeology as Anthropology' (Binford 1962), required living bodies whose actions could be observed in conjunction with

material culture in order to establish correlations that could be trans-
posed on to the archaeological record. Thus because behaviour requires
the actions of bodies, the study of human behaviour in the New Archaeology implicitly placed the body at the heart of its programme. Somewhat
paradoxically, as part of his belief in human rationality, Binford's apparent rejection of the body as a subject of interest, memorably expressed
in his statement on 'culture as man's extrasomatic means of adaptation'
(Binford 1964), in fact indirectly recognised the importance of the body
to action and identified a relationship between bodies and objects. The
emphasis on the behaviour of people's bodies thus differentiated the New
Archaeology and processualism from attempts to reconstruct social systems in the mould of Childe. To illustrate this further, it is useful to look
at a couple of examples of the ways in which the model building of the
New Archaeology placed the body at its centre.

In one of the best-known examples used to illustrate the value of ethnoarchaeology to the New Archaeology project, Binford (1983a) dis-
cusses the distances travelled by the Nunamiut on trips and the items
taken with, or deposited, at different distances from the camp. His aim
here is to explain the spatial distribution of objects around settlements
in relation to particular environmental circumstances as an analogue for
those found in archaeological contexts. Underlying Binford's description
of the spatial distribution of the objects is a concern with the needs, capabilities and limitations of the male body; how far he can go, how strong
or lazy he is, and what the needs of the body are for food or warmth.
Similarly, Binford's model of drop and toss zones around the Nunamiut
men's hearth (Binford 1983b: 153) discussed by Trigger in his account
of the history of archaeological thought in the context of the problems
of cross-cultural generalisations (Trigger 1989: 365) is an account of the
needs and actions of bodies in relation to the material world. This is particularly striking in Binford's illustration of the hearth which depicts the
bodies of the men in relation to the zones (Fig. 2.1).

Clarke's influential advocacy of models of time and space in prehistoric
contexts such as in his seminal paper 'The loss of innocence' (Clarke
1973) also highlights the role of the body in the development of the
New Archaeology agenda. In discussing model building as a method
for archaeological investigation, he argues that we need to use such an
approach to think about 'the meaning of time and space for the inmates
of particular systems. The mobile Palaeolithic band moving on foot with
limited external contacts and an extremely rapid generational turnover
presents a very different time and space surface from the Iron Age society
with elaborate transport' (Clarke 1973: 13). Key to this discussion is an
appreciation of the different ways that bodies move in time and space.

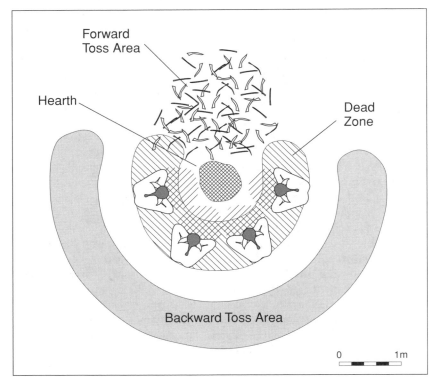

Figure 2.1   Binford's model of drop and toss zones around the Nunamiut men's hearth (redrawn after Binford 1983b)

The actions of people expressed through their bodies are what lend time and space meaning. Here it is the going by foot as opposed to going by cart that is important since the two modes of transport require the involvement of the body in different ways. The development of spatial archaeology as part of New Archaeology therefore had much to do with recognising the importance of the body.

New Archaeology also foregrounded the body through its strong emphasis on the investigation of mortuary contexts. The development of an explicit 'archaeology of death' (Chapman *et al.* 1981; O'Shea 1984) placed the dead body in a privileged position as a direct reflection of the past society to which it belonged. Through its association with objects, the body was categorised in terms of status, its 'social persona' (Binford 1972) acting as a metaphor for social organisation. The emphasis on the categorisation of the person in mortuary contexts also promoted the osteological study of the body within archaeology. As the post-war period saw a decline in interest in issues of race (Haraway 1988; Johnson and Mann 1997; Hamilakis *et al.* 2002b: 4), in conjunction with a move towards concern with processes of adaptation, health and demography at a population level (Johnson and Mann 1997), there was a surge in methodological interest in methods for sexing and ageing with the development of more accurate techniques (e.g. McKern and Stewart 1957; Krogman 1946, 1962; Hanna and Washburn 1953; Ferembach *et al.* 1980). This coincidence of interests between archaeology and biological anthropology meant that estimates of sex and age provided through the osteological study of the body became key variables and axes of analysis that could be juxtaposed with those of rank or wealth. Although skeletons had long been assessed for sex and age by individuals considered knowledgeable such as local doctors or teachers, with the New Archaeology it became important that the archaeological body both could, and should, be analysed scientifically as a matter of routine. The desire for such scientifically derived assessments on which to base archaeological explanations formed part of the wider emphasis on science in New Archaeology with its drive for accuracy through quantification and hypotheses testing.

New Archaeology therefore established a methodological use of the body through the principle of artefact association with specific kinds of bodies. However, while developments in human osteology enabled a new approach to archaeological theory, they were not in and of themselves explicitly included within it. As with other natural science elements of the discipline such as palaeobotany, faunal analysis or dendrochronology, the science was a way of illuminating culture and of serving the ideology of New Archaeology. It was therefore the recognition of the utility of the body through skeletal analysis, rather than the holistic integration of osteology into archaeological practice, that was a central contribution of the New Archaeology. Archaeologists became synthesisers of data provided by expert others, setting a trend that continues today.

My intention here is not to argue for or against the New Archaeology. It is rather, by way of examples, to illustrate the central role of the body in the radically different conceptualisation of the New Archaeology agenda. The contribution of New Archaeology to the study of the body was threefold. First, through its emphasis on ethnographic fieldwork it placed the observation of the living body and the results of the actions of the living body at the heart of archaeological interpretation. Second, it attempted to interpret the dead body in terms of social variables. Third, the emphasis on quantification and scientific modes of investigation encouraged scrutiny of the body as a discrete object of investigation. This threefold contribution, however, also left a legacy of three distinct strands of investigation of the body in archaeology – the living body in space, the dead body in mortuary settings and the osteological body – which was retained in subsequent archaeological thought.

Manipulated bodies

If the body was central to New Archaeology's initiative primarily as a focus for methodological discussion, it was vital as an illustrative device in the development of post-processual frameworks that exploited the body as a heuristic tool. Heavily influenced by the British and European classic tradition of social anthropology which had an historical interest in matters to do with the body (Turner 1991), post-processual archaeology took on the body in its programme and in its examples, although it retained many of the methodological insights of the New Archaeology, particularly the principle of artefact association. In order to illustrate this it is useful to look at a few key elements of the rather diverse post-processualist school, namely agency, symbolism, textual metaphor and context.

The post-processualist emphasis on actors and agency required bodies. Often described as a mechanism for stimulating internal social change, agency requires agents who in turn require bodies in order to act. More specifically, in the words of Giddens, 'Bodily discipline is intrinsic to the competent social agent' (Giddens 1991: 57). Though agency is considered to mean many different things (Dobres and Robb 2000), the agent in archaeology is often conceptualised in terms of an individual, a discrete unit conceptualised in terms of a single body (Barrett 2000). Gero (2000) argues that the social agent, though nominally neutral, can often be identified as a particular kind of body, that of the male, by implicit assumptions made through western associations between male behaviours, action and decisiveness. Furthermore, the relationship between the agent and structure is about relationships between bodies; 'A constant moving in and out of focus between the individual identifiable bodies and the body politic' (Morgan and Scott 1993: 15). The importance of agency and deliberate decision making in the treatment of the body has also been stressed (Chapman 2000).

The body was also important in highlighting the importance of symbolism to archaeology. Structuralist uses of the body in anthropology were particularly influential. Indeed, early examples that illustrated the significance and potential of symbolism to the discipline pointed to the body in the social anthropology literature and used body metaphors and differences between bodies as important analytical axes. Leroi-Gourhan (1968) identified the locations and associations of different animal species represented in Upper Palaeolithic caves in terms of myths dealing with male and female principles, while the symbolic principles identified in Hodder's (1982) work on the Nuba revolved around differences between bodies (male / female) or bodily states (clean / dirty, pure / impure, living / dead). Where archaeologists sought to investigate space and time, early post-processualist work often interpreted this by reference to the body in space (e.g. Moore 1986). Such an emphasis was not only about identifying and describing the reasons behind the distribution of material culture, but also specifically and explicitly about locating places for living bodies. In addition, the emphasis on symbols made possible the study of the representation of the human body in archaeology in both the past and the present through paintings, sculpture, museum dioramas and displays as well as other media with the aim of getting at meanings (Rautman 2000; Hamilakis *et al.* 2002a). Post-processualism took on the body as a powerful way of demonstrating cultural meanings by deliberately transforming it from biology to symbol or metaphor (cf. Tilley 1999a).

This is perhaps not surprising as the linguistic model that lies behind the interpretation of symbolism in material culture owes much to the way that the body was deployed as an example in the development of the model in other fields. In linguistics, Barthes's influential semiotic analysis of dress (Barthes 1985) explored the way that the body can be given meaning through a symbolic system. Similarly, the sociological insights of Foucault (1973, 1977, 1978) illustrated how institutional and discursive practices act on bodies subject to power, rendering them discursively constituted cultural productions or textual sites. Applied to archaeology, the textual model encouraged appreciation of cultural variability and the importance of context in interpretation as objects too became textual sites for the construction and communication of specific social identities of bodies (e.g. Thomas 1991; Yates 1993). The use of the body to explore archaeology's adoption of the textual model through its identification as a venue for signification and display that can be read through its association with material culture was therefore part of a more general trend towards the use of the body within the humanities in general.

If the application of social theory to the interpretation of bodies was crucial in promoting aspects of the post-processualist agenda – in particular the ways that archaeology took up semiotics and notions of cultural construction – this also had the effect of highlighting the body by emphasising its role in social practice. This is particularly noticeable in discussions of mortuary settings where the dead body was identified as being a primary reason for, and therefore at the centre of, depositional events. As the dead cannot bury themselves, the body was identified as being deployed in contextually specific strategies of power involving claims of social position and inheritance by the living (Barrett 1988) and acted as a 'central symbolic medium for the transmission of ritual' (Barrett 1994: 66). The body was seen to play a vital role in genealogies, kinship and social memory through its spatio-temporal location in a sequence of burial events (Mizoguchi 1992, 2000). The dead body was flagged as a highly visible social resource that could be appropriated to act as a focus for the communication of intended meanings related to the social perception of the deceased by others through material signifiers (e.g. Shanks and Tilley 1982). The ideological potential of the manipulation of the dead body and the paraphernalia surrounding it became an important demonstration of the complex and potentially deceptive character of the archaeological record (e.g. Parker Pearson 1982).

Despite this emphasis on the social construction of the body, post-processualist approaches to interpretation still required the skeletal body as the hook on which to hang interpretations. Post-processual archaeology took on board New Archaeology's methodological use of sex and age estimates in exploring the patterning of material culture in relation to the body. Thus, while the emphasis on symbolism and signification made possible engagement with the construction of social identity and contextual interpretations of patterns in a manner that differed considerably from New Archaeology, it too placed great emphasis on the osteological body as it required sex and age classifications in order to make associations between categories of people and grave goods. The body thus became simultaneously a remarkable source of tension, as well as a significant inspiration for archaeological practice, as it both challenged and relied upon objective biological determinations derived from examination of the physical body. In this sense post-processualism did not initiate a focus on notions of gender or age as it too relied on a method derived from New Archaeology. Rather, as Sørensen (2000: 18–19) has pointed out, it used and explored their articulation in new ways.

Post-processualism reflected a difference in the way that the body was viewed, used and even required in theoretical and interpretative arguments in order to promote the post-processualist agenda. Nonetheless, while the body was vital to the development of post-processual archaeology, its use of the body highlighted a growing gap between biological and social perspectives. The body became an explicit focus for debate over the ways and degree to which the body was culturally constructed, inscribed or subject to power relations. Such debate focused, however, on discussions of objects that only have symbolic significance through their relationship to the body, rather than through a focus on the body itself (Jones 2002b: 160). If the body was key to initiating and conveying the post-processualist message, attitudes to the body also fractured this school of archaeological thought, leading to the adoption of highly constructivist specific archaeologies of the body.

Archaeologies of the body

Recent years have seen the development of explicit archaeologies of the body as an important feature of archaeological discourse. The body has been seen as an experiential location through which living people encounter and understand the world, prompting archaeologists to experiment with the body as a means of accessing bodily experience. This emphasis represents a departure from previous approaches in its move away from a focus on the social body towards an emphasis on the singular living body and on the relationship between the body and the person. These archaeologies have particularly emphasised specific subjectivities using two main strands of thought: phenomenology and embodiment. Because both are often seen to represent strongly constructivist viewpoints that reject Cartesian dualism, these approaches are often collapsed, although in fact each is inspired by different schools of thought and is associated with different interest groups. They therefore represent two quite different approaches to the body, with contrasting notions of the relationship between the body and the person (Jones 2002b: 161) and differing emphasis on shared versus individual experience.

The adoption of the phenomenological approach in archaeology has largely centred on the generalised experience of living, moving bodies in relation to landscape, monuments or architectural space. Taken on primarily by British prehistorians (e.g. Thomas 1990, 1993a, 1993b; Richards 1993; Tilley 1994; Bender et al. 1997; Bender 2002), it was inspired largely by the Heideggarian brand of transcendental phenomenology. It emphasises notions of dwelling and being-in-the-world as sources for locating the description of actions of bodies in space, the body being the reference point around which space is ordered. In the words of Tilley (1994: 16) 'The very physicality of the body imposes a schema on space through which it may be experienced and understood. An experience of space is grounded in the body itself; its capacities and potentialities for movement.' In this sense, the world can be experienced only through the body since, as body and mind cannot be separated, we have no other means for sensing it. The universality of the human body lends people common or shared experiences which can also be used to move from present to past in the interpretation of archaeology.

The anthropological concept of the 'dividual self' (Strathern 1988, 1992) – in which people are constituted through social relations with others and the world – has recently been integrated into the phenomenological argument in order to bolster the premise of shared experience (Fowler 2002). Nonetheless, the way in which the body has been used in phenomenological archaeology has been subject to critique. In particular, the phenomenological emphasis on the physical body as the medium for experience neglects to specify the nature of the physical body (bodies being heterogeneous) and assumes congruent experiences to those held by the modern investigator by others in past and present in ways that may not be justified (Brück 1998). It has also been suggested that visual experience has been unduly prioritised over other forms of sensation (Hamilakis 2002), while the dividual person may be just as much of a culturally specific understanding as ideas of the singularity of the person that it seeks to replace (Jones 2002b).

Embodiment approaches in archaeology aim to foreground the experience of the individual as part of a methodological and interpretative interest in the self. They represent a move towards the sensual and experiential and represent a heightened recognition and interest in the humanity of past lives. The individual here is defined as a single person by the boundaries of the body. Heavily influenced by developments in sociology and anthropology (e.g. Shilling 1993; Csordas 1994; Turner 1984) and following developments in feminist thought (e.g. Butler 1990, 1993; Gatens 1996) (see Morgan and Scott 1993), they stress emotion and embodied agency, the latter often embracing notions of performance (e.g. Joyce 2000a, 2000b; Meskell and Joyce 2003; Bachand et al. 2003) as well as encompassing an interest in Queer Theory and sexuality as a source of body identification (Voss and Schmidt 2000; Dowson 2000). Advocates of embodiment argue that its emphasis on the experience of being in a body represents an alternative to what they perceive to be an undesirable Foucauldian treatment of the body as passive and manipulated in strategies of predominantly male control. They critique as superficial archaeological studies of the exterior or surface of the body, particularly archaeology's treatment of the body as a setting for display in mortuary contexts, such as studies of body positioning or costume, or a focus on the symbolic value of the body (Meskell 1996; Montserrat 1998). For many embodiment theorists, their perception that much of archaeology's work on the body has been superficial leads them to align this research with the depthlessness of post-modernism and to state that post-modern treatments of the human body are not about the body at all (Montserrat 1998). In order to give an impression of depth they are therefore careful to deny post-modernism and to emphasise a move away from theorising '*on the body*' (Meskell 1996: 1, original emphasis).

It is therefore paradoxical that the embodied body is frequently identified as entirely culturally constructed, itself a position strongly influenced by Foucault (1978) (Morris 1995). Critiques of embodiment have questioned the usefulness of emphasising the individual in archaeology through a focus on difference rather than commonality on the basis that it artificially isolates the individual from society and offers little recognition of society in terms of institutions and structures (Sørensen 2000: 56). Furthermore, with few exceptions (e.g. Joyce 2000a, 2003) the impact of accumulated experiences over the life course seems to be missing from accounts of embodiment, and individuals are presented as static (Birke 1999: 46). Arguing for particular emotional or sensory responses as part of the interpretation of archaeological contexts (e.g. Meskell 1994) may represent the imposition of the present and the denial of the very interpersonal and cross-cultural variability that embodiment theorists seek to promote.

Bioarchaeologies of the body

At the same time as this explosion of constructivist theorisation, there has also been the development of specific interest in the bioarchaeology of the body through the establishment of human osteoarchaeology as a distinct field of inquiry with its own interests and priorities. Here the body is the primary locus of investigation for science-based approaches in which human remains are understood as universal, concrete and essentially biological phenomena. Bioarchaeology tends to stress the interaction between the biology of the body and behaviour with a focus on the life-ways of modern populations recovered from archaeological sites (e.g. Powell *et al.* 1991; Grauer 1995; Larsen 1997). The emphasis often falls on the physical description of bodies be that through diagnosis-orientated case studies of palaeopathology (e.g. Buzhilova 1999; Roberts and Manchester 1995; Mays *et al.* 2001; Anderson 2003; Mitchell 2003), palaeoepidemiology (e.g. Roberts and Buikstra 2003), palaeodemography (e.g. Hoppa and Vaupel 2002; Sullivan 2004), analysis of diet and nutrution (Schoeninger and Moore 1992; Pate 1994; Sandford and Weaver 2000; Katzenberg 2000; Chamberlain and Witkin 2003), body modification (e.g. Robb 1997; Tiesler 1999), metric studies of normal variation (e.g. Howells 1973, 1989; Schillaci and Stojanowski 2002; Zakrzewski 2003) or studies at the molecular level (O'Rourke *et al.* 2000; Stone 2000; Kaestle and Horsburgh 2002), with repeated observation of a set of descriptions or descriptive elements used in order to build up a picture of past lives. While people are seen as creatures like any other who adapt to their environment, it is important to stress that bioarchaeological approaches differ from those of socio-biology in that biology is not held directly responsible for human behaviour and cannot be directly equated with genes. The aim is rather to elucidate the effects of past behaviour on the human body. Such work has enabled reassessment of traditional archaeological interpretations through, for example, studies of the health consequences of key transitions such as a move to agriculture or industrialisation (e.g. Cohen and Armelagos 1984; Bridges 1989; Peterson 2002; Larsen 1995; Lewis 2002), or comparisons between pre- and post-contact societies (e.g. Wright 1990; Larsen et al. 1992; Morris 1992; Larsen and Milner 1994). It also opens up the possibility of investigating a wide range of human actions and responses to physical experiences including disability (Hawkey 1998; Roberts 2000a), interpersonal violence (Robb 1998a; Brothwell 1999; Boylston 2000; Roberts 2000b; Walker 2001; Williamson et al. 2003) or childbirth (Cox and Scott 1992; Cox 2000a; Malgosa et al. 2004).

In modern osteoarchaeology, while methodologies for sexing and ageing remain crucial to the study of human bones – in contrast to the methodological emphasis of physical anthropology in the immediate post-war period – they are a means to an end rather than an end in themselves. The assessment of sex and age is thus used to make sense of archaeological patterns, enabling interpretations regarding, for example, the sexual division of labour (e.g. Larsen et al. 1995; Eshed et al. 2004) or demographic analyses suggesting infanticide or natural mortality profiles (Mays 1993; Smith and Kahila 1992; Gowland and Chamberlain 2002). The descriptive process in osteoarchaeology leads to the determination and categorisation of people through their bodies as male or female, infant, adolescent or adult, but this is usually only a first stage of analysis. Nonetheless, despite a few recent attempts (e.g. Robb 2002; Grauer and Stuart-Macadam 1998), osteoarchaeologists have, on the whole, failed to engage with recent developments in theoretical archaeology. This has led to negative perceptions of osteoarchaeology for treating the body as a specimen or object, particularly from those seeking to highlight embodied human experience.

Divided bodies

This brief account of bodies in Anglo-American archaeological thought clearly indicates that there is no one definitive body in archaeology. It is regarded as universal and specific, cross-cultural and culturally particular, social and individual, categorical and fluid, literal and symbolic, concrete and conceptual, passive and active, object and subject, shared (we) and singular (I), occupier and occupied, observed and experienced. There are many different kinds of competing and seemingly contradictory bodies that may be approached, constructed, interpreted and drawn on in different ways. Though we talk about 'the body', it is a fragmented and disputed entity.

Above all, the most serious fracture lies between notions of the bio-physical body and the culturally constructed body. Both New Archaeology and post-processual archaeology, while relying on the body and trusting in science, failed to develop theoretical insights into the skeletal body that would allow its more effective deployment in their analyses. Interpretative archaeologists have not yet made the most of developments in bioarchaeology, using results of the study of human remains in rather one-dimensional ways, rather than incorporating them into integrated analyses. Many see the provision of sex and age estimates as the primary reason for studying human remains. Despite increasing numbers of illustrations of the potential contribution of osteoarchaeology to reconstructing the past, they continue to look to their osteologist colleagues in much the same way as under the New Archaeology paradigm, relying on their estimates in order to link artefacts to people. Recent developments in archaeologies of the body, while exciting and stimulating, have headed in directions that exacerbate the gap. By emphasising the construction of identity and experience, they have distanced themselves from the material reality of archaeological bodies in ways that sometimes include rejection of its osteological description and classification, and thus research that focuses on the skeletons of the deceased people themselves. For their part, osteoarchaeologists have largely ignored (or occasionally denied) suggestions that the body is a contested site, preferring not to confront issues surrounding the cultural construction of scientific endeavour and osteological categories. On both sides there are serious misconceptions, distrust and concerns that their work would be undermined by accepting arguments belonging to the other.

Rejecting biology

Exposing biomedical approaches to the body, including osteoarchaeology, as cultural constructions that are part of changing historical conceptions (Laqueur 1990) is now commonplace (e.g. Meskell 1996, 1998a; Gosden 1999: 146–50; Conkey 2001: 344). In archaeology as elsewhere, such arguments often form part of a wider scepticism regarding scientific method which is seen as monolithic and determinist (Harding 1991). It is argued, often by reference to the ethnographic record, that the identification of the body as a scientific object is a modern western concept and is not necessarily the way that other groups in the past or present view the body, since science is itself a cultural construction. In such arguments, the explicit distancing of constructionism from naturalism and essentialism presents physiology as natural and unchanging; it is only the ways that we have analysed it that have changed over time and place. Hence physiology is distinct from culturally specific behaviour patterns which are fluid and changeable (Morton 1995). While it is certainly the case that the body may be perceived in different ways in different times and places, both the way in which biology is presented as static and the ways in which constructionists sometimes seem to advocate the free-floating of social categories are problematic as they create a space which is difficult to fill with anything genuinely human – a reality conditioned by, and participating in, organic processes (Morton 1995: 103).

The body is a dynamic developmental system and, as such, is not an unchanging entity simply waiting to be manipulated and socially constructed. It exists within an environment with which it has a recursive relationship (Ingold 1998). This means that the body cannot exist in some kind of natural pristine state as it both affects, and is affected by, its surroundings. The environment lends potentials and also places limits on the body. 'It is wrong to depict human beings as infinitely malleable by saying that "any" human organism can participate in "any" social or cultural environment' as some constructionists might have us believe (Morton 1995: 118). Rejection of biology 'allows the participation of persons in social relations only by removing the arena of such participation from the real world in which people dwell, situating it instead in a notional world of symbolic constructs' (Ingold 1991: 373). Furthermore, the production of osteoarchaeological knowledge does not preclude its interpretation in terms of social relations or what past people may have made of differences between bodies.

Morton (1995: 103–4) argues that exponents of constructionism still work with some universal notion of human nature, even if any such conception is overtly treated with suspicion. While they do generally tend to mean that 'difference' comes first, despite the rhetoric of rejecting biology they retain clear ties to biologism. Constructionism is still joined to a notion of the human being or of humanity that has in one way or another unified the discipline. 'It seems intuitively paradoxical to speak of the "cultural construction of human beings". And this is so . . . because human beings tend to be globally defined at the level of the species *Homo sapiens*, a strictly biologically defined entity. To what extent it is possible to distinguish a person from a human being is rarely discussed in the constructionist literature' (Morton 1995: 104).

Links to biologism are also visible in the way that constructionists have attempted to fight biology on its own ground, by using biology to undermine its own tenets. One example of this is the way that discussions of the genetic basis of sex have been used in the context of discussions about the cultural construction of sex and gender. It is argued that sex is not binary (male and female) as osteological categorisation would have it and that the ways that sex is perceived are socially constructed and learnt rather than natural. This is argued on the basis that the chromosomal sex indicators in humans – the X and Y chromosomes – are found not only in XX and XY combinations (commonly understood to indicate female and male respectively) but also as other combinations, including 47XXY (Klinefelter syndrome) and 45XO (Turner syndrome), suggesting a wider non-binary range of sex variation. Hence sex is seen as fluid and culturally constructed (Nordbladh and Yates 1990; Knapp and Meskell 1997; Gilchrist 1999; Hodder 1999). On one hand the constructionists seem to dismiss the relevance of scientific osteological sexing to the social understanding of biological sex (seeing sex itself as socially constructed), yet on the other hand they use highly categorical concepts of sex at the chromosomal level that are very much modern observations.

The most fundamental difficulty with the way that constructionists often refer to biology is, however, the conflation of biology with genetics (see Ingold 1998). The constructionist argument fails to recognise a distinction between developmental differences and genetic ones. The biology in question in much recent bioarchaeological work relates 'to development, not to genetics; and the social to the domain of lived experience rather than its categorical representation' (Ingold 1998: 25). This distinction is crucial because what lies at the heart of the osteoarchaeological study of the body is investigation of the relationship between people and the world. Nonetheless, this does not mean that we should be uncritical in our acceptance of osteoarchaeology. Rather, arguments need to be based on a specific awareness of its principles and practice and of the ways that it may be of value. Biology, as science in general, is not all 'bad' (Harding 1991) and it is certainly very difficult to do without.

Rejecting constructionism

Debates over the culturally constructed nature of the body are often alien to practising osteoarchaeologists who are used to working within broadly scientific paradigms. To those whose research involves constant engagement with the corporeality and physicality of the body through touching, measuring and observing it in a very physical way, notions of constructionism seem abstract and distant. Thus while the divide between cultural and biological approaches in archaeology forms part of a more widespread general increase in interest in cultural perspectives on science as part of a broader critique of modernity and its technologies of knowledge (Macdonald 1998), the notion of the body as a contested site has been largely ignored within osteoarchaeology. Where engagement with constructivist challenges has taken place, the reaction has often been to assert the superiority of scientific method and to deny the relevance of constructionist approaches to the body.

This rather defensive position is somewhat disappointing as many of the most exciting osteoarchaeological projects explore the ways that bodies are the products of contrasting cultural settings. Osteoarchaeologists are also increasingly aware of the potential ways that social relations – including those linked to status, class, sex and ethnicity – impact on the body. In this sense, the bodies of osteoarchaeology must be regarded as in part constructed through culture and prevailing discourses. Furthermore, scientific practice, including osteoarchaeology, is clearly a dynamic, historically situated cultural product and its historicism needs to be appreciated in order to situate current practice (see Jones 2002a). Even the tag 'archaeological science' is a fairly recent label within a constantly moving discipline.

Acknowledging the cultural specificity of osteoarchaeology need not undermine its contribution. Conceding that bodies and bio-disciplines, including osteoarchaeology, are discursive cultural formations does not lead inevitably on to what Morton (1995: 116) calls the 'potential excesses of the idea of "the impossibility of a pre-discursive encounter with 'nature'" (Wade 1993: 20)'. There are encounters outside of discourse which may also be described as social and cultural (Morton 1995). The organic constitution of people is an inescapable part of them and contributes to their development. 'To suggest otherwise is to unnecessarily limit human potential, paradoxically often in the name of liberation and freedom' (Morton 1995: 116). Bio-disciplines, of which osteoarchaeology is one, emerged because they are a way of making sense of, or investigating, observed patterns in the living world. They are inherently no better or worse than other widespread social assumptions that have appealed to groups with different and sometimes conflicting agendas (Harding 1991: 3).

An appreciation of constructionism can enhance understandings of what osteoarchaeologists do. It does not entail the rejection of the utility of biological understandings in terms of the processes by which the body meets and responds to social discourses. There are degrees of constructionism (Franklin 2002) and a key challenge is to explore the relationships between the discursive and the pre-discursive. Osteoarchaeologists need not be afraid of exploring the potential value of constructivism as a concept since it need not undermine the contribution of osteoarchaeological work.

Highlighting the body in archaeology

The relationship between constructionist and biophysical views of the body is complex and fraught with tension. Despite the palpable distrust of osteoarchaeologists among some archaeologists (Hodder 1999: 114) and the overt rejection of both the authority attached to science and its use as an appropriate methodology by others, constructionists still acknowledge and use biology. They retain clear links to biologism through essentially biological definitions of humanity, and by their use (and by implication acceptance) of osteological assessments in making associations between objects and people. The recent rise in explicit interest in archaeologies of the body cannot be described as a straightforward move away from the universal biological as the basis of experience to the culturally variable constructed body as is sometimes suggested (e.g. Hamilakis *et al.* 2002b: 4). Rather, current archaeological approaches to the body seem to reflect a methodological ambivalence, or even Catch 22, that contrasts with often well-articulated theoretical positions.

For their part, osteoarchaeologists have not always been reflexive in their practice and have only rarely engaged with developments in theoretical archaeology, seeing it as lacking relevance to them. Nonetheless, increased reliance upon osteological assessments within the discipline as a whole, as the hooks on which to hang interpretations, has privileged the field. Alongside recent methodological advances and an increasing appreciation of the range of information that can come from the study of the physical body, this has ensured the continuing importance of its study. There is expanding interest in the subject witnessed by a rise in demand for osteoarchaeology courses and blossoming osteoarchaeological research.

Highlighting the body in archaeology is therefore both stimulating and provocative. In common with the focus on the body in sociology and anthropology, on one hand it detaches and pulls out the body as an identifiable and discrete entity. On the other, it stresses fragmentation and constant change of the body, rendering it less stable and more mysterious (Frank 1990; Morgan and Scott 1993). The archaeological body has been fractured and its different components have been isolated and prioritised in a range of ways as if they are completely separate. While the range of approaches to the body in archaeology is perhaps a strength and sign of a dynamic discipline, underlining the importance of the body as an archaeological resource, it is also highly problematic. Archaeological practice cannot divide the physical, social or individual body into discrete boxes since each is dependent on the other – they are different facets of the same phenomenon – and archaeologists must make living bodies out of those that are dead. The body is the nexus between biology and culture.

   Such simultaneous tensions, conflicts and ambivalence between contrasting views and approaches are not unique either to the study of the body or to the discipline of archaeology but, as elsewhere, are products of prevailing social and intellectual currents. The divide between the two cultures of science and humanism is also manifest elsewhere within archaeology (see Jones 2002a; Knapp 2000, 2002), but with regard to the archaeological body their expression in terms of 'bio-text' and 'socio-text' (O'Neill 1985) is particularly keenly articulated. Though different archaeologists may be studying the same people, they identify them in contrasting ways. The biophysical body is deemed to be the province of the osteoarchaeologist, to be explored as a physical entity placed outside traditional material-culture-based interpretation. Osteoarchaeology is left behind in the quest for past social life (the social and individual bodies) because archaeology has traditionally identified sociality as the province of the humanities. Within archaeology, interrogation of current practice regarding the body is particularly pressing because it asks questions regarding the significance of the material basis of the skeletal body, thereby cutting to the core of a discipline which is based on the study of the material. As the body has itself become a context for investigation, it has become an important battleground in the establishment of interpretative responsibility and disciplinary authority.

3   The body and convention in archaeological practice

> Now I am ready to tell how bodies are changed
> Into different bodies.   *Ovid*, trans. Hughes 1997: 3

The socio-political implications of the historical and social conventions surrounding the division of the study of the body in archaeology that I discussed in Chapters 1 and 2, can be analysed and understood in terms of a series of perceived binary structural oppositions that sit beneath the divide between osteoarchaeology (science) and interpretative archaeology (humanism). These have had a profound influence on archaeological practice and it is these that I want to look at next.

Structuring the divide

The historical and social conventions that structure archaeological investigation have implications for the study of the body that go beyond an initial divide based on differences in material studied or methodology. Currently lying beneath the split between the science-orientated study of the body through osteoarchaeology and the humanist-orientated exploration of the body in interpretative archaeology is a problematic series of binary oppositions. They prop up this divide and themselves form elements intrinsic to the socio-political and investigative structure of the discipline.

The oppositions can be described as:

Osteoarchaeology	Interpretative archaeology
Atheoretical	Theoretical
Dead	Living
Inside (Unfleshed)	Outside (Fleshed)
Nature	Culture

These oppositions are linked to each other in a chain, each being related to others. Thus because osteoarchaeology is associated with science, its practice is often perceived as being technical and *atheoretical*, in contrast to interpretative archaeology which is identified as *theoretically orientated*. The focus of osteological investigation being the skeleton, the divide between osteoarchaeology and interpretative archaeology is underpinned by the all too rarely articulated, though nonetheless clear and implicit, distinction between understandings of the *dead* body and the *living* body, which also frequently corresponds to a dichotomy between *unfleshed* and *fleshed*. This latter also implies a contrast in the manner in which physical aspects of the body are made visible. The dead body is represented by the skeleton that forms the internal frame of the body and thus the *inside* of the body is seen. The living body is represented by flesh, blood and skin that interface with the world and thus the *outside* of the body is highlighted. In turn, these oppositions lead to what Ingold (1998: 22) has called the 'master division' between *nature* and *culture*, where the dead, unfleshed, skeletal body is regarded as the province of nature, while the living fleshed body is part of culture.

The tacit acceptance of these structural oppositions as a concealed part of the conventions that define the archaeological analysis of the body has important repercussions as they produce a series of conceptual, theoretical and methodological tensions. In order to expose these, it is useful to examine the character of each of these oppositions in relation to the specificity of the archaeological body. Engaging with such dichotomous thinking opens up the possibility for more active engagement with the middle ground (Jenks 1998).

Osteoarchaeology as atheoretical vs interpretative archaeology as theoretical

Earlier in this book I discussed how the categorisation of osteoarchaeology as science lends the knowledge it produces an authoritative and reliable status within archaeology (cf. Woolgar 1988; Macdonald 1998). Practitioners are often regarded as trustworthy experts or specialists to whom material is sent and from whom opinion is sought. These opinions frequently acquire a privileged status as, being invested with cultural authority (Macdonald 1998: 5), they are transformed by other members of the archaeological community into facts. Specialists are often unwilling to abandon their authoritative status, and problems and debates regarding the analytical process and the context of the specialist's knowledge are often unknown to those who use their reports (Jones 2002a). The reverence accorded to science on one hand, and a failure to convey the complexity of individual analytical questions within osteoarchaeology on the other, means that despite internal debates, the results of osteoarchaeological analysis are often viewed by the wider archaeological community as unproblematic.

The osteological specialist is seen as being a dry technician (cf. Coles 1995), on the basis that the study of the physical body is mechanical in nature and executed according to a prescribed 'recipe book' of ideas and methods. Furthermore, osteoarchaeology is a very tactile practice. Its study requires practical, hands-on work and working with one's hands is often seen as technical. Hence the study of the physical body through osteoarchaeology is seen to lack theoretical insights, in contrast to the more cerebral nature of interpretative archaeology which is seen to rely overtly on the construction of theoretical frameworks to make sense of past objects. Furthermore, the division of knowledge and expertise according to geographical location and period is a fundament of disciplinary organisation and, unlike interpretative archaeologists, the skills osteoarchaeologists possess can often be transferred from one place or period to another. This leads to a perceived lack of in-depth place and period knowledge which means that osteoarchaeologists are deemed unable to synthetically interpret. For both osteoarchaeologists and interpretative archaeologists, human remains are frequently seen as products sourced from excavation, their recording and reports passed on as commodities through a system of commercial contracts, thereby ensuring the place of osteoarchaeology at the bottom of the interpretative tree.

The archaeologist responsible for synthesising a site or body of data often expects the production of a standard form of bone report, usually consisting of information on sex, age and pathology. This may be partly for reasons of economy, but it has also become a disciplinary convention and many are uncertain how skeletal material might otherwise be treated. Osteoarchaeologists have tended to respond to such low expectations by providing basic reports, again partly for reasons of time and money. As a whole, osteoarchaeologists have been somewhat slow in being proactive. They have failed to demonstrate the wider potential of skeletal data outside their own community, and have been reluctant to take on archaeological theory in developing interpretations within the traditional ambit of material-culture-based archaeologists. Many osteoarchaeologists feel that they do not need to engage with theory in order to make sense of their data as investigation and interpretation are already defined by scientific parameters which are considered theory free. This only perpetuates and exacerbates outside perceptions of them as technicians, a label with which many osteoarchaeologists have become increasingly frustrated.

The identification of osteoarchaeology as purely technical and atheoretical is, however, to misrepresent the nature of the field. It establishes a false dichotomy between the practical and the theoretical by conflating the technical expertise required for the successful execution of method- ological strategies, with osteoarchaeological method itself, thereby failing to appreciate the theoretical foundations that underpin the latter. It is also problematic as it assumes that the analysis of the physical body is a form of knowledge which exists outside of social life, both in terms of the perception of the living body and in terms of the social practice of its investigation. Science carries with it theoretical baggage just as human- ist approaches do (Macdonald 1998). In osteoarchaeological work on the body, as with other forms of archaeological science, the theoretical framework in terms of assumptions, rationales and social contexts of the science is often hidden, disappearing into what Latour (1987) famously termed a 'black box' (see Jones 2002a). To say that osteoarchaeology is atheoretical is both to misunderstand its foundations and to do those who work within it a grave injustice. Though many osteoarchaeologists may not be aware of theory on a day-to-day basis and do not necessarily identify themselves as theoretically orientated, there is a great deal of tacit theory within osteoarchaeological practice.

Tacit theory in osteoarchaeological practice

The categorisation of osteoarchaeology as science relies on a series of key characteristics. The most significant of these are commonly held to be replication of results (experimentation), objective observation (the construction of categories which permit the development of common taxonomic knowledge and objectification of the subject of study), and explanation and prediction (an attempt to reveal or utilise underlying principles) (Chalmers 1982). Quantification (the use of instruments to measure and mathematical analysis of results) may also be important (Macdonald 1998). These characteristics can be broadly described as constituting scientific method (Chalmers 1982). The term 'scientific method' implies a single unified way of doing science that will almost inevitably lead to similar approaches and understandings no matter what is being studied, be it human bones or soil horizons.

Certainly, the osteoarchaeological study of human bones can replicate results in ways that interpretative archaeology cannot. The excavations from which osteological material is obtained cannot be rerun elsewhere as archaeological sites and depositional sequences are unique occurrences (Gero 1996: 252). However, no one paradigm unites osteoarchaeology. It cannot be defined through a single set of techniques or one overarching approach. Osteoarchaeological practitioners themselves express a range of opinions regarding what they perceive to be the prime focus and

definition of their work (cf. Coles 1995). There is considerable variability in approaches and analytical techniques within osteoarchaeology. For
instance, methods and understandings are vastly different between analysis at the molecular level and the recording of skeletal morphology. Some
approaches are confidently able to predict and explain, whereas others
suggest interpretations of past human activity and are therefore probabilistic rather than definite in character (Evans and O'Connor 1999). This
implies that, rather than science being a homogeneous activity, there may
be different levels of credibility within scientific practice. The practice of
science within osteoarchaeology is fragmented, reflecting wider debates
over the nature of science or whether science can even be said to exist in
any essential sense (Woolgar 1988; Latour 1987; Wylie 2000). Science is a
'highly variable animal' (Woolgar 1988: 15). In archaeology, as elsewhere,
science cannot be easily formalised. Tacit or craft knowledge plays a crucial role in generating data (Allison-Bunnell 1998), particularly in terms
of learning how to look at and discriminate salient information (Atkinson
1995). It is difficult to create an *a priori* definition of science that relies
on a privileged system of completely formal knowledge (Allison-Bunnell
1998).

Furthermore, though osteoarchaeologists are often seen to produce
facts, because the practice of science entails cultural assumptions and
social relationships (Harding 1991), science is part of, rather than separate from, culture. It plays an active role in the ongoing process of defining
cultural worlds and social difference (Harding 1991). This is especially so
in the archaeological examination of the body where the study of human
remains provides a means of constructing differences between individuals in the past which form the basis of categorisation necessary for interpretations and investigations of past lives. The questions that osteoarchaeologists choose to investigate and the data that they collect do not,
therefore, exist separately from theory, being collected within a particular remit. Osteoarchaeology is also dependent on outlooks, relationships
and results within archaeology as a whole. Nonetheless, different scientific fields do hold distinct cultural practices and produce distinct forms
of knowledge (Knorr-Certina 1999; Jones 2002a). Osteoarchaeological
research in general shares a number of characteristics that make it cohesive. The variety of methods employed are a means to a common end
rather than ends in themselves. We therefore need to look at osteoarchaeology specifically, rather than treating it together with science in general
(cf. Jones 2002a: 63) if we are to identify the tacit theoretical frameworks
that sit within it.

One of the key features of osteoarchaeology is an interest in human variation (Weiss 1998; Marks 1995). Themes through which this variation

may be examined include the study of sex differences, growth, population dynamics, disease or life-ways. Irrespective of the particular investigative techniques employed or skeletal elements examined, each of these require a comparative approach, whether at the level of fragments of a single individual compared to others within a single sample, or at a broader scale between populations. For example, some of the first aspects osteoarchaeologists frequently seek to establish when recording an assemblage is descriptive information regarding elements present, sex and age-at-death composition, and prevalence of pathological conditions, with the aim of establishing patterns of deposition, attitudes towards the disposal of different types of body or body parts, mortality patterns, the demography of human groups and health status. The collection of these descriptive data involves comparing the material under investigation first with an 'ideal' complete skeleton to establish which elements are present, and then an analysis of the relative sex and age composition of individuals within a site, which is in turn derived from a comparative understanding of the morphological characteristics of adult males and females, and of human development. The outcomes of analyses of single assemblages may be compared with other contemporary or local sites to build up a picture of the period or region. In large-scale population-level studies, cross-cultural or temporal comparisons are made between groups in order to examine transitions and contrasts between periods or contexts in terms of issues such as natural disasters and climate change (e.g. Wetterstrom 1992; Buckland *et al.* 1996; Bourbou 2003), differences in the health status of populations with contrasting life-ways such as urban and rural groups (e.g. Manchester 1992; Molleson 1992; Schell and Denham 2003), colonisation and contact (e.g. Larsen and Milner 1994; Steele *et al.* 1998; Baker and Kealhofer 1996) or subsistence strategies (e.g. Lukacs 1992; Lukacs and Walimbe 1998; Stock and Pfeiffer 2004).

The most fundamental comparison upon which all of these studies rests is between baseline data from individuals and samples whose parameters are known, and unknown samples. Such baseline data are available either as modern standards from living people (e.g. Maresh 1955, 1970) or from large skeletal reference collections such as from the sites of Christ Church, Spitalfields or St Brides, Fleet Street in London, where coffin plates indicate the name, sex, age and date of death of the deceased, in conjunction with historical documentation that provides a valuable picture of the life-way of the community of which they were a part (Molleson and Cox 1993; Cox 1996, 1998; Scheuer and Bowman 1995; Scheuer 1998). Some of the most accurate methods for ageing skeletally immature individuals, for example, are based on the dental development sequence (e.g. Schour and Massler 1941; Moorrees *et al.* 1963a and b; Gustafson and Koch 1974; Demirjian and Goldstein 1976; Ubelaker 1989). These methods are derived from examination and radiographs of the dentition of living children of known age. Osteoarchaeologists estimate the age of subadult skeletons by comparing their dentition with dental development charts. Similarly, the basic assumption that growth in juveniles is the best indicator of their health and nutritional status is derived from studies of living children where higher rates of illness and death are associated with stunting and wasting (Saunders and Hoppa 1993; Hoppa and FitzGerald 1999). This principle has been applied in archaeological contexts where metric studies of bone length and bone cross-sections in cohorts of developmentally similar children have been used as non-specific indicators of nutritional status within subadult skeletal samples (Humphrey 2000). Many of the diagnostic features of palaeopathology and disease in dry bones have been established through the efforts of medical practitioners, providing comparisons between patients who are known to have suffered from particular conditions in life and who were radiographed, or who were investigated post-mortem (Angel 1981; Roberts and Manchester 1995). It should, however, be noted that the criteria employed for clinical, radiological and dry bone diagnoses may differ, and the severity of conditions in living patients does not always correspond with the severity of changes in bones (see e.g. Andersen *et al.* 1994; Lovell 1994; Stuart-Macadam 1989).

Collections with known sex and age-at-death also provide the opportunity for establishing and cross-checking osteological methods (Bedford *et al.* 1993; Molleson and Cox 1993). For example, there are a number of osteological methods for sexing adult skeletons (see Mays and Cox 2000; Ferembach *et al.* 1980). Each is based on the identification of morphological characteristics, of which the most important are on the skull and pelvis (Buikstra and Ubelaker 1994), and in some cases metric observations of sex differences between males and females. Using the Spitalfields collection, Molleson and Cox (1993) tested the reliability of osteological methods of sex determination and found that they were correctly able to identify sex in 98 per cent of adult skeletons. The availability of large, well-documented skeletal collections, many of which have been excavated in the past few decades, has also made possible a move from case studies based on individual diagnosis to larger-population-orientated studies (Larsen 1997).

The comparative approach relies upon the identification of differences but assumes that the ways such differences manifest will always be constant, thereby allowing comparison to be made. The individual cannot therefore be understood as a useful unit of analysis in isolation, but must form part of a wider picture and contextual setting in order for observations to make interpretative sense. Individuals are studied as members of categories, and samples of categories are used to generate wider inferences about groups or populations. This understanding of osteoarchaeological practice lies in direct contrast to perceptions from outside the field which consider it to have an exclusive focus on the individual (e.g. Ingold 1998: 37). Only the establishment of patterns generated from observations of groups of individuals allow interpretation.

The basic theoretical formulation that sits beneath the comparative approach of extrapolating from known to unknown, and more especially of moving from observations of the living to understanding the dead, is a framework with many parallels to that described by the processual archaeology of the 1960s and 70s. Indeed, the explicit aim of much osteoarchaeological research to make 'behavioural inference' (Larsen 1997: 5) is strikingly similar to statements made by proponents of New Archaeology (cf. Wylie 1992: 28). As with middle-range theory, ethnographic and historical data provide the links that allow the move 'from bones to behavior' (Hudson 1993).

In order to understand patterns of skeletal change, emphasis is placed on adaptation and response as part of a system. This emphasis on human variability and its exploration through the identification of patterns based on assumptions of regularities in human responses to external stimuli, forms another point of similarity with the principles of processualism. In contrast to processualism, however, in osteoarchaeology the notion of regularity in human responses lies not in culture or behaviour as an adaptive response, but with the regularity of biological processes in terms of responses to the environmental and cultural stresses placed on the human skeleton.

For an investigation of human behaviour, osteoarchaeology's reliance on comparative method, universalism and generalisation from patterns of data open it up to a number of critiques. Given the similarities of its underlying theoretical framework to that of processualism, it is perhaps unsurprising that many of these critiques are similar to the by now well-rehearsed arguments addressed to the New Archaeology. In particular, while osteoarchaeologists often refer to hypothesis testing in their use of comparisons between known and unknown samples, when it comes to the inference of behaviour from human remains, as Hodder (1984) pointed out in relation to the study of objects, this cannot constitute a 'test' as archaeologists cannot go back into the past to check by direct observation. In this sense, the use of known data constitutes nothing more than a comparative reference point on which to hook interpretation. Archaeology thus shares the interpretative problems of other disciplines using scientific methods in the observation of past phenomena, such as geology and astronomy (Johnson 1999). Nonetheless, the strength of osteoarchaeology lies in the replicability of experimental results by different researchers and this differentiates it from results based on archaeological excavation.

In addition, the generalisation of interpretation from patterns poses a series of tensions. For example, although individuals may have differing susceptibilities to stress or propensities to form bone (Rogers *et al.* 1997a), it is difficult to take this individual variation into account in an empirical manner. In any given case, out of a group of individuals within a sample, the balance between the predisposition of that individual to be subject to skeletal change, and the effect of human behaviour and environment, is complex. All conclusions are therefore necessarily built upon generalised models. On a population level, interpretation tends to homogenise and simplify human behaviour, reducing it to a single explanation (for example, patterns of fracture occur because of an agricultural life-way). Furthermore, it is often assumed that skeletal changes are the response of human tissue to events outside the body (such as pathogens in the environment, patterns of work, cultural norms or pressures). On one hand, this implies that the stimuli for osteological changes are not of the individual's own making, but on the other hand, the use of human bones to discuss behaviour requires the person to act in such a way that the consequences of their actions are manifest in their bones after death.

Tacit theory in osteoarchaeology operates at a number of levels. It resides in the cultural assumptions and social relationships embedded within its identity and practice, the way that it describes the body, frameworks for moving from the living to the dead through the use of comparative data, assumptions of regularity in skeletal responses to external stimuli, and generalisation from patterns. Many of the premises of osteoarchaeology are similar to those of processualism. Since the existence of theory in the study of the body is often conflated with particular brands of post-processual theory (see previous chapter), a look at the principles underlying osteoarchaeological practice therefore suggests that a perceived lack of theory in osteoarchaeology is being confused with the use of a *different* body of theory. Some of the tensions between osteological and interpretative approaches to the body in archaeology may arise because, while the interpretative study of the body has taken on board post-processualist critiques, osteoarchaeology has not.

The dead body vs the living body

Archaeological bodies are fundamentally different to those in other disciplines dealing with the social. In archaeology we cannot see past people in action and the physical body is, by definition, lifeless. In examining the dead body, osteoarchaeologists strive to recreate a social being that is recognisable to all by describing a medical history borne by the body in a manner analogous to coroners and pathologists (cf. Hallam *et al.* 1999: 15). This becomes a starting point for a retrospective narration of a person's former life which, despite its specificity to the individual being examined, is necessarily derived through comparison and description by others rather than self-experience (Hallam *et al.* 1999). By contrast, many of the approaches recently adopted with the specific aim of exploring the body in interpretative archaeology derive from sociological, philosophical and anthropological approaches to the living body (e.g. Heidegger 1972; Butler 1990, 1993; Giddens 1991; Shilling 1993; Csordas 1994). They emphasise its agency or see it as an experiential location through which living people encounter and understand the world at any given moment. In particular, phenomenology and embodiment refer to self, 'the living body . . . with feelings, sensations, perceptions and emotions' (Ots 1994: 116). This creates a divide between osteoarchaeology and interpretative archaeology in terms of dead other vs living self that represents two different material and conceptual worlds corresponding to the distinction made in German between *Körper* (the dead body) and *Leib* (the living body) (see Ingold 1998: 27).

The dead body has come to be identified as a biological object and the living body with the cultural subject (Ingold 1998: 35). For osteoarchaeologists, the body is a constant biological phenomenon which observation and description allow categorisations, estimations or diagnoses. The body is therefore a resource to be exploited. Those who deal with the cultural subject emphasise its historical contingency. Advocates of the body as an experiential location critique other approaches to the body as essentialising and superficial for their failure to deal with the emotion, agency and experience of being in a living body (Meskell 1996, 1998a, 2000a; Montserrat 1998). They argue that bodies otherwise understood are, 'bodies cast adrift from their human occupants . . . [that] easily degenerate into ethnographic lists of bodily practices and prodigies, or present the ancient human body as a passive spectacle or museum artefact' (Montserrat 1998: 4). The implication is that the osteoarchaeological study of human remains represents just such a passive presentation, just as does archaeology's treatment of the body in mortuary settings in general (Meskell 1996, 1998a, 2000a; Montserrat 1998).

Yet, it has been argued that in dealing with the living body, many recent archaeologies of the body are not as well grounded in archaeological material as one would like (Sørensen 2000). The imported character of these approaches precludes consideration of the very particular physical nature of archaeological bodies. By focusing on the living body, agency, phenomenological and embodiment approaches which ostensibly aim to reinstate the corporeality of the body as a central theme in human experience, thereby linking materialist and discursive perspectives (see J. Thomas 2002), often fail to utilise information from the skeletal body in interpretations. Instead, they simply reiterate the dead vs living divide as they do not deal effectively with the specifically archaeological nature of the body as physically present but lifeless. In archaeological work on embodiment, the physical body is treated as a kind of shell for the person which is variously described as 'occupied' or 'inhabited'. The body is treated as a preformed container to be filled up with culture (Ingold 1998) and embodiment virtually becomes a synonym for cultural construction. In the words of Benthien (2002: 13), 'On closer inspection, the notion of living in the body always turns out to be a discourse about hollow space: the imaginary room created by one's own skin'. It is literally embodiment without bodies. As Ingold points out in relation to the use of the term 'embodiment', 'It would seem just as legitimate to speak of enmindment as of embodiment, to emphasise the immanent intentionality of human beings' engagement with their environment in the course of perception and action' (Ingold 1998: 27). Meanwhile, phenomenology's emphasis on the physical body as currently described in archaeology has failed to take account of the variation in bodies (Brück 1998) that is a major focus of osteoarchaeological research. Thus, though such perspectives represent welcome attempts to recognise and explore the relationship between social life and the body, they have so far failed to use the physical remains of the body itself as a basis for interpretation. Likewise, approaches to agency, while relying on the actions of the body, have neglected to explore the potential for its examination through the skeleton.

In order to bring living and dead bodies together we need to address a key archaeological question: how can we access the living body through the dead? To do this we need to explore in more detail the way that the divide between the living and the dead body in archaeology has been created.

The living dead: exploring the living body through the dead

One reason for the dislocation of tangible skeletal remains in recent archaeologies of the body lies in the perceived problem that such archaeologies are trying to solve. In particular, because advocates of embodiment and phenomenology are interested in experience, they aim to dissolve a Cartesian split between the body and the mind. This split is perceived as problematic since the living body is not just an instrument that simply carries out, almost by remote control, the orders of an insulated and 'disembodied' mind in which meaning and intention reside. Instead the body has a central role in human experience.

In recent years, it has become a common tendency in archaeology to swiftly and briefly reject the Cartesian model. However, while the split between body and mind may indeed be problematic, Descartes's model cannot be quite so easily dismissed. Not only has it been vital to elements of western thought over the past 350 years, but in a specifically archaeological setting the grounds on which it is rejected can be contested. Perhaps most challenging for attempts to combine mind and body is the notion that the osteoarchaeological body necessarily lacks a mind in both material and spiritual senses because it is dead; only the body remains. Playing devil's advocate, one might argue that as the skeletal body is devoid of life it cannot experience, experience being the province of the sensations and thus of the living. Furthermore, a critique of approaches to the human past that charges researchers with neglect of the body has been adopted from outside archaeology and completely ignores the osteoarchaeological tradition that has focused entirely on working with the body. Indeed, some might argue that its focus on the body has been to the detriment of the mind and notions of intentional action, in as much as the body is treated as a functionalist biological entity. On another level, the opposition between the body and mind in Descartes's thought may not be as extreme as many have presented it and oppositions may be largely produced in order to have a force against which to react (Sørensen 2000: 44–5).

The main difficulty with the division between mind and body in archaeology is not to do with the neglect of the body and the privileging of the mind. Nor is it to do with the need or desire to access meaning or human experience. Rather, the reason why Cartesian dualism is problematic stems from the very way that the distinction between body and mind mirrors the distinction between the dead and the living body. Accepting the veracity of a Cartesian approach means that it becomes difficult to work with archaeological bodies since it precludes a linkage between the living (identified as minds) and the dead (identified as bodies). Configured in this way, the challenge becomes not one of how to bring together mind and body but how to link two different kinds of bodies – the living and the dead.

While embodiment and phenomenology ostensibly seek to unite materialist and discursive perspectives, they fail to deal with this issue because, as Ingold points out, a desire to unify body and mind rests on the principle that the human being is a composite entity made up of separate but complementary parts – what Ingold calls 'the complementarity approach' (Ingold 1998). In other words, that human existence is made up of a series of different components – biological, psychological, social – that are commonly the subject of study of different disciplines, and that can be somehow bolted on to each other to understand the person. They cannot therefore bring into question existing disciplinary structures that arose within a Cartesian framework. In other words, that the body is traditionally the province of osteoarchaeology, and the mind is traditionally the province of interpretative archaeology.

Hallam *et al.* (1999) argue that current notions of embodiment assume the concordance of body and self through the elision of embodiment, agency and social identity. Harré (1991: 15) points out that the separation of the body from the person is 'routinely accomplished' by a series of 'separation practices'. Such processes include anaesthetisation for surgery, states of drug-induced disembodiment and murder. While acknowledging that lived social identity and experiences of the body are closely related (Featherstone 1982; Shilling 1993; James 2000), by concentrating on the living body, a focus on embodiment – to the exclusion of its counterpoint disembodiment – reflects the notion that the biological death of the body means that the individual has ceased to be (Hallam *et al.* 1999: 8). Such an emphasis, with its conflation of body and self, fails to deal adequately with situations where people have a social presence, yet lack a living body, as for example in the case of ancestors (Bloch and Parry 1982; Parker Pearson 1999b), a corpse in preparation for disposal (Kligman 1988), or even when a body becomes a focus for archaeological study.

Harré (1991: 35) suggests that a person's social identity may begin before their bodily identity has taken shape in the parental definition of the child to come and that it may persist long after the decay of the body. The importance of the social presence of the deceased for the living is familiar to archaeology in, for example, work on the funeral and the display of the corpse as an arena for the mourners (Barrett 1994). Though such archaeological studies are often presented in terms of the manipulation of the dead in the political strategies of the living, they also offer a clear challenge to current claims that people become social beings only through their living embodiment (cf. Hallam *et al.* 1999: 16). Here 'the biologically deceased can retain an influential social presence in the lives of others' (Hallam *et al.* 1999: ix). Tarlow's theoretically quite different work on the way that death impacts on the living, attitudes to death, and commemoration (Tarlow 1999) also illustrates how meanings and identity can detach themselves from the living body (Hallam *et al.* 1999: ix), while Gell (1998: 222) has argued that the biographical careers of people may be prolonged long after death through memories, traces, leavings and material objects. As Hallam *et al.* (1999) argue with respect to the social sciences, by failing to problematise who or what is embodied we have not adequately explored the nature of the body, its materiality and its boundaries in archaeology. Such an interrogation brings into question the boundaries between life and death and their assumed opposition. 'Just as the theoretical lines drawn between binary oppositions have been coming under fire, so the actual – living and breathing – boundary between life and death has become a matter of urgent debate, for both ends of the life cycle' (Bronfen and Goodwin 1993: 5–6).

Questioning the boundaries between life and death means that just as understandings of the living body cannot be taken as self-evident or given, nor can those of the dead body. The biological death of the body articulates a boundary that may be considered 'as an event-horizon, in which one form (myself) meets its potentiality for transforming itself into another form or forms (the not-self)' (Battersby 1993: 36). The difference between the living and the dead body is thus conceived of in terms of a process in which the potential for death always resides in the living, and the living become the dead, rather than a straightforward dichotomy that separates between live subject and dead object, or social presence and absence. 'Death . . . is everywhere encoded in life and life is encoded in death in a complex self-referential relationship' (Hallam *et al.* 1999: 12).

For archaeology, an approach framed in terms of continuity, transformation and the shifting potentiality of the body opens up the possibility for an investigation of the relationship between the living and the dead body. Not only can the body be identified in terms of understanding the potential continuity of the social presence of the person after death, but an appreciation of the material changes that accompany the biological death of the body can also be seen as part of a continuum that forms part of a complex relationship between life and death. At death, the turnover, replacement and production of cells ceases but there is no immediate dramatic material transformation at this point. The living and the dead can therefore be related to each other such that the body as found in the archaeological record represents only one point along a time-line of processes and horizons that include growth, life experiences, death, post-mortem treatment by the living and decay. A dichotomy between living and dead bodies does not adequately take into account the continuity that exists in terms of the skeletal body between life and death, instead assuming a sudden shift in the qualities of the body. While death constitutes one of the most profound events of the body, and the potentiality of the body may shift as it moves through another event horizon when the fleshed becomes the unfleshed, the skeletal body forms an important axis of continuity.

Although the changing potentiality of the body may imply changes in the accessibility of aspects of the physical and experiential body, the theoretical foundation of the investigation of the archaeological body rests upon the points of contact between the living and the dead body through the establishment and investigation of the references back and forth between the two sides of the death event horizon, creating the link between life and death. References between life and death may exist through grave goods surrounding a body, but are most direct in the skeletal remains themselves in modifications to the body that occur during life and that may remain visible in death. Such modifications are part of a series of different changes to the body, some of which may be deliberate such as dental modifications, while others may be accidental or inadvertent such as fractures or disease processes, or the result of inevitable agerelated processes such as degenerative changes to the joints. Though its potentiality changes, the living and the dead body are one and the same. The body does not merely reflect life but was once life itself. Osteoarchaeology thus becomes a way of knowing about the body that allows for the life experiences of people by exploring the form, pattern and origin of osseous changes, understanding these in terms of the skeletal consequences of what people did and how they lived.

Inside (unfleshed) vs outside (fleshed)

Just as the lifelessness of the archaeological body differentiates it from bodies in other disciplines dealing with the social, so does the expression of the body. While archaeological bodies are occasionally preserved with skin and hair as mummies or bog bodies, the archaeological body is epitomised by the unfleshed human skeleton. Hence the inside of the body, the body that is otherwise concealed and unseen, is exposed. A distinction between two forms of body, the unfleshed body and the fleshed body, can therefore also be conceptualised in terms of an inside : outside opposition.

As with the dichotomy between dead and living bodies, the inside : outside distinction is reflected in archaeological approaches that are split. This division mirrors two contrasting conceptions of the relationship between the body and the subject present in modern cultural history. First, the notion that what is authentic and essential to the subject lies beneath the skin, requiring decipherment through skills of reading and interpretation. Here, the skin is regarded as protective cover or, alternatively, as deceiving the observer by concealing the inner core of the person. Second, the notion that the essence and reality of the person is not hidden inside but is fully exposed. In this case, the outside of the body, its skin, is the subject that stands as a metonym for the whole human being and for life (Benthien 2002).

Osteoarchaeological approaches to the body fall within the first of these cultural models, with the focus of investigation lying beneath the skin and flesh by means of specialist decipherment of an osteological text. Osteoarchaeology sees the flesh and skin as a kind of wrapping for bones which is unpacked through processes of decomposition. Since skin and flesh rot away, the visibility of the person is understood through the skeleton alone, promoting its legitimacy as the only tangible, and therefore authentic, evidence of their existence. Here, the 'real' body is exposed, having been penetrated and stripped bare to its essentials. Indeed, osteoarchaeologists are frequently at pains to emphasise that they cannot access changes to the soft tissues (in other words to the whole body) and thus osteological analyses must, by necessity, focus only on the skeleton. In the case of palaeopathology in particular, osteoarchaeologists often point out that the manifestation of disease in bone is only a partial reflection of disease processes, most of which take place, either solely or in their initial stages, in soft tissue (Roberts and Manchester 1995). These kinds of statements serve to reinforce the authenticity of osteoarchaeological observations, in that they imply that for disease to be observable and to have penetrated beneath skin and flesh, the disease must have been severe or prolonged and, therefore, all the more real. However, in recognising the impossibility of investigating the outside of the body and therefore rejecting it because of its archaeological inaccessibility, osteoarchaeology has difficulties in linking fleshed and unfleshed bodies. With the exception of the highly specialised sub-fields of facial reconstruction and forensic anthropology, osteoarchaeology effectively ignores the outside of the body as it feels that it cannot deal effectively with it. Furthermore, an emphasis on the internal skeletal body alone seems to remove it from the social realm since it is not visible in life. Thus the body is often presented in terms of a medical case study.

By contrast, those archaeologists who work with recent archaeologies of the body, in focusing on living bodies also work with fleshed ones. Here, the second cultural model holds sway as flesh and skin are frequently used as metaphors for 'person', 'spirit' or 'life' as a *pars pro toto* of the entire human being (Benthien 2002: 13). Knowledge of external appearance, generated through flesh and skin, is axiomatic to many perspectives. This is particularly important for many archaeologies of sexuality (see Schmidt and Voss 2000) where genitalia and flesh are the media for communication and desire. Archaeological discussions of the body have explored the ways in which the fleshed body can be used as an arena for display and disguise in terms of public statements and the manipulation of categories of identity through clothing and ornamentation where the outside of the body is used as a venue for social expression (e.g. Sørensen 1997). Experiential understandings of the body including current uses of transcendental phenomenology and archaeologies of the senses also rely on the exterior of the body as the interface with the world and the means by which the world and sensations are experienced through vision, smell, taste, touch and hearing (e.g. Hamilakis 2002). The central metaphor of flesh and skin as life, and the primacy given to the exterior of the body, are, however, inappropriate to the archaeological body as it no longer has its living surface. In mortuary contexts archaeologists lack many of the most striking features of bodies that we recognise on a day-to-day level: skin, blood and flesh. They are devoid of those external features, such as breasts or genitalia, that have often been identified as vital to the recognition of corporeality and that form key features of much theorising about the body involved in other disciplines.

Theories of embodiment have explicitly attempted to transcend an inside : outside dichotomy, critiquing many traditional archaeological approaches to the body for their concern with describing only the surfaces of the body (e.g. Meskell 1996, 1998a, 2000a). Yet embodiment too sits within the inside : outside duality and, in doing so, presents a series of tensions. In order to identify a singular entity of the person who is said to inhabit the body, it relies on notions of the body where the individual is defined and bounded. Hallam *et al.* (1999: 11) point out that this forms part of a contemporary ethos within which the body is conceptualised as the finite container of a self defined primarily in terms of its separation from other bodies and is a highly localised reading of the body and its role in identity construction. Benthien expresses this in terms of the skin as the 'central metaphor of separateness' (Benthien 2002: 1); in as much as the skin implicitly provides a boundary, the outside of the body defines the person. For archaeology, the absence of skin means that archaeologists are attempting embodiment without defined bodies. The implication of this for accessing the individual is that, without the boundary of the skin, it becomes hard to locate the context of individual life. The lack of a physical boundary provided by skin and flesh to seal in the archaeological body means that its potential for fragmentation is greater, resulting in disarticulated and sometimes dispersed bodies. Furthermore, while the notion of the habitation of the body suggests that it is possible to access the core of the person in terms of, for example, emotions or feelings residing within, the substantive nature of that inside is unclear. The body becomes like an empty house, creating a disjunction between the subject who is said to inhabit the house and the environment, since the person seems to become sealed within their skin (Benthien 2002: 28).

Once again, the skeletal body poses particular theoretical and practical problems, leading to disjunction between the specific demands of the archaeological body, and theoretical and practical approaches to its interpretation. The archaeological unfleshed skeletal body is, in many respects, unique. Without skin it lacks what is perceived as the cultural border between the self and the world (Benthien 2002). It appears to be 'inside out'. There is a need for a specifically archaeological approach that takes as its starting point the notion of bodies without clear boundaries.

Inside out: reconfiguring boundaries

The inside : outside dichotomy is an historically emergent cultural construct (Hallam *et al.* 1999: 12). Familiar notions of the distinction between body interior and exterior with skin as the boundary of the individual emerged during the European Enlightenment. Pre-Enlightenment thought stressed the fluidity of boundaries with the skin as a porous non-closed surface that was open to the world (see Bakhtin 1984). Although the anatomical paradigm of penetration and uncovering was first established in the sixteenth century by Andreas Vesalius, the emergence of modern clinical-anatomical medicine in the eighteenth century brought with it understandings of skin as a boundary or place of passage into the inside (Bakhtin 1984; Benthien 2002). The distinction between inside and outside sees its culmination in the psychoanalytic tradition where the penetration of the inside of the body to unveil the hidden realities of the individual subconscious reflects a radical separation of inside from outside (Benthien 2002).

The interplay between the visible and the invisible, surface and depth, is subject to a great many strategies of interpretation and staging (Benthien 2002: ix). Elias (1978) argues that understandings of the individual in terms of inside and outside that are used in our culture to assert the independence of people as worlds in themselves separated from their surroundings, is not the experience of people in all cultures. Models of the body that focus on the individual reflect a particular western viewpoint rather than a generalised model of being (Strathern 1988, 1992; Busby 1997). They have difficulty in accounting for group dynamics such as agency as a group phenomenon (Becker 1995), or temporal solidarities (Sofaer Derevenski and Sørensen 2005). Though people may recognise the physical boundaries of their bodies they may not see their identities as also enclosed by their skin. Rather they may view themselves as being bound up with others through group membership and action (Strathern 1988; Sofaer Derevenski and Sørensen 2005). Becker (1995) describes a model of shared intersubjectivity where experience is contingent on how the self is situated in a relational matrix, that intersubjectivity and interaction with others being responsible for the construction of identity (Toren 1999, 2001).

In recent years, in disciplines other than archaeology, the distinction between the inside and outside of the body has been increasingly brought into question. The implantation of technological devices and transplant medicine have led to a forceful abolition of the classical distinction between internal and external, resulting in a political 'domestication of the body' (Virilio 1994: 108–9; Benthien 2002: 11; Rixecker 2000). Haraway's influential work on the interfaces between humans, machines and animals has played with disrupted and destabilised categories, exploring their implications and further undermining the inside : outside dichotomy by focusing on cyborgs as the fusion of the organic and the technical (Haraway 1991). Writing on cyberspace and cyberpunk has discussed the ways that people transcend their skin and reconfigure bodies and space through new ways of communicating (Featherstone and Burrows 1995). Performers such as Stelarc have sought to pierce and break the skin, reinventing and extending bodies through new technologies.

It is, however, debatable whether pre-Enlightenment notions of the porosity of the body were ever completely replaced, and thus whether the abolition of distinctions provoked by new technologies really represents a radically new view of the body. Pre-Enlightenment attitudes still hold sway in, for example, reactions to disabled or grotesque bodies which display unfamiliar boundaries and which are perceived as projecting out into the world through protruding body parts or the exposure of the inside (Bakhtin 1984; Benthien 2002; Porter 2001). The skeletal archaeological body is arguably in many ways analogous to the grotesque body in that it extends out into the world and lacks boundaries that are familiar, or indeed boundaries at all. As the skeleton has no skin or flesh, in archaeological settings the point at which the body ends is indistinct, merging with the grave, objects and context which surround it. Furthermore, as with the grotesque body, reactions to the skeleton may be ones of revulsion or loathing based on superstition and morbid associations. While recent technological developments would seem to have brought us full circle in realising the permeability and fluidity of the body, perhaps in the words of Latour (1993), 'We have never been modern'. Given the characteristics of the archaeological body, rather than a dichotomy between inside and out, reconfiguring its boundaries in terms of the 'pre-modern' extension of the body into the world may be a more appropriate model for reconciling and exploring its different aspects.

Latour (1993) argues that social life is not a pure construction of meaning but mutually constructed from 'heterogeneous materials' including bodies, technology, material culture and minds, each of which enrols and orders the others in fluid and shifting combinations (James et al. 1998). In doing so, the boundaries between bodies and other materials become blurred and the body is extended into the world through its association with material culture. A particularly pertinent example of this approach and how it can be used to explore the relationship between bodies and objects comes from the work of Place (2000). In an ethnographic study of a paediatric ward, Place describes the way in which bodies are intimately combined with material culture through tubes and other equipment connecting the body to medical apparatus. These enable detailed examination of the internal organs, which are symbolically monitored through signals or traces. The boundary of the body is extended and circumscribed by both corporeal (human) and non-corporeal (technological) elements. The body is, in this sense, 'technomorphic', and can grow and change shape by the addition of new technological artefacts. The boundary of the body is unclear. Is it enclosed by the skin or bounded by the technologies used to treat and monitor it (James et al. 1998)?

Archaeological contexts can be considered as parallel situations to that described by Place (2000). The body of a person lies in intimate contact with artefacts in a grave. The grave constructs and restricts, forcing the person and objects into association. It envelops the body and, as a human creation, is itself a form of material culture. In this setting one is again forced to question where the boundary between the person and material culture lies. As the skeletal body lacks the skin and flesh of the living, it becomes difficult to draw a unique line around it, sealing it off from the material world as the core of the body, itself composed of many separate bones, becomes exposed and externalised. Here too the body is technomorphic as the boundary of the body is extended and unclear in relation to the world. It is also being symbolically monitored through a process of cultural negotiation. Just as the doctor in Place's study constantly maintains the relationship between the patient and the symbols and signs produced by the medical technology through interpretation of those signs, the archaeologist has to maintain the relationship between the body and objects through the study of the skeleton as well as through reference to the interpretation of symbolic elements of material culture linked to the perception of the fleshed living body. Each mutually explicates the other (cf. James et al. 1998). The relationship between body and world can potentially take many forms and a variety of associations be created. 'The issue becomes not whether there exists a "real" body as distinct from social constructions of it – because this would be taken for granted – but how many different claims to "speak for" this body and enrol it in the service of intentional social action are made' (James *et al.* 1998: 168). The body thus becomes an interpretative resource which is all the more powerful because it is extended outside itself. Both living and dead bodies are technomorphic.

In archaeology, the extension of the body can be identified not only in terms of the symbolic monitoring of the skeletal body through the association of specific objects with particular individuals or categories of people, but also through the interpretation of the skeletal remains themselves. As human bones are potentially affected by the environment and behaviours of the living, they represent the extension into the world of the living subject. Here the body can clearly be understood as a porous entity. What is commonly regarded as the 'interior' of the body holds the potential to become a site for inscription, just as does the 'exterior' of the same body. The ontological difference between inside and outside of the human body is thus less apparent and the dichotomy between them is destabilised. Instead, the difference between the two becomes one of degree and form of inscription rather than a debate over the existence of its connections with the world and its status as a sealed unit. As with the dichotomy between living and dead bodies, the inside and outside of the body are, in fact, inseparable aspects of the same entity.

Nature vs culture

The division between nature and culture is one of the most fundamental distinctions in archaeology. As the discipline that explores humanity through the medium of material culture, archaeology assumes that human beings are unique in their ability to elaborate the world. This belief is often transformed into a celebration of transformation and triumph over nature. Indeed, it is in the transcendence over nature that the essence of humanity has been said to lie (Ingold 1998: 24). Claims for a distinct social domain made by Durkheim have provided further grounds for the separation between the natural and the cultural (Franklin 2002; Macnaghten and Urry 1998). The distinction between the natural and the cultural lies at the source of the idea that archaeologists study artefacts (Ingold 1998: 34), and the disciplinary structure of archaeology is firmly rooted in a division between the study of the natural (biological, physical and chemical) and the cultural (people and objects). In archaeology, the biological body has become synonymous with nature as an equation is made between osteoarchaeology as a branch of investigation linked to the biological sciences and the investigation of the biological body as a natural entity. By contrast, the social, interpreted and discursively orchestrated body is regarded as the province of culture.

The origins of many of the internal tensions that sit within dichotomies between perceptions of osteoarchaeology as atheoretical vs interpretative archaeology as theoretical, dead vs living bodies and inside vs outside can be traced to the recurring 'master dichotomy' (Ingold 1998: 22) between nature and culture. The dualism nature : culture renders the natural world an object for study (Brück 1999) in which the deceased and skeletal archaeological body has come to be identified as a residual biological object of nature to be investigated and observed by means of scientific paradigms. This focus on the body as organic is reinforced by the assumption that the individual is no longer present from the moment of death and what remains is a shell or husk (Hallam *et al.* 1999: 64–5). Identification of the dead body as natural is the legacy of the Enlightenment where a focus on understanding natural laws deadened nature itself by changing it 'from a life giving force to dead matter, from spirit to machine' (Macnaghten and Urry 1998: 10) as part of Descartes's vision of the body as a machine directed by instructions from the soul (Turner 1996: 9). This contrasts with the culturally constructed body of the living subject (Ingold 1998: 35) whose actions (resulting in and from material culture) are studied through the humanities. It remains a paradox that, in the words of Ingold (1998: 24)

humans – uniquely among animals – exist simultaneously in two parallel worlds, respectively of nature and society; in the first as biological individuals (organisms) and in the second as cultural subjects (persons). As organisms, human beings seem inescapably bound to the conditions of the natural world. Like other creatures, they are born, grow old and die; they must eat to live, protect themselves to survive and mate to reproduce. But as persons, humans seem to float aloof from this world in multiple realms of discourse and meaning each constitutive of a specific historical consciousness.

In recent years, however, the general validity of a division between nature and culture has come under increasing general scrutiny and attack. Researchers have sought to reassess the relationship between them, often by identifying either nature or culture as the key axis, fixing investigations within one or the other. The nature : culture division has been exposed as a particular product of western thought which is not always cross-culturally applicable (Descola and Pálsson 1996). Perceptions of the world are culturally specific and cosmologies are contextually variable (Ingold 1992; Olwig 1993; Bird-David 1993; Descola and Pálsson 1996). The distinction between humans as cultural and animals as natural has been increasingly problematised as the continuities between them have been made visible in, for example, the transmission of spongiform encephalopathy from cows to humans which attacked the human mind, the part of human beings that supposedly makes them distinct from other species (Dickens 2001: 93–4). The difficulties involved in distinguishing between the natural and the human environment have also been stressed (Ingold 1993a; Evans and O'Connor 1999) and the relationship between them has been problematised (Thomas 1993b; Tilley 1993; Duncan 1996). On a more prosaic level, human interaction with the environment is widely perceived both as the source of environmental problems and as the key to their solution (Milton 1993; Weeratunge 2000). People do not live in isolation from the world but are involved within it (Thomas 1993b), and in a purely physical sense the world cannot be considered entirely wild or untouched. Increasingly, nature is no longer seen as an external independent variable (Franklin 2002).

Despite their considerable value and the range of insights emerging from such critiques, they have had relatively little impact on perceptions of the body in archaeology. The body as nature is understood in terms of essential qualities, inherent forces and tangibility (cf. Williams 1983; Franklin 2002). An emphasis on human ecology has drawn osteoarchaeology into environmental archaeology through an integrated exploration of the human niche and the ways in which human groups related to the environment around them (Sofaer Derevenski 2001). Thus the kinds of questions that are traditionally asked within osteoarchaeology are to do with external forces that act on the human organism, and discussions are concerned with how it responds to such pressures. This position is closely linked to a Marxist-inspired form of ecology in which the body, as part of nature, has independent causal properties of its own that are involved in the structuring of the social in a dialectic between the real and the abstract that links nature and culture, while retaining a distinction between them (Benton 1989; Franklin 2002). In such a perspective, the social is embedded within nature, thereby offering a solution to the dichotomy between nature and culture.

In practice, however, the human ecology perspective often simply converts humans into entirely biological phenomena that adapt to their circumstances (Ingold 1996). Consideration of the nature of the relationship between nature and culture seems to occur almost entirely through a re-evaluation of understandings of the natural environment. The identification of the body as natural is taken to an extreme in evolutionary psychology and allied Darwinian approaches to archaeology which identify humans as organisms with common, stable hard-wiring whose behaviour is solely the product of their genetic inheritance (e.g. Dunbar *et al.* 1999;

Pinker 1999). Biology thus becomes responsible for all forms of human behaviour through the conflation of biology with genetics. The ways in which the body is modified and adapts through use in specific settings are ignored, although many features of organisms are not straightforward products of evolution (Dickens 2001; Rose and Rose 2001). In archaeology, confidence in the authenticity of the biological body has also led to the use of biological metaphors in the discussion of human social life, such that nature has become a metaphor for culture (e.g. Shennan 2002).

This position can be contrasted with arguments for the social construction of nature in which the body is a cultural production. In contrast to claims for the authenticity of the body, here the body has been the focus of post-modernist and post-structuralist thought that often seems to deny the physical and genetic reality of the body (Dickens 2001: 96). Here bodies are fluid, shifting, multiple and fragmented. Foucault is often regarded as a primary exponent of the constructed body. In his discussion of sex and desire in *The History of Sexuality*, Foucault (1978) emphasises the importance of discourse in the construction of historically specific attitudes towards the body through the articulation of ideas surrounding sex in writing and speech. For him, notions gain reality only through this articulation, which intersects with discourses of power that prohibit and allow the expression of desires. Notions of the 'natural' and discussions of sexual practices regarded in the nineteenth century as 'contrary to the laws of nature', illustrate for him the transience and instability of claims for the existence of nature outside of such discourse. In archaeology, Foucault's influence can be seen in a wide range of work, much of which has largely focused on representations and ornamentation of the body (Meskell 2000a), rather than skeletal remains. Its emphasis on power has been subject to strong critique (Meskell 1996; Montserrat 1998), although others (e.g. Hamilakis *et al.* 2002b) still see an important place for Foucauldian writings as analytical tools in archaeology. In relation to the study of the physical body, however, a Foucauldian perspective poses particular and different problems as it becomes difficult to understand corporeality in terms of both social and organic processes. For example, although disease may be constructed within a particular set of social relations through the clinical gaze of modernity (Foucault 1973), people are not simply dupes and disease has an organic reality (Anderson 1995).

In archaeology, the body seems to be aligned either as an organism on the side of biology or as a person on the side of culture. In the first case, the body as object is separated from the subject. In the second case, 'the subject is split off from the organism as object, leaving the latter bodiless, reduced to an inchoate mass of biological potential' (Ingold 1998: 27). An appreciation of the physicality of the body as an organism leads to the displacement of culture while 'the embodiment of culture leads to nothing less than the disembodiment of the organism!' (Ingold 1998: 27). An emphasis on the human body that focuses on biological mechanisms leaves out the influence of the world. Conversely, in many archaeologies of the body, humans often seem to remain categorised as intangible, essentially cultural, phenomena.

A central tension therefore exists 'between the thesis of humanity's separation from the world of nature, and the counter-thesis that humankind exists alongside other life-forms on an uninterrupted continuum or chain of being' (Ingold 1990: 209). Much of the conceptual exchange across the nature : culture divide serves only to underline the pitfalls of this dichotomy and the ways that each camp continues to practise its own form of reductionism (Descola and Pálsson 1996: 11), exaggerating the parallel science : humanism divide within modern archaeology. Given that osteoarchaeology is the study of the physical remains of past people in archaeological contexts, it forms an important site for the interrogation of this tension.

Between nature and culture

The subtext that lies beneath a distinction between natural and cultural bodies and that forms one of the most 'tenacious mental habits' (Duden 1991: vii), is the notion that the biological osteological body is immutable, unchanging and stable in contrast to the culturally constructed body, which is temporally variable and flexible. In this scheme, the biological body, while seen as a vehicle of social and cultural activities, is differentiated and divorced from culture and society, implying the existence of some kind of biological entity that is separate from the cultural life of the body (Duden 1991: vii; Ingold 1998). Importantly, this perception of the stability of the biological body lends it a reality or authenticity that the changeable, and perhaps more fickle, cultural body is seen to lack. Furthermore, this notion of stability is taken to mean universality in the human body, such that bodies are everywhere regarded as similar. This is further extended to an association with the impersonality of the biological body, which, separated off from culture, not only is seen as common to all, but cannot hence be regarded as in any way individual or personal in the way that the fluid culturally constructed body is. This underlying belief in the biological body as fixed even permeates feminist thinking, although this is ostensibly denied by statements that we cannot understand our biological selves except through culture, thus perpetuating an 'additive model' of culture superimposed on to nature (Birke 1999: 44).

Assumptions of stability operate at a number of levels. At the molecular level, the natural biological body is often conflated with genes on the basis that genetics are seen as determining who we are, and are therefore given and stable (Ingold 1998; Birke 1999; Fox Keller 2000). Ingold (1998: 29) points out that in standard accounts the genotype is identified as the locus of organic form and that it provides the formal specification of the organism in terms of its phenotype. However, the stability of the body can be questioned here as genetics do not provide a straightforward blueprint for the organism to follow. There is no reading of the genetic code that is not part of a process of development, and genetics are active in processes throughout the life course in that they may contribute to a propensity to develop particular characteristics under certain conditions (Ingold 1998: 30).

Birke (1999) considers assumptions of stability inherent in discussions of physiology. She points out that a central principle of the systems of the functions of the body (the nervous system, the endocrine system, the immune system and so on) is homeostasis: the body's ability to maintain a constant state. Such systems are, however, always on the go. In healthy individuals they continually undergo minor changes and corrections, while in disease states they may fluctuate more widely outside of normal gross limits. For Birke, the biological body is changing, changeable and transformable (Birke 1986, 1999). This insight is of particular significance for an osteoarchaeological approach to the body. As with all cells, bone cells renew themselves. This turnover of bone cells means that, assuming normal rates of adult turnover, cortical bone has a mean age of twenty years and cancellous bone one to four years (Parfitt 1983). Bones grow and their structure changes with age (Brickley and Howell 1999; Carter et al. 1987; Currey 2001; Jee 2001). Bone is also plastic and responds to the direction of stress placed upon it by remodelling when loads are placed upon it through exercise or repeated activities (Ruff and Runestad 1992; Knüsel 2000; Cowin 2001; Jee 2001). This means that over time the skeleton is transformable. The systems of the body are interlinked so that changes in one can impact on, or be expressed in, another. Thus alterations to the endocrine system can lead to morphological changes expressed in the skeleton (Jee 2001). Similarly, the build-up of muscle tissue through exercise can lead to enlarged bone growth at their attachment sites (Dutour 1986; Robb 1998b). Constraints are nonetheless imposed by one part of the body on another, so that overall appearance in adulthood may change relatively little (Birke 1999).

Over the whole life course the body changes dramatically. The perceived constancy of the body is often implicitly understood in terms of stasis but represents only part of a continuum of processes of growth, maturity and senescence from birth to death. For example, while people are born with genital sexual characteristics, the skeletal expression of sex changes over the life course as a result of changing levels of hormones. Hence skeletal determinations of sex can only be reliably obtained following the development of adult sex characteristics (Mays and Cox 2000). Changes to the body form the basis upon which age estimates can be made, such as the sequence of dental development or epiphyseal fusion in the subadult skeleton (Scheuer and Black 2000). Changes can also take place over time through everyday activities as the body is affected by specific life-way choices and repeated activities that can cause modifications and accelerate inevitable degenerative changes to the skeleton (Larsen 1997; Kennedy 1989). A significant corpus of the osteoarchaeological literature deals with the possibilities and difficulties provided by changes to the body over the life course as well as their use, misuse and calibration. Indeed osteoarchaeology relies on the interrogation and understanding of human morphological change as vital to its method and is increasingly interested in examining the complex interaction between human physiology and life-ways.

The biological body does not, therefore, conform to notions of stability, constancy and independence often associated with ideas of nature. Throughout the life course the body is both subject and product of processes and is constantly modified. Structures of the body are constantly changing from the moment of conception until death. Process and structure are inseparable (Toren 2002). The mutability of the body is a physical reality that arises not only from inevitable physiological changes but also from the relationship between such processes and social life. The speed and the end point of processes of the body are not always predictable (Dickens 2001), particularly if one takes into account the potential for interaction between different processes and human intervention in them. Furthermore, individuals are unique in the degree to which they may (or may not) display evidence of such processes. 'If it is worth using the term at all, "nature" is no more than the provisional outcome of local processes, the current state attained by a universe of systems whose ultimate states will always defy prediction' (Clark 2000: 12). Rather than being static, the biological body is fluid in life and death. It is never pristine. However, the balance between inevitable physiological processes of growth, maturation and senescence and interaction with the world may change at different points of the life course (Crews and Garruto 1994). The challenge then becomes the identification of the relationships between different causal entities, configurations of contingencies, and time spans (Franklin 2002: 45).

There are, of course, limits to how fluid the osteological body can be. For instance, a disabled body cannot 'cure' itself (Birke 1999). Nonetheless, given that the changeability of the human body is one of its key features, how does the mischaracterisation of the osteological skeletal body as stable arise? Jones (2002a: 21) argues that attempts to use 'social physics' (Bourdieu 1990) or an empiricist philosophy to understand society places artificial constraints on understanding and turns it into a static object in order that it can be measured. In terms of the study of human remains, osteoarchaeology sees only the end point in a series of processes in the life–death continuum. It is often difficult to order events in the biography of an individual from their bones and so it seems safer to relate only to this end point rather than to think in terms of process. An additional reason may be confusion between notions of *stability* and *regularity* of the physical body that can be linked to Descartes's legacy of the body as a machine, and understandings of machines as stable and repeating. Stability ought to be distinguished from regularities that exist in processes such as the development of human morphology or in disease where biological processes follow particular patterns or stages defined by the limited range of responses of human tissue and regulatory mechanisms (cf. Lovejoy *et al.* 2003). Regularity is vital to the practice of osteoarchaeology as it allows estimates and diagnoses to be made, and comparisons between individuals and groups to be carried out. It is because of this regularity that exceptional bodies, such as those of the deformed, become all the more striking.

The identification of regularity in local processes common to individuals offers the opportunity to distinguish a series of fixed points in the recognition of the body derived from the identification of stages within these processes. At the most basic level, regularity allows the universal identification of a body as a body, in that the features of the body are present (for example, the head, arms and legs) to distinguish between the sexes, or to say that someone is relatively old or young. This principle also lies behind the ability to reconstruct faces and the estimation of stature (Prag and Neave 1997). Since the biological body is common to all humans, the identification of common points between otherwise unique individuals means that regularities in patterns and common features of the osteological body are seen as impersonal and formal properties. This can be contrasted with ways in which the cultural body is seen as personal and subjective through its identification in terms of the construction of social identity. Implicit in this association is the assumption that the identification of the personal is meaningful, whereas the commonality of the biological is not.

This assumption does not hold up under closer scrutiny. In as much as regularities form part of and 'belong' to individuals, they are also personal. Indeed, the biology of individuals can be considered their most personal aspect. In a study of ageing ballet dancers, Wainwright and Turner (2004) demonstrate how the physical processes of ageing or injury mean that the failure of the body to accomplish tasks that were once 'natural' requires the renegotiation and reinvention of self-identity in relation to changing bodies. The processes of ageing and injury are regular in that they happen to all individuals sooner or later and, when they occur, follow the same biological 'rules'. The regular thus becomes the personal as social relations are referenced to the experience of common biological processes (Rival 1993; Franklin 2002). Here, the regularity and commonality of biological processes enable social understandings (Birke 1999), while at the same time the constraints placed on human lives by the physical limits of the human body challenge radical social constructionist views.

While what is made of regularities of the body may be variable in time and space, the culturally constructed body is not necessarily entirely fluid. It too relies on a degree of stability to build constructions upon. Indeed the limitations of the biological body are prerequisites for construction to take place as constructions and discourse require fixed points in order for that discourse to be meaningful to others. Discourse cannot float free from observation and the stability of discourse allows shared understandings of the body at particular points in time and space. Cultural understandings of the body rely on the identification of regularities in form and process which are socially meaningful, although the form taken by those meanings can vary. Thus the identification of physical differences between people has been held to form a key aspect of the construction of identity in terms of what people make of the body. This has been extensively discussed in archaeology with regard to the relationship between sex and gender (see Hill 1998; Gilchrist 1999; Sørensen 2000; Meskell 2001), but is also vital for distinctions made in terms of age and ageing through the growth and senescence of the body (see James et al. 1998; Sofaer Derevenski 2000a, 2000b; Joyce 2000a), as well as being pertinent to the social exclusion of disabled bodies (Shay 1985; Roberts 2000a; Waldron 2000; Porter 2001). On this basis, interpretative archaeology relies heavily on investigating patterns hooked on to fixed points, particularly in the identification of regularities of sex and age, hence the emphasis given to sexing and ageing in archaeology. Categorisations of the physiology of single bodies are culturally negotiated on a collective level as biological changes are incorporated into social life. Social relations are understood to be natural, as the natural becomes cultural and the cultural becomes natural.

The biological body has a social presence (Turner 1984). In particular, the osteological body is directly implicated in the construction of identity as the skeleton forms the supporting framework around which the body is hung, giving shape and form to bodily features, thereby permitting categorisations. The skeleton shapes the body, and the lives of people are shaped by their bodies (Turner 1996; James 1993; James *et al.* 1998). The biological body is not separated and external to the person. In as much as the body has a physical presence and the processes of the biological body are regular, the body also has an extra-discursive reality. In other words, it is not formed purely through patterns of discourse. This reality, however, need not be conflated with an idea of nature. To assert the importance of biology and biological fluidity does not mean one heads inevitably towards biological essentialism (see Birke 1999). Similarly, as Franklin (2002: 43) points out, it is important not to confuse the identification of social constructionism in nature with its simultaneous denial as an extra-discursive entity. The body may be a focus for discourse, and disciplinary practices may be cultural constructions, but this does not mean that the world is an undifferentiated mass that is brought into focus only through the lens of discourse. The body is a physical reality amenable to the senses *and* discursively ordered that is embedded within space and time (Franklin 2002: 38), and these concepts are not mutually exclusive (Birke 1999). At any point, and in different circumstances, the body may sit within degrees of biologism and degrees of cultural constructionism. The reason why human remains are so complex and fascinating is precisely because local biological processes and human cultural life are inextricably intertwined at the single location of the body. The methodological basis and usefulness of osteoarchaeology for archaeological interpretation rest on a philosophical and 'real' relationship between people and the world. An absolute division between nature and culture is therefore unhelpful to archaeological interpretation.

For the body, it is not always possible to see where nature begins and culture ends. Nonetheless, asserting the complex character of the body does not mean that people themselves recognise a relationship between the body, society and the world, or make particular explicit philosophical statements that link nature and culture. As Astuti points out, living people do not necessarily see the world in non-dualistic ways and investigating or describing 'natural dualism' as how they see themselves in relation to the world as 'a socially and cognitively practicable form of thought does not amount to endorsing its philosophical validity' (Astuti 2001: 431). We therefore have to separate frameworks for archaeological practice in the analysis of the body, from how past people may have perceived their bodies and relationship to the world. We need to use a framework that rests on an explicit exploration of the relationship between biological processes and social life in order to investigate how people organise their relationships, whether this is natural dualism or alternative forms of constructions. As Harding (1991: ix) says, 'if natural sciences and their preoccupations in reporting on nature are embedded in and complicitous with social projects, then a causal, scientific grasp of nature and how to study it must be embedded in – be a special area of – causal, scientific studies of social relation and how to study them'.

Unconventional bodies

The binary conventions of archaeological practice sit uneasily with the archaeological body. The skeletal body and its investigation have particular characteristics which suggest that oppositions between theory and lack of theory, living and dead, inside and outside, nature and culture are difficult to sustain. In this sense, archaeological bodies are 'unconventional'. If we insist upon binary conventions, either we cannot incorporate osteoarchaeological insights, or we cannot access meanings given to the body. Neither purely biological nor purely interpretative approaches adequately represent its specific character and potentials.

Destabilising the conventional oppositions that structure the archaeological analysis of the body leads to an ontological shift in archaeological understandings. In particular, it brings the divide between the inanimate and the animate, objects and subjects, the material and the cultural into question, and traditional distinctions between bodies and things into the spotlight. This does not mean, however, that we need to see the body in unstructured terms. In the next chapter I want to build on some of the issues raised here by exploring their implications, and to propose a framework that links osteoarchaeological and interpretative approaches to the body.

4   Material bodies

> The body is a most peculiar 'thing', for it is never quite reducible to being merely a thing; nor does it ever quite manage to rise above the status of thing.
>
> Grosz 1994: xi

The separation between objects and people is deeply ingrained in the discipline. This distinction traditionally rests on a division between animate subjects that belong to the cultural world and inanimate objects that are part of the material world (Jones 2002a: 65). Accordingly, the living body is regarded as a person but as soon as the transition to death is made, the body becomes an object. Death not only describes an event horizon, but precipitates an ontological shift in the perception of the body that assumes a sudden change in its qualities.

If, however, as I have argued in the previous chapter, there need not be any sudden dramatic material transformation at the point of death and, in addition, the human skeleton may retain a social presence in death even though it becomes inanimate, then there exists some continuity on either side of the death event (Hallam *et al.* 1999). The porous character of the body means that it is difficult to identify clear boundaries between the body and the world. Furthermore, the divide between the living body as cultural and the skeletal body as natural cannot be sustained as bodies will always be both, albeit in different and changing configurations. An ontological shift in perceptions between the living body and the dead body, based on an assumption of a clear distinction between the cultural subject and the material object, is called into question.

Rather than treating the body as given, the particularities of the archaeological body demand that its materiality be made explicit, and the specific form taken by that materiality explored in relation to the division between bodies and artefacts in archaeology. As Grosz (1994) suggests, in relation to the body we need to think more closely about what a 'thing' is. Interpretations need to take account of the potential and limits of the material on which they are based. We need to consider how it is that we formulate interpretations as we move back and forth between observations and theoretical assumptions (Jones 2002a: 61). This chapter therefore explores the material specificity of the archaeological body.

Bodies and objects

The traditional distinction between bodies and objects can be problematised on a number of levels (see Tilley 1999a and b; Jones 2002a; Fowler 2002; Knappett 2002). Most frequently, the distinction between objects and people has been questioned from the side of the object, the concern being to establish how like people objects can be. Bodies act as metaphors for objects whose parts may be named after those of the body (Tilley 1999a; Caiger-Smith 1995). They can also take on qualities associated with human bodies. Objects, like people, are said to have histories, biographies and social lives (Appadurai 1986; Kopytoff 1986; Hoskins 1998), or act as metaphors for the self, standing in for people in the absence of a body (Hoskins 1998). Objects are said to be 'active' (Tilley 1999a). More recently they have also been identified as 'animate' and 'social' in the same way as people, since they are always bound up in their social projects (Jones 2002a: 35).

Less archaeological attention and explicit theorisation have been devoted to illustrating how like objects people can be, although the identification of excavators on archaeological sites as 'digging machines' who are functionally equivalent to objects has been pointed out (Lucas 2001; Yarrow 2003). This may be because when the body is discussed as an object this is understood to be real rather than metaphorical and is consequently deemed to be disturbing, dangerous and open to accusations of essentialism. The effect has largely been to deter theorisation and investigation of bodies as objects in archaeology and, influenced by feminist thought to which critiques of the subjugated and objectified body have been central, to react against the categorisation of bodies as objects by encouraging politically ideal perceptions of the body that impose a universal equality. A basic distinction between people as sentient beings and inanimate objects is thus reinforced rather than investigated.

Nonetheless, in society at large and in the modern global economy, the body is frequently identified and treated as an object (Scheper-Hughes 2001: 1), while metaphors used for the organic are frequently material (Haraway 1976). Furthermore, despite claims that the Enlightenment turned people into objects through developments in medicine and science, the commodification of the body has a considerable genealogy (Scheper-Hughes 2001) which is not limited to the West (Lock 2001). Diverse and widespread forms of the objectification of the body both pre- and post-dated Descartes. The ways in which bodies and body parts are treated as objects by being bought, sold, stolen, made captive and inherited, have been explored through work on, for example, the commercial trafficking of human organs, tissue and genetic material (Scheper-Hughes 2001; Pálsson and Harðardóttir 2002), grave robbing to supply a sixteenth- and seventeenth-century demand for corpses for dissection (Richardson 1987; Lock 2001), the collection of medieval relics (Bynum 1991; Lock 2001), colonialism and the native body (Creed and Hoorn 2001), slavery (Walvin 2001), bodies and body parts taken as trophies of war (Bass 1983; McCall 1999), prostitution (Schwarzenbach 1998), apprenticeship (Murray and Herndon 2002) and an 'economy of substances' in the British Neolithic that saw elements of disarticulated and defleshed bodies exchanged as gifts in cycles of reciprocity (J. Thomas 2002: 42). Such commodified bodies differ from the deliberate deployment of bodies and body parts as material statements. The latter may also be commodities but differ in as much as they are elaborated and materially transformed with the deliberate aim of turning them into objects through manipulation and transformation after death as in, for example, mummification (see Meskell and Joyce 2003), or the use of human bones for musical instruments, tools or ornaments (Gould 2002; Hester 1969; Mclean 1982). However, like material statements, commodified bodies may be regarded as real rather than metaphorical objects.

Interpretations that identify the body as an object do not require that their authors endorse them as sociological or political statements. Rather, they illustrate that the categorisation of people as objects is significant and allows the acknowledgement of difference. Investigations into the commodification of bodies and body parts through their exchange, for example, avoid the pitfalls of essentialism by recognising that these bodies also hold symbolic and ideological meanings (Scheper-Hughes 2001). Archaeologists who follow the lead of social theorists may 'all too easily fall prey to an uncritical moralizing rhetoric, a knee-jerk reaction against body commodification to which still attaches fairly "primitive" sentiments of bodily integrity and sacredness which demand that the body be treated as an exception' (Scheper-Hughes 2001: 3). Commodities are material and the commodification of the body highlights its material foundation. People can become objects *because they are material*.

The materiality of the body

The materiality of the body has been increasingly recognised and referred to as a source of inspiration in archaeology (e.g. Hamilakis *et al.* 2002b; J. Thomas 2002; Meskell and Joyce 2003). The use of the term 'materiality' in relation to the body would seem to imply a concern with its material basis. On the whole, however, identifying the materiality of the body has not meant interrogating the material basis of that materiality or investigating it in terms of its material composition. The specific physical forms that materiality may take are rarely explored and it is most often taken as self-evident. Where explicit discussions of the materiality of the body are carried out they are instead frequently concerned with the production and effects of meanings (Hallam *et al.* 1999). In archaeology, as in other disciplines, while the body has been extensively discussed in terms of its significance, its ontological status has received little attention (Hallam *et al.* 1999: 63).

Following on from Foucault (1978) and Butler (1993), materiality is often identified as constructed. Archaeology's recent concern with text and textual models for material culture have meant that Foucault's philosophy and Butler's comparative literary analysis have been easily absorbed into archaeology. A concern with text in archaeology and the use of a textual model for material culture where relationships between signifiers and signified are arbitrary (Hodder 1991), and meanings play within an endless web of signification (Tilley 1991), make the material 'pawns in a more important game where what really matters are concepts, symbols, ideologies and human agents' (Boivin 2004: 63). This desire to react against the perceived limits of the material, such that the material is the 'other' of the 'discursive' (Bapty and Yates 1990), would seem to imply that the study of material is not enough and that it is in some way impoverished, leaving archaeology the poor cousin of other disciplines.

The body is frequently understood as being given meaning through historically specific forms of power articulated through discourse and language, allowing the expression of different understandings of bodies and persons in different times and places. J. Thomas (2002), for example, works with this notion which allows him to suggest that disarticulated Neolithic bodies in British long barrows need not be understood in terms of discrete individuals but as 'partible persons' (Strathern 1988). J. Thomas (2002: 37) cites a key passage in Butler (1993: 2): 'What constitutes the fixity of the body, its contours, its movements, will be fully material, but materiality must be rethought as the effect of power, as power's most productive effect.' Here the material basis of the body (its 'fixity') is distinguished from its materiality (an 'effect'). The focus on its constructed materiality allows escape from determinism and ethnocentrism as it situates the body within a social frame. The importance of specific social and historical contexts to the study of the body (described here in terms of power relations that constrain and enable perception and action) is an important insight. Yet, this focus also leaves the material basis of the body unproblematised by regarding it as set. In archaeology the investigation of the material forms the foundation of the discipline and it therefore ought to be precisely what is in question.

Previous attempts to recognise the body as a tangible entity have seen the use of 'materiality' in the sense of 'corporeality' or the 'lived reality' of experiences of, and through, the body. Here materiality is seen as the foundation of embodiment where the effects of the materiality of specific bodies lead to particular embodied experiences of individuals. Drawing on Butler (1990, 1993), Joyce (2000a and b, 2003) and Meskell and Joyce (2003) see the enactment of cultural practices as leading to the materiality of the body. In Joyce's work on the construction of gender in Aztec children (Joyce 2000a), gender is performed as a constant reiteration of regulatory norms, and it is in the performance of these norms that the materiality of the body emerges through the production of the gendered body by means of dress, the use of gender-specific objects, and the disciplining and regulation of the body in life-cycle rituals that include permanent modification and marking of the body. In performance, the actors become their roles and are produced by them.

This approach is exciting and inspiring in many ways, particularly in terms of its temporal dimension, exploring the creation of particular forms of living subjectivities through performance. What is missing again, however, is an appreciation of the physical characteristics of the body that underpin these human experiences. This gap is also present in allied approaches that build upon the physical characteristics of the body to take account of senses, sensations and movement (e.g. Hamilakis 2002). An insistence on bodies first and foremost as living persons means that, while bodies are identified in terms of their materiality, they are not understood in terms of their 'material'. To emphasise the material, as opposed to the materiality, of the living body is seen to reduce its humanity. The study of the physical body is seen as the province of biology which is, in turn, seen as part of an undesirable Cartesian legacy of the body as machine separated from the mind. Yet to state that the materiality of the body is the basis of the corporeality of the cultural subject without considering the material grounding of the body itself seems unsatisfactory.

For the archaeological body, a more detailed scrutiny of its material composition seems appropriate. Renfrew (2001, 2004) stresses that material reality takes precedence over words, in that the material reality of the substance precedes its symbolic role. Substances therefore come before the concepts associated with them and some material symbols are constitutive in their material reality. The physical properties of material items bear on how they are incorporated into symbolic schemes and social strategies (Boivin 2004: 64), in terms of both their potentials and their limitations. Indeed, the properties of materials are what allow them to have symbolic value.

To illustrate this point, Boivin (2004) draws on the work of Connerton (1989) who uses the example of Victorian clothing to show how the social meaning of clothes is connected to their physical properties. The heavy, constricting and complex clothing worn by women not only symbolised their inactivity, frivolousness and submissive nature but also produced these behavioural attributes, while men's clothes signified that they were serious, active and aggressive and allowed them to be so. Extending Connerton's argument to archaeological settings and a specific concern with soil and clay as materials, Boivin (2004) suggests that the inherent physical properties of materials used to build houses in the Neolithic of south-east Europe and the Near East, not only shaped the form that the houses took by permitting and constraining new forms of material culture, but that in doing so they also contributed to new social and cultural patterns through the codification and elaboration of categories of difference, as the creation of walls and pots encouraged division and compartmentalisation.

The material properties of clay also make it particularly suitable for marking time through plastering and replastering of floors and walls to highlight particular points and rituals in the human life course (Boivin 2000). This line of thought can be applied to other materials. As a further example, metal has particular qualities as it can be recycled, reused, transformed from one form into another, bent, twisted and incised (Needham 1998; Sofaer Derevenski 2000b; Sofaer Derevenski and Sørensen 2005). In the Copper Age of the Carpathian Basin, copper was made into spiral arm rings. The pliability of the material and the design of the rings allowed them to expand with the physical growth of the individual who wore them, and to be removed at a given point in the life course. Here people drew on the material properties of metal through metallurgical technology to articulate changes in age–gender identities (Sofaer Derevenski 2000b). Material symbols are therefore not arbitrary, and the properties of materials need to be taken into account when considering past meanings (Boivin 2004).

Since the social meanings attached to the body cannot be separated from its physical reality, arguments regarding the importance of the properties of materials imply that we need to return to the body as a tangible entity with its own particular properties. If we take on board the general point that physical qualities and material consequences are an inseparable dimension and defining parameter of semiotic significance (Malafouris 2004), and we accept that bodies do have such significance, we might ask why an exploration of material qualities should apply only to objects and not to bodies, especially since objects can be regarded as bodies and bodies as objects.

This point applies equally to living and dead bodies. As with living bodies there is a need to ground the materiality of the dead body in an appreciation of its material qualities. The human skeleton is often taken as a material given, a view grounded in an assumption of the organic nature of the body which will deteriorate and rot like other dead matter (Hallam *et al.* 1999: 64–5). Thus the skeletal body becomes a point from which to start analysis (cf. Armstrong 1987), rather than a focus of exploration in terms of its constitution and the basis of materiality. Hallam *et al.* point out that the materiality of dead bodies is not obvious but has to be made evident through description of its physical features. These may be responsible for the strangeness or 'otherness' of the dead body and predominate in the absence of attributes such as warmth, muscle tone, facial expression and speech (Hallam *et al.* 1999: 61). Using the examples of neonatal death, Persistent Vegetative State (PVS) and attitudes towards the dying on a geriatric ward, they demonstrate how the binaries 'alive' and 'dead' can be destabilised through varying descriptions of the body which bring into question its once unequivocal material qualities. The constitution of the body becomes key to its perception and categorisation as dead. For sociologists Hallam *et al.* (1999: 62), material qualities have to be spelled out in order to define the status of a body.

These insights take an important step towards relating the materiality of the dead body to its physical qualities. In archaeology, however, the antiquity of the bodies in question, and their skeletal rather than fleshed form, mean that the same emphasis on the material description of bodies as physically living or dead is not seen as methodologically necessary. Here the issues at stake in terms of relating materiality with material are different, in as much as archaeologists try to access the living from the dead. The material qualities that are described archaeologically are therefore to do with reconstruction of a past state rather than establishing a present one, and hence are necessarily of another sort. A discussion of the materiality of the archaeological body needs to take into account the material qualities of the body in life.

To reinstate the material in the archaeological study of the body by proposing the importance of its physical qualities is not to identify materiality in terms of irreducibility and determinism, but rather to ask what the particular physical qualities of the body are that lend it to manipulation and construction. The materiality of the body can be brought into being only on the basis of material qualities, while the special characteristics of the archaeological body demand appreciation of the particular ways in which materiality is anchored to material. The relationship between material and materiality underpins the interpretation of the body and to understand it we need to examine the relationship between the material and the biological.

The material and the biological

Archaeological accounts of the material foundations of the body are somewhat inconsistent. On one hand, the body is situated in the classical distinction between nature and culture described in Chapter 3, with the dead body on the side of nature because it is biological, and the cultural seen to confer animation through living bodies and objects. On the other hand, the material and the biological are seen as mutually exclusive categories rooted in a division between inanimate objects and animate subjects, where the material is associated with lifelessness and the biological is seen to confer animation. The classification of bodies as biological, and objects as material, precludes the possibility of an explicit exploration of the material foundations of the body that links materiality, material and meaning. The division between the biological and the material is problematic because while bodies move from subjects in life into the realm of objects in death on account of being inanimate, they continue to be identified as once living people on account of being biological. In death, the archaeological body continues to be seen as a biological phenomenon that needs to be treated differently. In recognition of this problem, skeletal bodies are commonly regarded as 'biological objects', somewhere between the biological and the material. This forms a rather awkward resolution as it sets the skeletal body apart from other foci of archaeological interest and seems to create a special category within which ideas of what constitute the biological shift. Here the biological is not what *is* animate but what *was* animate.

Outside archaeology, however, the concept of biology refers to process, not to substrate (Birke 1999), and is concerned with mechanisms of the body in life. Biology is also a very broad concept. Substances may be biological (in other words subject to biological processes) but there are many different biological substances with many different biological qualities. Furthermore, the categories biological and material are not mutually exclusive. The substances of the body can be regarded as simply a subset of the wider category that encompasses all materials. In other words, biological substances are material. The biology of the body refers to the specific material qualities of the body which are related to biological processes that form and renew the matter of which it is made. In order to explore the specificity of the body in archaeology, we need to be clear about its material constitution and its material qualities.

Material constitution and material qualities

While various substances of the body can be analytically distinguished at a number of levels, bone – the primary material of the skeletal body – is a composite material (Lucchinetti 2001). In this sense, bone is analogous to other archaeological finds such as pottery which is made up of a range of clay minerals, temper and water. While each of these single constituents can be separated out, they are usually considered to be part of a single material which has a range of physical properties. Similarly, mud bricks are made from a mixture of straw and mud and have their own range of material properties. These properties are, of course, dependent on the particular mix of ingredients, but it is the potential and limitations of the material, rather than its individual component substances, that are of interest. The skeletal body can be understood as *a material* with its own suite of physical properties.

Like other materials, human bone has mechanical properties that are related to its composition. When dry, it is about 70 per cent mineral (hydroxyapatite) and 30 per cent organic (collagen) (Mays 1998). The mineral component lends bone rigidity while the organic component allows a slight give which lends bone its strength (Mays 1998). Living bone and dead archaeological bone differ, however, in that the decomposition and degradation of the organic component mean that dead bone is much more brittle than living bone (Mays 1998). In life, bone is a living tissue that forms part of a complex network, responding and communicating with other parts of the body. Bone constantly degenerates and is renewed. Bone is therefore dissimilar to other common materials found on archaeological sites, as living bone turns itself over by producing more bone. Teeth are also frequently preserved as part of archaeological bodies and consist of three hard tissues: enamel, dentine and cementum. Enamel is almost entirely inorganic with a chemical composition similar to that of bone mineral, while dentine is about 75 per cent inorganic and 25 per cent organic. Cementum has a composition similar to that of bone (Mays 1998). Dentine and cementum are living tissue while enamel is not. The human hard dental tissues lack a blood supply and are not turned over.

A key material quality of the skeleton, and of the human body, is its plasticity. The principle of plasticity underlies the bioarchaeological approach to the study of the human skeleton. Plasticity is a key concept in contemporary human biology (Roberts 1995; Hulse 1981) and is defined as 'systematic changes within the person in his or her structure and / or function' (Lerner 1984: xi) or 'the capability of being moulded' (Roberts 1995). It affects both the soft tissues and the bony structures of the body and refers to a process of functional adaptation to the environment, where the notion of environment is understood as comprising both so-called natural and cultural phenomena (Roberts 1995). While plasticity is an adaptive response, it differs from acclimatisation (a short-term reversible adaptive process) and evolution (genetic adaptation over generations) (Garruto 1995; Schell 1995). Here it is used as a concept related to dynamic irreversible ontogenetic modifications that are not heritable (Lasker 1969). Plasticity begins in utero. Thus it is increasingly understood that effects of the mother's environment in relation to the class and health status of pregnant women influence the child's intrauterine experience and the body of the foetus. Mothers who eat poor diets, use drugs and consume excessive alcohol during pregnancy are more likely to have intellectually impaired children (Dickens 2001), while smoking, poor maternal fat stores and heavy weight-bearing activity in late pregnancy lead to a lower neonatal bone mass and increased risk of osteoporosis later in life (Godfrey et al. 2001; Cooper et al. 2002). The effect of nutrition on human growth has been the subject of numerous studies showing that improved nutrition leads to greater body size (Boldsen 1995; Bogin 1999, 2001), as exemplified in studies of migrants and their children (see Roberts 1995; Coleman 1995).

The notion of plasticity also provides a framework for understanding synchronic and diachronic contrasts between otherwise similar human groups through skeletal responses to damage, mechanical stress or disease. Following traumatic injury, over time bones may heal, sometimes with considerable deformity (Roberts 2000b). Conditions of prolonged and continued stress imposed by habitual or occupational activity can cause bone to deform with the development of irregularities of osseous and dental tissues (Kennedy 1989; Rubin et al. 1990). Bone remodelling is a functionally adaptive skeletal response to applied stresses in order to maintain integrity in support and movement (Rubin et al. 1990; Goodship and Cunningham 2001). Wolff stated that 'the form of the bone being given, the bone elements place or displace themselves in the direction of the functional pressure and increase or decrease their mass to reflect the amount of functional pressure' (Wolff 1892 cited in Kennedy 1989:134). The mechanical load applied to living bone through, for example, weight-bearing or muscular tension therefore influences the structure of bone tissue, in terms of both morphology and density (Lanyon et al. 1982; Lanyon 1987; Cowin 2001), although the complexities of the relationship between stress trajectories and trabecular architecture have been increasingly recognised and form a focus of investigation (Cowin 2001). Remodelling is greatest under cyclical loading, as in movement (Martin and Burr 1989).

One of the most well-known and frequently cited examples of bone remodelling is Jones *et al.*'s (1977) X-ray study of the arm bones of professional tennis players. They found that the thickness of the cortical bone in the humerus of the racket arm of the players was on average 30 per cent greater than in the non-playing arm (Mays 1998). Stirland (1993, 2000) identified an increase in the dimensions of the left shoulder of male individuals from Henry VIII's flagship the *Mary Rose* along with reduced asymmetry compared to contemporary individuals, and non-union of the acromial epiphysis, and interpreted these people as archers. Weiss (2003) found that male ocean rowers had more robust humeri than river rowers or not rowing at all, although humeral robusticity was difficult to attribute to specific activities as the upper limbs are used for a range of actions and differences may be related to overall activity levels. Bone mineral is lost when the physical strains on bones are decreased (Goodship and Cunningham 2001). Patients who are confined to bed for some time lose bone mineral but regain it when normal activity is resumed (Donaldson *et al.* 1970; Uhthoff and Jaworski 1978). For bone remodelling, stressful or strenuous activities that begin early in the lifetime of an individual elicit the greatest osseous response as the bones of children are more plastic than those of adults (Knüsel 2000; Currey 2001), although the potential for remodelling, as for plasticity in general, exists throughout the life course (Roberts 1995).

Bone may also respond to stress with accelerated degenerative changes to joints (osteophytosis and osteoarthritis), which result not only from the inevitable process of ageing but for which, in general terms, the primary contributing factor is mechanical stress on the skeleton (Radin *et al.* 1972; Radin 1982; Peyron 1986; Larsen 1997). Stress may be activity or lifestyle induced (Dutour 1993) and the skeleton may therefore be affected by changes that are produced through a lifetime of interaction with the world, including learnt actions, labour, habits and states. Repetitive motions integrated into a technical gesture that are the product of occupational or sporting activities are liable to evoke anatomically elective adaptive reactions of the osseous tissue (Dutour 1993). Such skeletal markers of occupational stress are well described in the sports medicine and occupational pathology literature (e.g. Claussen 1982; McMurray 1995; Cooper *et al.* 1994; McKeag 1992). On the basis of these examples, given that the general biomechanics of the considered gesture have not varied appreciably over the course of time, the observation of identical lesions may enable inferences to be drawn regarding the type of gestures (and hence activities) undertaken by skeletal populations (Dutour 1993).

There is a growing body of literature which has examined activity-related change in skeletal samples with varying degrees of success using musculoskeletal stress markers, nonpathological articular modifications, directional asymmetry, cross-sectional geometry of bone, and pathological lesions, the latter including degenerative changes to joints and trauma (e.g. Merbs 1983; Ruff *et al.* 1984; Kelley and Angel 1987; Robb 1994; Baud 1996; Pálfi and Dutour 1996; Sperduti 1997; Stirland 1998; Steen and Lane 1998; Mays 1999; Peterson 2002; Ciranni and Fornaciari 2003; Eshed *et al.* 2004; Stock and Pfeiffer 2004). Kennedy (1989) describes 140 markers of occupational stress reported in published medical and anthropological sources, while Capasso *et al.* (1998) published an *Atlas of Occupational Markers on Human Remains*. At one end of the spectrum, researchers have examined and identified particular skeletal changes related to specific activities such as horse riding (e.g. Pálfi 1992), canoeing and kayaking (Lai and Lovell 1992; Lovell and Lai 1994; Hawkey and Street 1992), or postural and upper limb modifications associated with grinding foodstuffs (Ubelaker 1979; Molleson 1989, 1994; Miles 1996; Bridges 1989). At the other, observed skeletal modifications have been regarded as more general and non-specific indications of lifestyle (e.g. Cohen and Armelagos 1984; Kennedy 1998).

Controversy exists regarding the extent to which it is possible to specifically identify such changes in terms of particular activities (Jurmain 1990). Some researchers remain sceptical about the ability to identify activity-markers in skeletal material (Jurmain 1990; Stirland 1991; Rogers and Waldron 1995; Knüsel *et al.* 1997). Many workers emphasise that the precise aetiology of many traits are currently poorly understood and that 'a specific modification . . . may not be attributable to a single activity pattern, but rather a wide range of habitual behaviours' (Capasso *et al.* 1998 cited in Knüsel 2000). The effects of stress on the skeleton are often described anecdotally and there is a need to accumulate more base-line data on the impact of known activities on the skeleton by examining historically and ethnographically documented populations where possible (Sofaer Derevenski 2000c). Where musculoskeletal stress markers are used, preferential consideration of groups of muscles that function together is desirable (Stirland 1998). In the case of both musculoskeletal stress markers and pathological lesions, not all work done by individuals may be sufficiently stressful to produce an effect on the skeleton. In order not to over-interpret skeletal observations it is necessary to take into consideration the current limits of osteoarchaeological knowledge. In some cases, however, it is possible to identify skeletal responses to particular culturally specific deliberate and sustained attempts at modification and deformation. For example, intentional cranial deformation through head-binding has been practised by a range of human groups, often to visibly express social class or ethnic affiliation, and can be seen in a range of modified head shapes (Ortner and Putschar 1985; Kustár 1999; Lorentz 2003).

Responses to disease also illustrate the plasticity of the skeleton. Disease processes are a form of stress and have a synergistic relationship to the total environment in which people live and work (Kelley 1989; Roberts and Manchester 1995; Roberts and Cox 2003). The prevalence of types of infectious diseases has changed as human life-ways have altered, a classic example of this being the domination and spread of pathogens causing smallpox and cholera in urban communities with a high population density (Kelley 1989; Roberts and Cox 2003). Metabolic diseases, including those related to nutritional deficiency, can give rise to skeletal modifications as in rickets, scurvy and iron-deficiency anaemia (Stuart-Macadam 1989; Roberts and Manchester 1995). Palaeopathological bone changes represent an adaptation by forming bone (proliferative changes), destroying bone (destructive changes), or a mixture of the two (Roberts and Manchester 1995). Proliferative changes may result in the formation of woven bone, indicating that the disease process was still active at time of death, while older lamellar bone may suggest that the process was quiescent or had been overcome (Roberts and Manchester 1995). The so-called 'osteological paradox' (Wood et al. 1992) means that a lack of bone changes in a skeleton need not necessarily imply a healthy constitution. Rather, an individual may have died before bone changes could take place.

While teeth do not remodel in the same way as bones, they too respond to stress and mechanical forces. Stress during tooth formation can result in disturbance to the growing tooth enamel, resulting in pits or a band of thinner enamel known as dental enamel hypoplasia (Goodman and Rose 1990). Dental enamel hypoplasia has been related to a wide range of conditions including fever, low birth weight, starvation, congenital infections and weaning (see Goodman and Rose 1991; Hillson 1996; Larsen 1997), although in some cases, the significance of weaning for their formation may be coincidental (Blakey et al. 1994; Larsen 1997). The rate of tooth wear is related to diet, and patterns of dental macrowear and microwear reflect the relative consumption of foodstuffs (e.g. Smith 1984; Schmidt 2001; see Larsen 1997), as well as the use of teeth for grip in daily tasks (e.g. Turner and Anderson 2003).

The plasticity of the body means that the body is never pre-social and is contextually dependent. There is no gene for plasticity. It is not pre-coded. Plasticity is a developmental phenomenon that exists from birth to death (Lerner 1984: 3). For the skeleton, plasticity, as a material quality of the body, rests upon the physical, chemical and mechanical properties of bone (Knüsel 2000; Cowin 2001) which are, in turn, a function of biological processes. The biology in question here is that of contextually contingent development and phenotypic variation (Ingold 1998; Dickens 2001), where the phenotype is defined as an expression of the genotype in a particular environment (Knüsel 2000), not inherited nor just of genetics and genes (Ingold 1998; Schell 1995; Knüsel 2000). The form that changes to the body take is affected by the life-ways of the body. Thus, while the plasticity of the body arises out of the biology of the body, the two are not the same. Although the material qualities of the body and its potential plasticity are common to all, the experiences and interactions of each person will vary, so different outcomes will emerge. The plastic skeleton has the potential to be altered through human action, even if this is the unintentional consequence of past lives.

Plasticity is not, however, limitless. Nor does it deny the regularities, constancies and continuities that characterise people's experiences. Indeed, to be able to identify plasticity one also needs to identify its constraints (Lerner 1984: 4). Because processes of modification of the human skeleton are governed by its physical properties, types of modification are not infinite, although individual skeletons may manifest it to different degrees. The degree to which the human body may be influenced is complex and multifactorial, being affected by a wide range of parameters including age, sex and predispositions (Bridges 1991; Larsen 1997). Researchers have highlighted that interaction between factors such as nutritional disturbance or disease may influence the real or apparent manifestation of skeletal markers (e.g. Jurmain 1977). One example of this is the observation that osteoporosis and osteoarthritis are rarely found together, leading to suggestions that osteoporosis can protect against osteoarthritis (Dequeker *et al.* 1983; Mays 1996). Constraints are imposed by the organismic features of the human, by the context in which s/he is situated and by his or her experiences (Lerner 1984: 4). Some changes to the body may be temporary, but others may permanently alter skeletal tissue.

Mindful of the resistances in the data there is, nonetheless, broad consensus that osteoarchaeological studies retain potential for yielding insights into the identification of human life-ways (Knüsel 2000). Understanding the plastic quality of living bone is therefore significant for a consideration of dead bone, as its ability to renew and remodel allows consideration of past life-ways from the human skeleton. Osteoarchaeological method rests on an understanding of material qualities by employing a reconstructive approach 'from trace to function' in order to infer processes from their results in the exploration of past life-ways in

archaeological samples (Dutour 1993: 59). This inference is not a perfect reflection of past processes as there are many processes that are not
manifest in the skeleton and leave no trace. Nonetheless, the notion of
plasticity links the living and the dead body as it allows a study of the living from the dead. It also links the humanities and science as it provides
a framework for relating human experience, behaviour, development and
the expression of the body; experiences become explanatory causal constructs in their own right (Sperry 1982).

Materiality

The material qualities of the human body are key to its materiality. The
materiality of the archaeological body, in other words the particular form
that a body may take, can be understood as the material outcomes of
human plasticity at a given point in time. The materiality of the archaeological body is not therefore given and immutable, but follows from the
specific material qualities of the human skeleton that permit or constrain
its change and development. The materiality of each body is context
dependent, temporally described, produced and unique. Nonetheless,
because the plasticity of the body is not limitless, and people have common experiences, or are situated in contexts with common social values,
bodies may have common expressions (albeit to different degrees). The
materiality of the body is the product of social relations in that the traditions, values and skills of the living may be expressed as a result of
the plasticity of the body, but it is not produced in a purely discursive
manner. It exists in a very real way where actions have the potential for
often predictable material consequences. In this sense, the materiality of
the body incorporates culturally specific life-ways that are, in the words
of Ingold, 'literally *embodied* in the organism, in its neurology, its mus-
culature, even in features of its anatomy. Biologically, therefore, English
speakers *are* different from Japanese speakers, cello players *are* different from sitar players, lasso throwers *are* different from archers' (Ingold
1993b: 470 original emphasis). Such an understanding of materiality is
a matter of incorporation rather than inscription (Ingold 1998: 26–7).

In a discussion of the relationship between biology and culture, Ingold
(1998: 26) gives the example of walking as a further case of how social
traditions are incorporated into the body. Drawing on Mauss's famous
essay of 1934, *The Techniques of the Body* (Mauss 1979: 97–123), Ingold
points out that although the capacity to walk is universal, people in different cultures are brought up to walk in very different ways. Learning to
walk is not just expressive of social values imposed on the body, but is an
acquired skill that develops in specific settings in particular ways through

walking caregivers, a range of supporting objects and a certain terrain. It is not therefore possible to separate learning to walk from learning to walk in a socially approved manner (Ingold 1998). For Ingold, walking is biological, in that it is part of the *modus operandi* of the human, but it is also social – not because it is expressive of values that somehow reside in an extra-somatic domain of collective representations, but because the walker's way of walking is responsive to others in the immediate environment. 'The making of meaning is . . . a social process but . . . it is also a function of the anatomy of human being' (Toren 1999: 86).

Materiality is thus brought into being over the life course, emerging over time as a developmental process, and is contextually dependent because the expression of plasticity is contextually dependent. Such a contextual view of development means that the body is constantly reworked and is never finished; 'throughout life the body undergoes processes of growth and decay, and . . . as it does so particular skills, habits, capabilities and strengths, as well as debilities and weaknesses, are enfolded into its very constitution' (Ingold 1998: 26). The materiality of the skeleton is brought about through a lifetime of culturally defined activities and skeletal responses to them, as well as unavoidable universal biological change.

The materiality of the body is the *materiality of process*. It can be identified as expressive of social values and habits, but the body is not a pre-existing passive biological container to be filled with culture (Ingold 1998: 26–7). Both Ingold (1998) and Toren (1999, 2001) point out how humans grow in an environment provided by the presence and activities of others. There is a growing corpus of literature showing that social relations affect how a child develops in later life (Dickens 2001), suggesting that those early experiences become 'biologically embedded' (Keating and Miller 1999: 232). Our experiences are thus related to those of our parents and carers. We literally embody our history and because our history is created through our relations with others, we also embody the history of our relations with them, thereby tapping into their histories too (Toren 1999: 2). As Connerton (1989: 72) puts it, the pasts of people are 'sedimented' in their bodies.

Toren (1994, 1999) makes this point in relation to the spatial disposition of children's bodies in her ethnographic work on child cognition and the learning of hierarchy in Fiji. Here, hierarchical relations are described by people's relative position on an above–below spatial axis within buildings. Children learn routine behaviours that are performed by adults concerned with maintaining the rules of hierarchy and who enjoin youngsters to follow the rules. Children have to accommodate adult concerns by sitting, crawling, walking, clapping or taking food in the prescribed manner. The embodiment of behaviour is key to the process by which these behaviours are understood over time, and to the reproduction of ritual and ritualised behaviour. Toren's concern is with building a theory of mind where cognition is not abstract, but part of an autopoietic (self-creating) organism whose development is a material phenomenon. This is a function of a certain kind of biological organisation, but one that is mediated by intersubjectivity and an artefact of the way that humans embody the history of relations with others (Toren 1999: 127). Traditions and conventions do not exist in any external sense but are bodily phenomena which practice (or rejection) actively leads to particular kinds of bodies. Because materiality is brought about through intersubjectivity, body and mind are linked in a material way (Toren 1999).

One might extend this notion to a consideration of the body where histories and value systems are made material in the skeleton. The health risks run by individuals are related to the culturally specific social categories to which they belong, be that in terms of status (e.g. Robb *et al.* 2001; Kelley and Angel 1987), age (e.g. Chavez and Martinez 1982), gender (e.g. Grauer and Stuart-Macadam 1998; Judd and Roberts 1999; Sofaer Derevenski 2000c), class (e.g. Mascie-Taylor 1990) or combinations of these. Despite the potential problems posed by diagenesis (Radosevich 1993; Nielsen-Marsh *et al.* 2000), trace element or stable isotope work on diet (e.g. Richards *et al.* 1998; Schutkowski *et al.* 1999; Coltrain *et al.* 2003), human mobility (e.g. Sealy *et al.* 1995; Cox and Sealy 1997; Price *et al.* 1998; Bentley *et al.* 2004) and weaning (e.g. Herring *et al.* 1998; Schurr 1998; Fuller *et al.* 2003) have also highlighted the ways that the histories and traditions of individuals and groups are expressed in the body in a particularly vivid manner, adding a new dimension to the axiom, 'you are what you eat'. The skeleton embodies the history of social relationships and is an artefact of those relations. The life experiences of people have consequences for the ways that their bodies and those of others are formed, those experiences driving future actions. Descriptions of skeletal modifications or bone chemistry do not just represent lists of processes or events that happened to a particular individual, but are histories of relations between that person and others created through the constant alteration of skeletal structures and bone composition from the moment of conception until death, interacting with the inevitable age-related processes of growth and degeneration.

The materiality of the body is brought into being in a concrete manner. Emphasising histories, social relations and the dynamics of development in relation to the materiality of the body means that archaeological accounts must take account of its dual character as biological and social. Culture is not a superficial addition to the body, but is part of it in a developmental process that sees the incorporation of cultural norms into the body. Since human ontogeny is a biological process in which sociality is given (Toren 2002), the materiality of the body implies that 'cultural differences *are* biological' (Ingold 1998: 28 original emphasis), or, rather, that we cannot distinguish between biology and culture (Toren 2002; Dickens 2001). This is not to say that the biological and the cultural, or even the sociological and psychological, are indistinguishable as concepts. Rather, because the body is a developmental system, here they overlap and their boundaries are unclear. For Ingold in particular, the body is a living organism whose development forms part of an organic continuum, just as other organisms also develop within the context of their environments; '[T]he social life of persons is an aspect of organic life in general' (Ingold 1990: 208). For Toren, both the biological and the social are required aspects if we are to achieve our respective poises since the behaviour of human beings is a function of intersubjectivity (Toren 2001: 159). The body cannot be understood other than as a whole with an embodied mind that cannot be considered separately from the workings of the body, and a body that cannot be considered separately from an embodied mind (Toren 1999: 4).

This perspective shifts away from mechanistic assumptions about genes *per se* and towards the causal powers of organisms, albeit genetically inherited causal powers (Dickens 2001: 101; Farnell 2000). But this emphasis on what archaeologists might be more used to calling 'agency' does not necessarily require conscious articulation to be expressed as the materiality of the body. As Toren points out, the notion of mind as an embodied phenomenon draws attention to mind as a function of a certain kind of biological organisation, 'but embodiment refers too to the fact that mind is not exhausted by knowledge processes that are or can be articulated by subjects; these are only "the tip of the iceberg" as against those unconscious processes we constitute as knowledge in the body – e.g. particular ways of moving' (Toren 1999: 103).

Materiality and objects

The materiality of the body as a history of relations between people is also a history of relations to objects. Objects are key to social practices and social traditions are thus intimately connected to objects. Without objects and associated actions, social relations have little substantive reality (Renfrew 2001; Sørensen 2000), as there is nothing through which these relations can be mediated. Objects form a focus of shared understandings to which common references are made, allowing our own perspectives to include an understanding of the perspectives of others (Toren

1999). People are defined through people–object relations (Kirkham and Attfield 1996; Sørensen 2000) and, as objects provide the means by which such relations are visualised, they are the basis for practices that result in repetition, reproduction and tradition (Sofaer Derevenski and Sørensen 2005). Experiences are held through the material world (Sofaer Derevenski 2000a) and objects therefore play a vital role in the creation of people's histories. Since the development of people is defined through historical intersubjective relationships, and such relationships necessarily involve objects, the body is also literally created by objects.

In the French anthropological tradition, the relationship between people, objects and body actions has long formed a significant focus of study. Leroi-Gourhan (1945) pioneered work on how the '*technique*' of doing things – in other words the actions of bodies – is related to the objects that people use. He was interested in how the significance of tools is in the gesture which makes them effective, and how different kinds of objects can be linked with different forms of actions (Fig. 4.1). He recorded a variety of ways that objects falling within different classes are used, such as objects used for hunting and fishing, objects used for grinding and pounding, objects used for carrying, or objects for fire making (Leroi-Gourhan 1943, 1945). This approach has had a significant legacy, being employed to analyse in detail the gestures and skills required to learn crafts (Roux and Corbetta 1990; Roux 2000), or ergonomic studies of the complexity of muscle actions involved in seemingly mundane activities such as sitting or brushing teeth (Arcadio *et al*. 1973). With few exceptions, such as Ingold's work on skill and attention (Ingold 1993b, 2001a and b), this approach has been somewhat neglected in Anglo-American archaeology, perhaps because it has tended to focus more on meaning and process, and less on underlying mechanisms of social transmission. However, it is precisely because of the latter that the insights provided by the French tradition offer a way into thinking about the potential ways in which the material world is literally involved in creating the physical body. Since objects are involved in skills performed by the body, and different objects require different skills, this leads to different kinds of bodies (Ingold 1993b, 2001a and b). It is therefore through the study of technique and body gestures that the skeletal implications of the use of objects in contextually specific social relations can be explored.

In terms of the skeleton, it is possible to see this in, for instance, the potentially contrasting skeletal implications of different methods of carrying (Fig. 4.2). Merbs's (1983) study of the Inuit indicates that carrying burdens using a tumpline may increase the frequency of lesions in the neck that are associated with high frequencies of disc herniation as well as accessory articular facets at the sacroiliac joint (Trotter 1964;

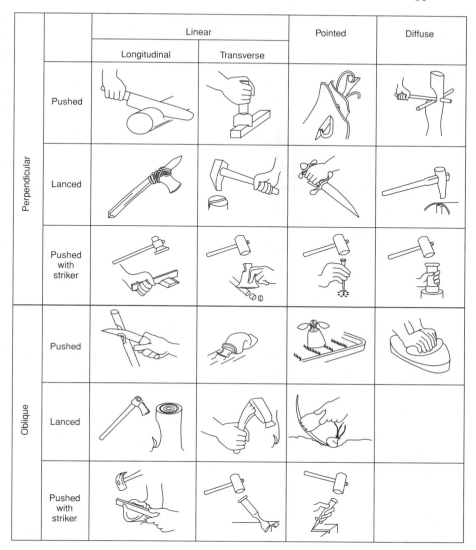

Figure 4.1 The relationship between gestures and objects (redrawn after Leroi-Gourhan 1943)

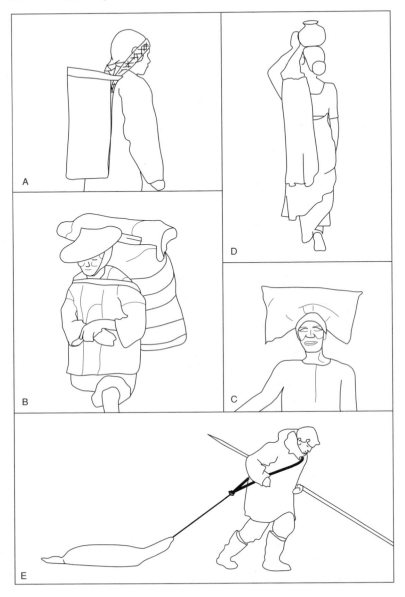

Figure 4.2 Different methods of carrying: a) Using a tumpline b) Using a band across the chest and shoulder to support a basket c) On the head without additional support d) On the head supported with one hand e) Dragging

Merbs 1983; Lai and Lovell 1992). Using a band across the upper chest increases the frequency of lesions in the thoracic region (Merbs 1983). Women carrying creels supported by a strap across the breastbone and round the shoulders on the Scottish island of Ensay show joint remodelling and eburnation on the facets in the upper thoracic segment of the spine and progressively increasing prevalence of osteophytes on the anterior vertebral bodies in the lumbar region (Sofaer Derevenski 2000c). Levy (1968) and Scher (1978) report on spinal cord injuries in porters who commonly carried up to 200 pounds (>90 kg) sacks of grain or other produce on their heads for short distances. Injuries were found to affect both the upper and lower cervical regions. Women who typically carried bundles of firewood or pots in the course of their household duties were also found to be affected (Scher 1978). Flexion-rotation injuries were the most common, followed by evidence of either vertical compression or hyperextension injury. Neurological consequences such as paraplegia typically resulted when the lower cervical region was involved. In archaeological samples, severe joint changes in the cervical spine have been related to the practice of carrying loads on the head (Lovell 1994). Pickering (1979) found that the degree of osteoarthritis in the spine and left arm of females was greater in prehistoric agriculturists than hunter-gatherers and speculated that this pattern may have resulted because agricultural products were carried by females on the head as in south Asia today. In her study of the sample from Abu Hureyra, Molleson (1994) suggested that load-bearing on the head led to the development of a buttressing support in the upper vertebrae, osseous remodelling being a response to activity-induced stress. Among the Sadlermiut Inuit, a high prevalence of severe joint changes in the lumbar segment conforms with ethnographic records which indicate that men often lifted or dragged heavy objects such as animal carcasses or building materials. Such behaviour may have tended to stress the lower back, especially since the Inuit habit was not to bend the knees when lifting (Merbs 1983). In each of these examples, who does the carrying is situated within a social framework that variously relates to gender, age, ethnicity and class.

Day-to-day, people may use a range of different objects that combine to produce the materiality of the body. The roles of specific objects are not therefore always easy to identify in the skeleton. It is also difficult to approximate the frequency or intensity of activities (Jurmain 1990: 92). On a general level, however, since objects are material resources and hence form part of the material conditions of existence, it is possible to extend arguments surrounding the relationship between objects and the materiality of the body to suggest that the body is modified by capital (cf. Dickens 2001). Those with few material resources, such as the homeless or unemployed in our own society, are more likely to suffer poor health and disease (Dickens 2001). Epidemiological work that identifies the environment or way of life as having major direct effects on human well-being asserts the social as well as the biological causes of illness and short lives (Dickens 2001: 103). Thus changes in lifestyle over time and major historical transitions can be related to parallel shifts in health and disease (Hawkey and Merbs 1995; Roberts and Cox 2003). Palaeo-demographic work using skeletal samples also illustrates the relationship between social conditions and human welfare. For example, Grauer and McNamara (1995) suggest that children entering the nineteenth-century Dunning Poorhouse in Chicago with its crowded conditions and dynamic migrant population were more likely to die than those in the city and county in general. In these examples, 'Body and mind, the biological and the cultural, the material and the ideal, are aspects of one another, rather than separate and dialectically related phenomena' (Toren 1999: 4).

The idea that people are materially created through their relationships to other people, to objects and to material resources in general, offers something of a challenge to traditional archaeological thinking. As archae-ologists we are familiar with the idea that objects are created by people. So, for example, people make pots and we consider the meanings, ideas and attitudes that people put into material culture. We are perhaps less routinely aware of the ways that people are literally created by objects and the material world, although the implications of this are profound. It becomes impossible to separate what is natural and what is cultural, what is inside the porous body and what is outside it. The boundaries between bodies and objects break down as they are mutually imbricated in com-plex networks (Latour 1993; Jones 2002a; Knappett 2002). Bodies are constructed from a vast array of resources (Prout 2000) as the materiality of the body is brought into being over time.

This complexity, instability and contingency of the archaeological body suggests, following Latour (1993), that it is a hybrid formed 'in and through patterned networks of heterogeneous materials; it is made up of a wide variety of shifting associations and disassociations between human and non-human entities' (Prout 2000: 14–15). Bodies are 'quasi-objects' and 'quasi-subjects', 'where the boundary between the human and the non-human is shifting, negotiated and empirical' (Prout 2000: 14–15). While such hybridity is not without limits (Strathern 1996), this is of sig-nificance since it implies that we cannot make one kind of entity alone – bones or objects, osteoarchaeology or interpretative archaeology – do the explanatory work. What we need to do is to try to tease out the relation-ships between different aspects involved in the construction of the body in specific contexts and to distinguish between different forms of hybrids

(Van der Ploeg 2004). The materiality of the body can be identified in terms of slippages between the categories of object and body, just as in the previous chapter we have seen that the archaeological body also brings into question the dichotomies dead and alive, inside and outside, nature and culture. Such a perspective on the materiality of the body, with its emphasis on networks and development, dispenses with the biological: social opposition (cf. Ingold 1998: 26) as the plasticity of the body allows it to change through interaction with the world. For archaeology, this means that it is impossible to separate the osteoarchaeological study of the body from its interpretative study. People interact with the world and both form, and are formed by it. Furthermore, because the materiality of the body is a historical and material phenomenon (cf. Toren 2002), it not only forms a topic for archaeological investigation, but archaeology has a particularly apt and distinctive contribution to make to its study. The question then arises as how one might work this through methodologically, and it is to this that I now wish to turn.

Material bodies

In order to consider the methodological implications of the materiality of the body we need to take a step back from materiality and return to material. The body is material, and mind and body are inseparable precisely *because* they are fundamentally material. This suggests that, while it is important to acknowledge that the body is an organism whose development forms part of an organic continuum (Ingold 1998), for analytical purposes it is possible to substitute notions of the body as an organism with that of 'material'. As Harré (1991: 33) puts it, 'A great part of what it is to be just this person is to be embodied as just this material thing.'

This reconfiguration has a number of implications for archaeology. Bodies are *material* and *social*, just as objects are. This further blurs the boundaries between bodies and objects and, in doing so, offers a methodological equivalence to bodies and objects situated within networks since it no longer assumes a pre-given division between material objects as extra-somatic and bodies as somatic. It thus resolves a central tension in archaeology arising from the perceived dichotomy between persons as biophysical entities and objects as socio-cultural entities. The distinctive status of the body in terms of a separation between bodies and objects becomes less clear.

Foregrounding the material places the body within a specifically archaeological frame of reference since the study of the material is the foundation of the discipline. From a methodological perspective, bodies and objects fall into the same archaeological domain and a distinctive archaeological contribution to the body grounded in an appreciation of the material becomes possible. Osteoarchaeology becomes the study of a particular form of material (the human body) sitting firmly within the discipline, on a par with the investigation of pots, flints, soils or any other find. This shift of emphasis towards the material also allows us to relate living and dead bodies together in terms of a common denominator, that being their material foundation. Once the material is highlighted, the ontological status of the body as living or dead is not what matters, but the trajectory of the developmental process and the form that the materiality of the body takes for any given individual. From this angle, what is important about the body from an archaeological perspective is not just whether the body is an organism, or social, or both, but how the specific material potential of the body is expressed in a contextually dependent and archaeologically accessible manner.

Although archaeology has traditionally concentrated on the production of social meaning through the interpretation of artefacts, the explicit identification of the body as material reinstates it in the archaeological project. If bodies and objects are both material and social, because the processes that bring them about are both material and social, and we cannot separate bodies and objects because they are mutually implicated in those processes, then from a methodological perspective the body may be understood as a form of *material culture*.

The body as material culture

By dissolving the perceived dichotomy between persons and artefacts, the notion of the body as material culture provides a potential vehicle for reconciliation between science and humanism on a meta-theoretical level. Indeed, it radically changes the subject–object relationship; the body becomes the object of study but, as a person, is also an active subject. From this perspective, the study of the body does not aim to illustrate the uniqueness of the human being set apart from nature (see Ingold 1998: 25), but to reveal the complexity and interconnectedness of human relations.

Treating the body as a real material object is often regarded as a dangerous move, being allied to attempts to identify essential truths or basic ontological certainties (Scheper-Hughes 2001: 2). Yet, as we have seen, the very contingency of the body resides in its materiality. In this sense, the notion of the body as a form of material culture is not simply a heuristic device. Identifying the body as material culture represents a way of thinking about the body that refers to a specifically archaeological approach resting upon its specific material qualities. It recognises the need for interpretation of the body, but is not an endless play of signs or the 'add culture and stir' model of material culture that Ingold suggests is often meant by the term where 'to make an artefact you first take an object with certain intrinsic material properties and then add some culture to it' (Ingold 1998: 35). Rather, it is used here to indicate that the skeleton is a site of articulation of the material and social (cf. Haraway 1991).

Identifying the body as material culture aims to access the particularities of the body in a specifically archaeological manner by understanding the development of individual bodies in contextually specific social settings. The emphasis is on the processes by which bodies are formed (considered analogous to processes involved in the production of other forms of material culture), agency and action, through the ways that the social lives of people are implicated in the creation of their bodies. The transformation of bodies over the life course involves acts of fabrication and destruction (cf. Featherstone and Hepworth 1998: 164) and one might add to Douglas's famous statement that 'what is carved in flesh is an image of society' (Douglas 1966: 116), that what is made in bone is also part of that image. The body is the 'ground of human action' (Gatens 1996: 68), enabling acknowledgement of cultural and historical specificities, moving beyond traditional assumptions of bodies as given.

Such an approach is about accessing what people literally made of their bodies in the broadest sense, irrespective of whether this was consciously articulated or not, within a framework that is meaningful to twenty-first-century archaeologists; this version of the body, studied through the methods of osteoarchaeology, is meaningful only in terms of transmitting knowledge to the archaeologist, rather than as a medium for past individuals for whom this avenue of communication was inevitably inaccessible. It does not necessarily mean that people were aware of modifying their bodies, that moulding the body is part of a deliberate social project of the self (sensu Giddens 1991), or that people set about creating particular forms of bodies demanded by society (Foucault 1977), although this may sometimes have been the case and people may have deliberately done so (see Lorentz 2003).

In common with other forms of material culture, the body is not the product of unmediated individual intentionality (Shanks and Tilley 1987: 98). Since bodies have common material properties, and broadly similar effects upon it will result from similar social arrangements, the emphasis on process that lies at the heart of the notion of the body as material culture moves away from recent theoretical understandings of the body that have seen it in terms of methodological individualism. Individuals are structured in terms of the social, and hence material culture is socially, rather than individually, constructed (Shanks and Tilley 1987: 98). Such an approach sits easily within established osteoarchaeological methods where, precisely because of individual variation and the need to look for patterns, studies of the skeleton can be meaningful only if they are situated within the context of a wider sample, or a comparison with other populations.

In addition to the theoretical insights generated by recognising the body as a form of material culture, this approach also has a number of immediate practical advantages. If bodies are regarded in the same way as objects, then they can become foci for archaeological investigation using archaeological methods targeted at understanding material culture. The empirical nature of the process of knowledge acquisition from the skeleton is not much different to that applied to other more readily recognisable artefacts, such as pots or flints, in terms of the recording of objects by measuring, drawing, photographing, identifying and classifying morphological differences (cf. Shanks and Tilley 1987: 114). As Jones (2002a: 21) points out, the rigorous application of precisely defined scientific methods should be regarded as a strength.

An archaeological tendency to split the study of the body, with the body as artefact on one hand and the body as lived experience on the other (Meskell 1998a, 2000a), is an artificial division on which to take sides. There is a middle ground that identifies the body as an object from a methodological perspective in order to *do* archaeology but that aims to explore experiences of life through an appreciation of the physicality of the body. Recognising human bodies as material culture does not preclude the acknowledgement of difference but aims to explore this through their materiality. If we believe in the value of archaeology, and archaeology takes as its focus the study of the past through the material world, then expansion of the remit of material culture to the body should hold a positive, rather than negative, connotation.

In the following chapters I want to explore the utility of the body as material culture to inform on contextually specific relations between people, taking gender and age as axes of investigation. The sex and age of the body have become dominant features of the skeleton for archaeologists. However, current archaeological practice in the examination of gender and age holds significant tensions between method and theory.

5   Sex and gender

It is not that our bodies naturally evince gender differences, or any other
form of difference, it is rather that these differences are produced as an
effect upon them.
                                                                Moore 1994: 85

Archaeologies of sex and gender are key locations for contesting the
body as they are arenas in which the relationship between bodies differently regarded as biological or social comes to the fore. Here, the divide
between osteoarchaeology and interpretative archaeology has almost
inevitably led to tensions arising primarily from the practice of associating artefacts with bodies, and the consequent superimposition of cultural gender on to biological sex. This chapter examines the implications
of these tensions in terms of the relationship between method and theory, and the potential for integrating the study of the skeletal body into
the study of gender without falling back on biological determinism. It
explores how the idea of the body as material culture may be useful in
helping to resolve the tensions between method and theory in the archaeology of gender.

Sex, gender and the skeletal body

The body has a pivotal role in the archaeology of gender as its ontological
status is debated through contrasting and varied theoretical notions of
the relationship between sex and gender, and the ways that these may, or
may not, be linked to the physical body (Sørensen 2000; Meskell 1996,
1998a, 2001, 2002a and b; Joyce 2000a and b, 2002b; Gilchrist 1999;
Conkey and Gero 1997; Gibbs 1987; Nordbladh and Yates 1990; Knapp
and Meskell 1997). In practice, however, the relationship between biology and culture seems to create peculiar difficulties for archaeologists
in separating gender from the logic of natural difference, particularly in
burial contexts. Associating artefacts with particular categories of bodies
tends to lead to the superimposition of culturally constructed gender on
to biological sex, resulting in the de facto conflation of sex and gender

(Sofaer Derevenski 1998). There are therefore two levels at which the relationship between osteoarchaeology and interpretative archaeology becomes crucial for archaeological interpretations of gender. The first is the identification of what sex and gender are as categories and the connection between them. The second relates to methodologies used to access sex and gender in mortuary contexts.

It is not my intention here to provide a history of gender archaeology. This has been well described elsewhere (e.g Sørensen 2000; Gilchrist 1999). Nonetheless, because the role of the body revolves around the relationship between sex and gender (Sofaer Derevenski 1998; Sørensen 2000), it is necessary to start by addressing these notions in archaeology.

The articulation of sex in archaeology

Most commonly, sex is understood in terms of biology. It is used as a term to emphasise the innateness and fixity of essential unchangeable biological characteristics. Sex is defined by differences between males and females that are determined at conception and enhanced in subsequent physiological development (Armelagos 1998: 1). Sex differences include chromosomal differences, genitalia, and morphological contrasts in the skeletal anatomy of men and women that are related to hormonal differences between them (Mays 1998; Mays and Cox 2000). At the most fundamental level, sex is based upon observations of the physical characteristics of the body (Sørensen 2000: 45).

In archaeological contexts, sex is most frequently derived through examination of the features of the skeleton. The establishment of sex through the classification of individual bodies as male or female is therefore primarily seen as the province of osteoarchaeology. Reaction against the prioritisation of grave goods has seen the emergence of a commonly expressed concern with accuracy that identifies the use of osteological sex determinations as being more secure than a potentially ethnocentric identification of objects as male or female without reference to the skeletal body (cf. Tarlow 1999: 12). Such accuracy is important for both osteoarchaeology and interpretative archaeology since sex is used as a basic axis of analysis, according to which patterns of skeletal change or distributions of objects are examined; sex differences are not only important to society in terms of human reproduction and the influence they may have on biological processes, but highly visible and socially meaningful. Determination of sex is seen as a vital service provided by osteoarchaeologists for interpretative archaeologists.

Determination of sex in adults normally takes the form of the visual assessment of morphological characteristics, based on observations of sexual dimorphism in skeletal samples of known sex and of radiographs of living people. Osteoarchaeology identifies what is seen in the skeleton as a proxy for what is observed in life because the skeleton is the frame for the flesh. The pelvis and skull are generally considered to be the single most reliable areas for sex determination, the former reflecting functional differences between men and women related to childbirth (Mays 1998; Mays and Cox 2000). Thus although the whole skeleton should be assessed, where just pelvis and skull are available for analysis, morphological methods can have an accuracy of 97% (Meindl *et al.* 1985) with 96% for pelvis alone and 92% for the skull alone (Meindl *et al.* 1985). In a study to assess the accuracy of osteological sexing methods, Molleson and Cox (1993) reported that 98% of the eighteen- to nineteenth-century skeletons of known sex from Spitalfields, London were correctly identified using morphological methods. Although there are schemes based on discriminant function analysis of measurements of the skull and pelvis (Giles 1970; Ditch and Rose 1972), these do not generally offer improvements in reliability over morphological methods (Mays 1998). Sex determination of immature skeletons is more complex. While there are several methods for the assessment of sex in non-adult teeth and bones (see Mays and Cox 2000), these tend to focus on foetal and perinatal infants rather than older pre-pubescent individuals, they have often been applied to small samples and are frequently controversial. For non-adult bones in particular, sexual dimorphism forms a relatively small component of morphological variability, the majority being due to growth (Mays and Cox 2000: 126). However, for both adults and non-adults, sex is identified in terms of regular differences between men and women, or boys and girls, which have universal characteristics. Although DNA analysis is seen by some as the way forward, particularly as a solution to problems of sexing immature skeletons (Brown 1998, 2000; Stone 2000), this currently plays a limited role in archaeology.

Biological understandings of sex as either male or female have, however, been increasingly questioned by archaeologists (e.g. Nordbladh and Yates 1990; Knapp and Meskell 1997; Gilchrist 1999; Hodder 1999; Arnold 2002). Influenced by developments in sociology, the male : female distinction has come under fire in three main areas: first it is argued that that sex is not binary, second that it is not stable, and third that it is a construction rather than a given.

In Chapter 2 I described how critiques of sex as binary argue that it cannot be comprehended through two categories alone as there is a range of variation in the expression of sex characteristics at both genotypic and phenotypic levels. They point to the existence of individuals with chromosomal, gonadal, endocrine and phenotypic conditions including

Klinefelter syndrome (47XXY), Turner syndrome (45XO) and Testicular Feminisation syndrome (46XY). Such arguments verge on biological reductionism in the manner in which they identify sex. Furthermore, the skeletal implications of such configurations are unclear so it is difficult to know how they could be recognised in past populations (Mays and Cox 2000), especially given their relative rarity in living groups (non-XX or non-XY combinations, including Klinefelter syndrome and Turner syndrome, are estimated to average 0.193 per cent of total live births) (Blackless *et al.* 2000: 159). People do not see each other as genes but as bodies in the world.

Such critiques also point to the way that osteoarchaeologists record skeletal material to argue that this suggests that it cannot be classified into simply male and female. For example, both British and US guidelines to the standards for recording human remains advise the use of five categories from which to choose when recording adult innominates (pelvic bones) and cranial features, on the following scale: typical male, probable male, sex unknown, probable female, typical female (Buikstra and Ubelaker 1994; Brickley and McKinley 2004) (Fig. 5.1). In determining sex, osteoarchaeologists record features on the body in terms of a range of options and on the basis of the category in which the majority lie assess the sex of the individual. It is argued that this reflects a continuum of variation in sex that ranges from hyper-male on one hand to hyper-female on the other, and so sex is a spectrum rather than a binary division (Nordbladh and Yates 1990). While there is a wide range of phenotypic variation in skeletal expression of sexually dimorphic traits even within normal XX or XY chromosomal combinations, such an argument, however, misconstrues the principles that lie behind osteological recording which are to do with degrees of certainty in determination, rather than absolute correspondence with a range of sexes. Overall, males and females do fall into two distinct groups because they are dimorphic (Fig. 5.2). What is of importance for sex determination is the strength of dimorphism at a population level since some populations display a greater degree of dimorphism than others. By using a method based on rank scoring, osteoarchaeological practice explicitly recognises potential variation in the expression of sex and, by using a multifactorial approach that takes into account a range of different characteristics, acknowledges the complexity of the process of classification. Scoring methods thus represent a potential range of permutations, but in reality observations fall into two clusters. The variation in expression of sex that exists is not evenly distributed along a spectrum, but exists primarily within two distinct categories. As Sørensen (2000: 47) points out, what is at stake here is not whether sex exists but our ability to classify it.

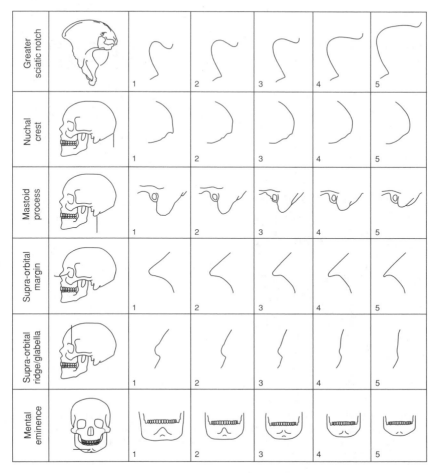

Figure 5.1   Recording categories used to estimate sex in adult innominates and sexually dimorphic cranial features. 1 = typical male, 2 =
probable male, 3 = unknown, 4 = probable female, 5 = typical female
(redrawn after Buikstra and Ubelaker 1994)

Arguments critical of the stability of sex contend that sex is not fixed
at birth and instead focus on the ways that people are able to manipulate
and alter perceptions of their bodies. They are based on an increasing
awareness of changes in understandings of sex in the history of medicine
on one hand (e.g. Laqueur 1990), and on the complexity of sex identity particularly in terms of transsexuals, transvestites, and historical and
ethnographic accounts on the other (e.g. Blackwood 1984; Herdt 1994;

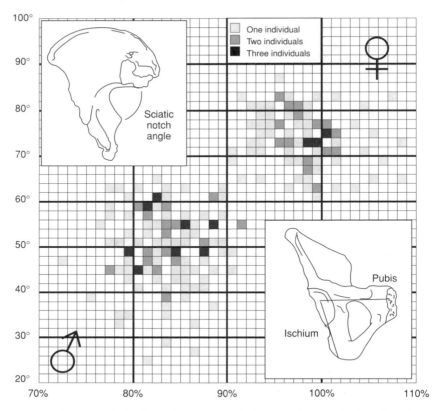

Figure 5.2 Angle of the greater sciatic notch (degrees) plotted against the ischium-pubis index (per cent) illustrating sexual dimorphism in the human pelvis (redrawn after Hanna and Washburn 1953 and Brothwell 1972)

Roscoe 1998). Drawing on influences from psychoanalysis and the work of Butler (1990, 1993), concern with sexuality as an aspect of individual sexed experience has been emphasised alongside the idea that what people make of sex is not just reproductive (e.g. Nordbladh and Yates 1990; Voss 2000; Meskell 2002a; Gilchrist 1999; Hollimon 2000a and b). Arguments for the instability of sex argue that pigeonholing people as men or women fixed from birth on the basis of sex characteristics does not allow for potential fluidity and choice in the expression and experience of sex.

Such critiques, however, do not necessarily mean that with regard to the body sex is changeable. While discussions surrounding the stability of sex have highlighted the ways in which the relationship between the body and desire is complex, historically contingent and culturally understood, variation in attitudes and desires does not mean that recognition of the body as sexed necessarily changes with the construction of sexuality. In osteoarchaeology there is a particular need to retain a distinction between sex and sexuality as it is not possible to determine sexuality from the skeleton. Furthermore, critiques of the stability of sex are to do with the relative importance of the physical features of the body in given situations and the potential complexity of the relationship between self-identity and the body. In the case of transvestites, the deliberate attempt to mask sex in the process of dressing and become another may indeed be said only to reinforce the fixity of body sex characteristics. By removing themselves from the category 'reproductive male' or 'reproductive female', individuals need not necessarily leave the category 'male' or 'female' altogether and become another sex as physiologically they may still appear as men or women. Transsexual changes are a recent medical phenomenon with dubious relevance to archaeological contexts, although pre-pubertal male castrates might potentially be identifiable owing to delayed fusion of the long bones (Leroi 2004).

Critiques of sex as stable tend to ignore osteoarchaeology's implicit and explicit concerns with the ways that the physical expression of sex changes over the course of people's lives as bodies mature and senesce, including the development of sex characteristics in puberty. Interest in these changes arose largely out of a desire for more accurate sexing and an appreciation of the limitations of osteological methods. Nonetheless, this emphasis on expression as dynamic remains radically different to perceptions of osteoarchaeology as simply pigeonholing people as male or female. Within archaeology there appears to be some confusion between sex as a category to which people belong, and the expression of sex within that category which can change over the life course.

Arguments for sex as a cultural construction follow on from an interest in the instability and fluidity of sex. It is argued that, because sex can be fluid it is a produced representation rather than real, and that a binary division of sex into male and female is a regulatory ideal that is the product of discourse (Nordbladh and Yates 1990; Conkey 2001: 344; Meskell 1996, 1998a, 2001; Joyce 2000b; Gosden 1999:146–50; for a discussion see Sørensen 2000: 47; Houston and McAnany 2003: 34). According to this line of thought, biological notions of sex are specific cultural statements created through particular cultural practices that, in archaeology, are those involved in the osteological determination of sex (Claassen 1992). Following Foucault (1978), the process of sexing bodies thus produces sex, which does not exist prior to its description. As evidence of this construction, bias in sexing towards males is pointed out (Arnold 2002). The logical extension of this approach is that osteological determinations of the sex of the human body are redundant to archaeological practice since they are based on universalist principles that are incompatible with arguments concerning the discursiveness of sex. Most of those workers who emphasise the construction of sex do not deal with skeletal material or mortuary contexts, but with studies of the body using textual records or traditional material culture, thereby avoiding the skeletal body.

The idea that sex is a construction because the method that leads to it is a construction would seem to conflate two quite different arguments. It is possible to acknowledge that the particular notion of sex as it is understood in osteoarchaeology is the product of a particular contextual and historical perspective on the basis that the act of creating scientific knowledge is a social act (Harding 1986; Jones 2002a), without suggesting that observable differences between men and women are some sort of irrelevant mirage, or that osteological determinations do not form a useful axis of analysis. The aim of osteoarchaeology is to find ways of analysing the difference and variation that are already observed in the skeleton; osteoarchaeology is not a form of alchemy that is able to create something from nothing. Sex differences also have implications for other aspects of skeletal biology (Armelagos 1998). For example, while a range of factors including diet and exercise may contribute to low bone density (osteopenia) and osteoporosis, these are more commonly found in women due to pregnancy, lactation and menopause (Weaver 1998). Osteoarchaeological efforts at sexing human remains are practices concerned with understanding categories and variability within categories where what is at stake is not the existence of differences between bodies – because this is taken for granted – but the assessment that understanding bodies in this particular way is of importance. As Sørensen (2000: 49) says, 'The essential issue is not whether sex is subject to social categorization, but to what its construction refers, and therefore how sex may have different social foundations and emphasise specific differences between people as it is created and recognized personally and socially.' There may then be many different ways of understanding what sex is under different historical conditions, but this potential plurality does not undermine the relevance of osteological ideas of sex for archaeology.

Sex has a material reality. It is not simply a representation. It therefore seems difficult to do without osteological notions of biological sex. While an osteological approach may be culturally constructed, it has a clear contribution to make as an effective way of dealing with differences between bodies by providing categories that can be investigated in terms of their social relevance in the past. Osteological categorisations of the physical body do not prohibit or remove the need to examine how sex is socially understood and regulated. 'Sex as an analytical concept is not *per se* a prescriptive term establishing either how societies should be or necessarily revealing the variation which social concepts of sex suppress' (Sørensen 2000: 48).

The articulation of gender in archaeology

The development of gender as a concept arose in the social sciences from an awareness of the complexity of relationships and behaviours surrounding the lives of men and women, suggesting that they are not contingent solely upon biology (e.g. Ortner and Whitehead 1981; Collier and Yanagisako 1987; Hess and Ferree 1987; Shaver and Hendrick 1987; Moore 1988, 1994; del Valle 1993; Cornwall and Lindisfarne 1994; Lorber 1994). It was therefore considered necessary to maintain a distinction between sex and gender, as observation of biological difference alone cannot describe or explain social life. As Moore (1994: 71) points out:

the obvious fact of biological differences between women and men tells us nothing about the general social significance of those differences; and although human societies the world over recognise biological differences between men and women, what they make of those differences is extraordinarily variable. We cannot deal, therefore, with the observable variability in the cultural construction of gender across the world or through historical time simply by appealing to the indisputable fact of sexual difference.

Gender is generally considered to be socio-cultural and learnt, although the meaning and application of the term 'gender' is not universal and its relationship to sex is debated (see Sørensen 2000; Sofaer Derevenski 1998; Gilchrist 1999). Differing emphasis has been placed on gender as a structure and organising principle linked to sex, or as the way that individuals understand themselves (see Sørensen 2000). Where archaeology has been influenced by anthropology, gender is seen in terms of relations and interactions, often between broad categories of people (e.g. kin categories such as sister, wife, son, brother). Sociologists often tend to collapse concepts of gender with sexuality and class, and reference to this literature in interpretative archaeology has increasingly coloured the treatment of gender with growing fragmentation and focus on the individual. This divergence in the study of gender is mirrored in the frequent division of gender into ideology, role and identity, the first two of these often being interpreted as referring to gender in relation to society, and the latter in relation to given individuals. These concepts therefore reflect differences in meaning and scale of analysis in discussions of gender, and have become topics of debate in terms of whether gender 'belongs' to groups or individuals.

A contrast in focus between society on one hand, and individual identities on the other, leaves open a middle ground that sees gender in terms of social practice and agency (McNay 2000; Sørensen 2000; Sofaer Derevenski and Sørensen 2005). Here, gender as practice emerges through what people do, while agency allows women and men to negotiate problems and uncertainties with the potential restructuring of gender relations over time (McNay 2000). Such a perspective identifies gender as a social institution where sex is only one of many potential reference points for gender. Gender is a process (Sofaer Derevenski 1998, 2000b; Arnold 2002) that changes over the life course in a socially recognised manner; people are constrained by society's view of who they are but are able to negotiate and alter their perception in relation to pre-existing configurations (Sofaer Derevenski and Sørensen 2005).

Understandings of gender as a cultural construction distinct from sex but related to recognisable physical differences of the sexed body have, however, been increasingly questioned. Following Butler (1990, 1993), the concepts of sex and gender have been deliberately collapsed with both being identified as cultural constructions (Gilchrist 1999; Meskell 1998a, 2001). As part of this trend there has been a move towards seeing gender as a redundant category on the basis that, because biological sex is not binary, sex is culturally constructed and so gender is no longer required (for a discussion see Sørensen 2000). By arguing that sex is also a cultural construction and that the cultural identification of sex and sexuality leads to the cultural construction of gender (e.g. Knapp and Meskell 1997; Meskell 1996, 1998a, 2001; Joyce 2000a and b, 2002b), this position resolves a perceived clash between culture and biology, but it has pitfalls in as much as it needs to take account of the way that biological sex acts to create socially sanctioned 'normalities' (Sørensen 2000: 48). Similarly, although the embodiment of a range of forms of identity has been seen as an alternative to the use of sex and gender (Fisher and Loren 2003), such a solution is problematic, as I have argued earlier in this volume, since, despite its welcome emphasis on corporality, it fails to take account of the physicality of the skeletal body.

Arguing that both sex and gender are culturally constructed does not mean that gender is an invalid notion, or indeed that sex and gender can be used interchangeably. As Sørensen (2000) points out, sex and gender need not be equivalent and maintaining the possibility of both sex and gender allows for a range of possibilities in analysis that collapsing sex with gender as a single form of construction seems to preclude.

While joining sex with gender is a methodologically tempting path as it would seem to get away from the troublesome distinction between biology and culture by placing it all under the umbrella of culture, it then seems difficult to account for the body and morphological differences between the sexes in the skeleton that are effectively out of the deliberate control or manipulation of people. We need to consider gender otherwise we run the risk in archaeology either of falling back into biological determinism, or of cutting ourselves off completely from the possibility of accessing the full range of potential ways that differences between bodies may be socially regulated and understood. The utility of gender as a concept is therefore as it was originally conceived: it provides an explicit distinction between the biological and the cultural. Such an approach does not deny that people have to come to grips with their sexed bodies and that they have sexual experiences, but by allowing for the possibility of gender, a potentially greater complexity of human life can be explored.

In contrast to trends within interpretative archaeology, in osteoarchaeology there is increasing awareness and insistence on the distinction between sex and gender, with specific discrimination between the terms (Pearson 1996; Armelagos 1998; Walker and Cook 1998; Mays and Cox 2000; Grauer and Stuart Macadam 1998; Sofaer Derevenski 2000c). Interpretative archaeology and osteoarchaeology are thus pulling in opposite directions. There remain, however, many more references to sex than gender in osteological papers (Walker and Cook 1998). It is only relatively recently that osteoarchaeologists have engaged with gender, more often being explicit regarding an awareness of the analysis of data in terms of sex distributions in a field where determination of biological sex is seen as a fundamental parameter. In addition, some workers have felt alienated by the language of constructionism often used in the gender literature. Where gender has been tackled it is often conflated with sex by default rather than by design, and workers have failed to identify the distinction between sex and gender in their material. This apparent failure to engender skeletal material (as opposed to the identification of sex differences) may be because there has been a lack of a theoretical frame of reference within which sex may be distinguished from gender with regard to the study of the body itself.

Rigid political positioning by some practitioners of gender archaeology has not been helpful. Too often there has been a tendency to label individuals with gender and to see it as an answer to archaeological questions, rather than to use it as an exploratory analytical tool. Often this is reflected in terms of efforts to classify individuals in terms of gender (in other words to say that grave 'a' is male and grave 'b' is female), or to identify members of third or even fourth genders. While categories are important, their identification may be more useful as a means to an end that allows the exploration of social dynamics, rather than an end in themselves. Furthermore, in practice the classification of gender often tends to assume that gender is stable thereby precluding the fluidity that is a particularly useful element of the concept and that is inherent in understanding it as culturally dependent and learnt. Rather than considering gender in relation to a range of other social factors such as age, status, socio-economic position, ethnicity or religion in order to account for the range of variation in any given archaeological sample (cf. Meskell 1998b; Sofaer Derevenski 1998), gender is often seen as an *alternative* interpretation. Assessments of the importance of gender to a given society are rare. This results in an implicit concentration on fertile adult individuals (automatically excluding children who may comprise one-third of a population (Acsádi and Nemeskéri 1970)), and the presumption that sex and gender are static throughout the life course. The impact of biological change on perceptions of individuals and social categories is rarely discussed. However, responding to the problems of classification by moving away from it altogether also has its difficulties. A focus on individuals in terms of embodied subjectivities that is not tied to sex runs the risk that they become free-floating from meaningful social discourse which works by reference to mutually understood social categories. The problem is how to 'forge an understanding of gender that neither underestimates nor neutralizes its relationship to sex, while at the same time, neither reducing nor negating its social dimension' (Sørensen 2000: 57).

Sex, gender and archaeological practice

Clearly there are a number of potential ways of configuring sex and gender. Yet it is important to recognise that both osteoarchaeological and interpretative approaches share a common concern with diversity, differences and variation, with what generates difference and, most important, what constitutes meaningful differences, albeit using divergent strategies (Worthman 1995). Nonetheless, debates regarding the relationship between sex and gender, and thus about the link between characteristics of the physical body and social life, have potentially serious methodological implications in terms of the relevance of the osteoarchaeological study of the skeletal body to archaeological interpretations. They should fundamentally affect the practice of archaeology, particularly in terms of how we access and understand associations between bodies and objects.

If, for example, one argues that sex is a construction, then the osteolog-ical determination of the physical body becomes less critical to interpreta-tion. Collapsing sex and gender renders associations between bodies and objects unproblematic and it becomes possible to legitimately make links between the two. But we ignore the physical body at our peril because then we disregard how features involved in the sex determination of the body may be involved in making identities. As we have seen, the physical body does have a reality of male and female, and some of the features used by osteoarchaeologists for sex determination are related to those observed by living people. If, however, we accept that it is useful to main-tain a distinction between sex and gender as two meaningfully different concepts, then this presents methodological challenges, particularly in mortuary contexts, and the question becomes how they can be worked through in archaeological practice in order to access the articulation of sex and gender in the past.

One might therefore expect the relationship between osteoarchaeology and interpretative archaeology to have received significant attention with regard to gender. However, while debates over the role of the body are by now well rehearsed within theoretical approaches to gender archaeology, and essentialist links between the sexed body and social life have long been exposed as untenable, the methodological significance and implica-tions of these debates have received relatively little attention. A recurring issue is the ambivalence with which archaeology treats the biology of the body. On one hand osteoarchaeological determinations are deemed methodologically necessary, but on the other hand they are treated with suspicion because the wide range of theoretical approaches to gender aim to disassociate themselves from biological determinism. It is worth exploring this dilemma in relation to current archaeological practice in further detail.

Tensions between method and theory in the archaeology of gender: implications of archaeological practice

As sexed and therefore 'known', the skeleton is often accorded a privileged status in the study of gender and archaeological interpretation. Osteoar-chaeology is relied upon to determine biological sex in order that pat-terns of grave goods can be associated with male or female bodies. Since archaeologists cannot observe living, fleshed individuals interacting with the material world or with other individuals, archaeologists tend to equate gender as a social and cultural construction with biologically sexed bodies through the practice of artefact association. Objects are divided into two mutually exclusive categories relating to male and female. Artefacts which cannot be associated in this manner are frequently dropped from the analysis and are implicitly regarded as non-gendered. Young individuals who cannot be anthropologically sexed are also excluded, although there is no *a priori* reason why they too may not be gendered. Thus biological sex, determined and ascribed through osteological analysis, continues to act as the foundation for much archaeological interpretation as archaeologists directly infer gender from sex in mortuary contexts by associating artefacts with sexed individuals.

This seems to indicate methodological uncertainty in how to approach gender as a cultural construction and a failure to successfully adapt the study of gender to the unique investigative parameters surrounding the discipline of archaeology. While the concept of gender appears to set out a cultural agenda, it frequently conflicts with a methodology that relies on sex. Although it is commonplace to identify bodies as 'sexed' and grave goods as 'gendered' (Whitehouse 2002), the practice of associating objects with sexed bodies would logically seem only to conflate sex and gender by using the same variable to examine both (Sofaer Derevenski 1998; Sørensen 2000). Archaeological practice is thus problematic because while it sets out a theoretical distinction between sex and gender, it simply ends up categorising people through sex, and so returns to biology. This results in methodological and epistemological confusion regarding the character of gender. An *a priori* division of grave goods into two categories corresponding to anthropological definitions of male and female that links the duality of the sexes with a universal assumption of the bimodal distribution of grave goods assumes a high degree of congruence between the identity and the activities of the deceased in life. But, given that gender is a social and cultural construction, it does not make sense to equate such a complex aspect of social life with the single variable of sex. By associating gender with sex through an exercise that matches objects with sexed bodies, with few exceptions (e.g. Joyce 2000a; Sofaer Derevenski 2000b) gender is assumed to remain constant throughout the life course.

A gap exists between the theoretical perception of gender as a cultural construction and the practice of archaeological data interpretation. Unable to observe the actions of living individuals, archaeologists continue, in practice, to infer gender from sex in mortuary contexts. This mapping of gender (a cultural construction) on to sex (the biological sexed skeleton) results in severe tension between the apparent inferential simplicity of method and the complexity of theory on a number of levels. The body acts not as the focus of interpretation, but as a reference point around which interpretations of surrounding artefacts are made. In other words, interpretations focus on the patterning and distribution of grave goods in relation to bodies, rather than on the bodies themselves. In cases where there are no objects with bodies, this approach implies that it is not possible to access gender in the past, or even that gender was not important, thereby potentially conflating burial traditions with social structures.

While there have been some recent attempts to examine gender using osteoarchaeology (e.g. Grauer and Stuart-Macadam 1998; Hollimon 1992, 2000b; Peterson 2000; Sofaer Derevenski 2000c), gender often seems to be located outside the body, constructed external to the person who was gendered in life. Current practice leaves the impression that identity resides in objects rather than in the people themselves. Archaeological methodology sets up a dichotomy between person and object that mirrors the disciplinary divide between osteoarchaeology and interpretative archaeology, although gendered individuals made and used those artefacts, and the material world is crucial to the construction of gender through practice (Sørensen 2004). This leads to tension, for without gendered individuals there can be no gendered meaning. The body becomes a stepping stone to interpretation, rather than central to the project of an engendered archaeology. Yet how can archaeologists access gender through the body when gender archaeology relies on the assumption that gender is accessible through the study of material culture in order to escape from determinism?

Tensions can also be traced to the use of culture in relation to the concept of gender. It has been argued that our very dependence on 'culture' as our primary analytical framework is a discursive power that homogenises and constructs a unified whole, rendering social relations invisible (Handsman 1988). Indeed, in using 'culture' in the archaeological identification of gender, a central problem becomes apparent; as archaeology is unable to define cultural differences between groups in the past other than through the lens of material culture, then it is forced to render gender visible by relying upon sex dichotomies in the construction of models of difference from which to find patterns in the past.

Furthermore, the emphasis on finding gender and categorising people according to gender based on a methodological exercise that looks at associations between objects and men and women in terms of presence and absence, as many studies do, implicitly attributes the same degree of meaning to all objects and the same strength of association for men and women, although this need not be the case (Sofaer Derevenski 2002). Material culture is not a single symbolically homogeneous construction. As the product of living societies, it carries a variety of interlocking and inseparable meanings. Objects imbued with gendered symbolism may therefore be simultaneously loaded with other socially constructed

nuances such as sex, age, status, religion or ethnicity. These may be experienced concurrently with gender and affect the development of gendered
perceptions or identities. A variety of factors may affect the construction
of gender, coming together in the creation of a material culture which
is not less gendered, but more complex and multidimensional than has
previously been recognised. Moreover, not only may objects vary in the
strength of gendered meanings attached to them, but a single object
may hold various meanings for different people. Sørensen (1989) calls
this the 'fluidity of meaning', suggesting that objects cannot therefore be
understood completely. Understandings of how gender may be encoded
in objects are frequently poor and archaeological interpretations have
often been based on ethnocentric assumptions. This results in severe tension between the investigation of meaning, which should be the object of
archaeological investigation, and the existence of a predetermined understanding.

The methodological relationship between sex and gender mirrors the
relationship between osteoarchaeology and interpretative archaeology.
Not only does it set up a distinction between nature and culture, where
sex is most often positioned as nature in relation to gender as culture, but
it is also analysed as representing a distinction between body and mind,
where sex is regarded as equivalent to the body and gender is regarded as
being the realm of the mental (Sørensen 2000: 44; Gatens 1996). Sex is
thus physically expressed and concrete, whereas gender is abstract. This
conceptualisation is problematic because, as I suggested in Chapter 3,
the basic oppositions involved are problematic. If one takes on board the
argument that both body and mind are physical entities that change as
part of social life, it becomes difficult to regard the sexed body as pristine
and natural in opposition to cultural gender as fluid and cultural, since
both sex and gender require anchoring in the materiality of the body.

Within the archaeological community there is a lack of clarity in terms
of the relevance of the physical body to understandings of gender in mortuary contexts, particularly if sex and gender are not regarded as equivalent. The study of gender becomes problematic since an uncertainty about
what to do with the physical body makes it difficult to decide upon widely
understood strategies for the study of gender. The practice of mapping
gender (a social construction) on to sex (the biological sexed skeleton)
results in a number of serious tensions between the apparent inferential simplicity of method and the complexity of theory. These tensions
can be further related to the relationship between osteoarchaeology and
interpretative archaeology. Without an attempt to resolve the tensions it
may be difficult, in practice, to reduce the current archaeological need to
rely on sex as an equivalent to gender. Lacking the direct ethnographic

observation of person–object interaction, archaeologists can neither dis-associate objects from the biology of the individual without loosing a point of reference, nor associate objects with the body without falling into the trap of biological determinism. Since the body and its relationship with objects is at the heart of methodological tensions in the archaeology of gender, we need to re-examine their role in archaeological analyses if we are to attempt a resolution. It is here that the identification of the body as material culture may be of use.

Resolving the tensions: material gender

One of the key assumptions that sits within tensions in the archaeology of gender is that, within archaeological method, the physical body is synony-mous with sex. Despite a methodological reliance on the skeletal body, its other aspects are rarely taken into consideration. Although skeletons have been studied in terms of burial position and burial type, and as symbolic entities, they have rarely been understood as contexts or sites of gendered interpretation in their own right. The implication is that the sexed body is passive in the expression of gender.

The skeleton is, however, much more than sex. The concept of plastic-ity, discussed in the previous chapter, emphasises how the body is related to social life and environment in the broadest sense. Skeletal remains can be regarded as the product of human action in much the same way as other forms of material culture, with gender materially articulated in the skeleton. Thus the Chinese tradition of foot-binding women lead-ing to deformation of the bones of the feet (Ortner and Putschar 1985; Blake 1994) is a skeletal expression of gender. The gendered division of labour can also produce gendered bodies. Food preparation may involve strenuous, repetitive work such as pounding or grinding. Carried out on a regular basis from a young age, this places repeated physical stress on par-ticular locations on the body. Molleson (1989, 1994) found that female skeletons from the Mesolithic and Neolithic site of Tell Abu Hureyra, Syria showed metatarsal-phalangeal modifications in the first metatarsals with degenerative changes to the margins of the joint facets in older indi-viduals. She suggested that alterations to the joint were probably the result of prolonged hyperdorsiflexion of the toes while kneeling. Such a posture while grinding cereal is depicted in Assyrian and Egyptian dynastic tomb art (Molleson 1989).

Bridges (1989) suggested that pounding corn with long wooden pestles held with both hands may have led to an increase in diaphyseal bone thickness and strength, along with a reduction in bilateral asymmetry of the humerus in Mississippian females compared to Archaic females.

Most people preferentially use one hand over another in skilled tasks contributing to a tendency towards asymmetry in bone morphology and mineral density in paired skeletal elements in the arms and shoulder girdle (Steele 2000). As both arms were used in pounding, the forces on both arms would have been equivalent, resulting in reduced asymmetry. The major motions involved in this activity were flexion and extension at the elbow as the arms were first drawn up together and then forcibly straightened to drive the pestle into the mortar (Bridges 1985, 1989).

Other gendered activities have also been implicated in changes to the human skeleton on the basis of their socio-cultural and archaeological context. Merbs (1983) identified osteoarthritis of the ulnarcarpal and radioulnar joints, especially on the left hand of Inuit women, as a result of holding skins in the right hand and cutting them with the left. Lovell and Dublenko (1999) suggested that lesions on some of the skeletons of men from the cemetery at the nineteenth-century trading post at Fort Edmonton, Canada were consistent with 'mushing' (driving a dog sled), while those on the single preserved female from the site may have been related to the arduous domestic chores documented at the fort including milking cows, churning butter, stirring lye soap, and harvesting grain and root vegetables by hand.

A further example of the material skeletal expression of gender comes from the sixteenth- to nineteenth-century site of Ensay in the Outer Hebrides (Sofaer Derevenski 2000c), where the gendered division of labour between men and women is known from ethnographic sources and historical documentation. The people of Ensay led a self-sufficient crofting lifestyle that remained unchanged from the first records of interment in the cemetery on Ensay in the sixteenth century until the indigenous population left in about 1875 (Martin 1703; Sinclair 1794; Macdonald 1978; Miles 1989). Both women and men participated in work in the fields, but most of the outdoor agricultural work was considered the responsibility of the men. Men dug plots of land, harvested the crops with scythes, looked after livestock (including milking), made ropes, fished and hunted for birds (MacGregor 1952). Task specialisation such as carpentry, net-making or shoe-making began in the nineteenth century and then only among a minority of men in towns. Although men did odd jobs around the house, women were responsible for the majority of domestic tasks such as cooking, sewing, knitting, spinning, weaving, grinding meal at hand querns and 'calanas', the preparation of wool for the manufacture of cloth. They were also responsible for the majority of heavy labour, including transporting peats for fuel and wet seaweed for fertiliser (Cameron 1986). Small island ponies were occasionally used but, in most cases, women carried loads using a form of basket known as a 'creel'

Figure 5.3 Woman carrying a creel

(Fig. 5.3). A creel full of peats weighed approximately 80 lb (Murray 1966) or 36 kg. The gendered division of labour was strictly regulated by a system of social censure. If transgression in gendered labour activities occurred, then ridicule and shame resulted (MacGregor 1952; Macdonald 1978: 63).

Table 5.1 *The prevalence of osseous change in the regions of the spine and their statistical significance in men and women from Ensay. (In all cases d.f. = 1. *Where one or more of the expected frequencies is less than or equal to 5, Fisher's exact test has been used.) (Data from Sofaer Derevenski 2000c)*

Type of osseous change	Segment of spine	Number of affected individuals, aspect				% of affected individuals, aspect				χ^2, aspect		Significance ($P \leq 0.05$)	
		Left		Right		Left		Right					
		Male	Female	Male	Female	Male	Female	Male	Female	Left	Right	Left	Right
Facet remodelling	Cervical	3	3	2	3	15	12	10	12	0.087	0.045	1.000*	1.000*
	Upper thoracic	14	17	17	21	64	63	77	78	0.002	0.002	0.961	0.966
	Lower thoracic	10	3	11	5	45	11	50	19	7.335	5.463	0.007	0.019
	Lumbar	4	0	3	1	20	0	15	4	5.488	1.660	0.033*	0.309*
Facet osteophytes	Cervical	6	5	6	5	30	20	30	20	0.602	0.602	0.500*	0.500*
	Upper thoracic	12	6	11	12	55	22	50	44	5.450	0.150	0.020	0.698
	Lower thoracic	15	10	12	14	68	37	55	52	4.705	0.035	0.030	0.851
	Lumbar	9	12	7	15	45	48	35	60	0.040	2.779	0.841	0.096

Facet sclerosis / eburnation	Cervical	2	2	2	2	10	8	10	8	0.055	0.055	0.815*	0.815*
	Upper thoracic	6	8	12	12	27	30	55	44	0.033	0.495	0.856	0.482
	Lower thoracic	6	1	8	3	27	4	36	11	5.499	4.440	**0.036***	**0.046***
	Lumbar	1	2	2	3	5	8	10	12	0.161	0.045	1.000*	1.000*
Osteophytosis	Cervical	4	6	3	5	20	24	15	20	0.103	0.190	1.000*	1.000*
	Upper thoracic	7	5	5	7	32	19	23	26	1.160	0.067	0.282	0.796
	Lower thoracic	11	13	12	14	50	48	55	52	0.017	0.035	0.897	0.851
	Lumbar	11	22	11	21	55	88	55	84	6.188	4.549	**0.013**	**0.049**

Differences between the sexes in the prevalence and distribution of osseous changes at Ensay can be related to highly structured differences in activities, in particular the load-bearing done by women. Creels were supported by a woven strap across the breastbone and around the shoulders with the weight resting on a 'dronnag' or creel pad just above the pelvis. These arrangements resulted in a characteristic posture while using a creel which modified the normal S-shaped curvature of the spine, turning it into a hook with the curves of the lower thoracic and lumbar regions straightened out. The way in which weight was transferred down the spine was thus altered, disrupting normal patterns of osseous change. Weight was spread over the chest and upper back with little involvement of the vertebral articular facets in the lower thoracic segment, while there was increased stress on vertebral bodies in the lumbar region as a result of the lack of the moderating influence of curvature. Ensay women are therefore significantly less affected than men by facet remodelling, facet osteophytes and facet sclerosis / eburnation in the lower thoracic vertebrae, but are significantly more affected by osteophytosis in the lumbar vertebrae with a characteristic skirt-like distribution at the base of the spine (Table 5.1; Fig. 5.4). Comparison of distributions of bone remodelling and vertebral degenerative change between the sexes at Ensay can be interpreted in terms of interplay between natural and activity-induced stresses on the spine, and accord with hypotheses suggested by the ethnographic and historical information (Sofaer Derevenski 2000c).

In addition to skeletal changes produced through gender-specific tasks, a range of studies has identified more general overall differences in the degree of skeletal stress and traumatic injury suffered by men and women, particularly at key transition periods in human history, and have related these to a redistribution of workload or changes in activities and gender ideologies (e.g. Goodman *et al.* 1984; Cassidy 1984; Cook 1984; Bridges 1983, 1989; Robb 1998a). In a recent study of the transition to agriculture in the Levant using musculoskeletal stress markers of the upper limb, Eshed *et al.* (2004) found that changes in activity patterns between Natufian hunter-gatherers and Neolithic farmers led to an overall increase in stress in the farming population, with women taking on a greater proportion of subsistence activities compared to Natufian females. Differences in diet between men and women have also been a focus of investigation. In an early examination of the links between food and gender relations, Hastorf (1991) used botanical and isotopic data to suggest differential access to foodstuffs that she related to changes in Andean women's political position during Inka rule. More recent work has explored the relationship between gender, group membership and status through diet (e.g. White *et al.* 1993; Schulting and Richards 2001; Privat *et al.* 2002;

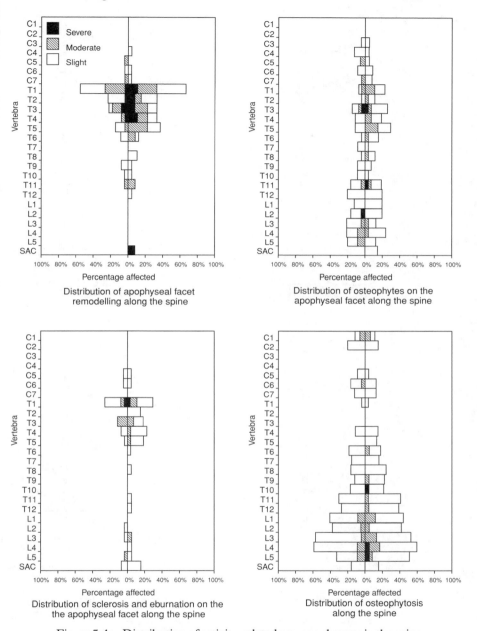

Figure 5.4a Distribution of activity-related osseous changes in the spine
of Ensay females (data from Sofaer Derevenski 2000c)

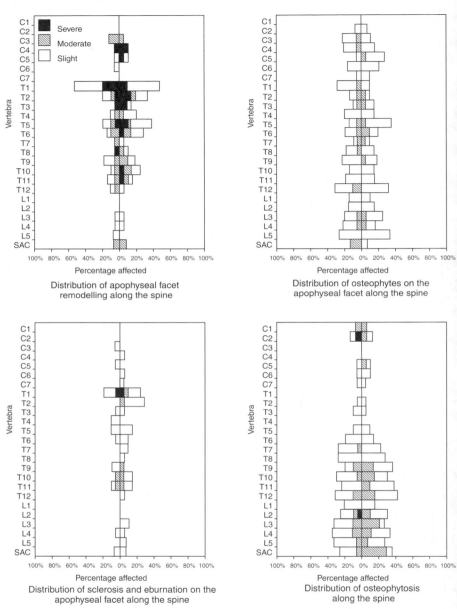

Figure 5.4b   Distribution of activity-related osseous changes in the spine of Ensay males (data from Sofaer Derevenski 2000c)

Cucina and Tiesler 2003; Ambrose *et al.* 2003), indicating the relative importance of gender for patterns of food consumption, as well as the potentially complex ways in which gender was played out in a range of archaeological contexts.

Rather than inferring gender roles through grave goods, changes to the skeleton can be related to the ways that gender as a social institution impacts on the body. This produces bodies that are not more or less gendered, but rather bodies that are gendered in socially and temporally specific ways. Particular forms of gendered bodies are created through practice with the health consequences that this entails, as people express their social position and relation to others by way of their bodily *hexis* (personal manner and style of the body including deportment, gait, stance and gestures) (Bourdieu 1977), which itself becomes part of the body. Since skeletal change occurs in both males and females and there is, as yet, no convincing evidence to suggest that one sex has a greater propensity to activity-induced change than the other, gender is not accessed through assumptions of natural and immutable sexual differences. Instead, gender can be examined independently of sex-based assumptions with sex regarded as one of a number of elements of gender. The skeleton may be affected by changes that are deliberate expressions of gender ideology or which are inadvertently produced through a lifetime of gendered activities.

A first step in addressing the tensions between method and theory in the archaeology of gender can be taken by recognising the potential of the body for the material expression of gender, where gender is the outcome of human agency and related to social practice. An infinite variety of potential forms of human action exist and individuals may accept or reject different forms and levels of gendered action which may result in different manifestations on the skeleton. The plasticity of the body means that the expression of gender is not fixed and may change over time. The body is not solely a site of production, but acknowledges the effects of gender, and can be regarded as a form of material culture which, manipulated by human activity, is both involved in, and acknowledges, past practice. As with other forms of material culture, the body does not just reflect cognitive systems and social practices, but is actively involved in their formation and structuring (Shanks and Tilley 1987: 85).

This perspective generates a specific understanding of gender such that it is identified in terms of modifications to the body distinct from aspects that can be understood as sex. The skeletal body is culturally constructed – moulded by action – but this is in the most fundamental *material* way. For the human body, gender is not just a mental construction but is materially expressed social practice. The material and the ideal are aspects of each other (Toren 1999). Sex can be regarded as influencing gender perceptions, but gender is not inevitably determined by sex and can be methodologically distinguished. As Moore (1994: 85) puts it, 'It is not that the material world, as a form of cultural discourse, reflects the natural division of the world into women and men, but rather that cultural discourses, including the organisation of the material world, actually produce gender difference in and through their workings.'

Social practices require interaction between people, being negotiated between them as part of a social context (Bauman 1973). The material expression of gender explored in individual skeletons lends insights into the wider social regulation of gender, while allowing for an appreciation of similarity and difference between individuals. Modifications identified in a single individual are difficult to identify as gender but need to be situated within patterns explored at a group level. Such an approach situates the corporeal expression of gender in terms of a range of potential materialities as it allows consideration of individuals whose bodies may have differing propensities to respond to gendered actions. It represents a distinct understanding of the means by which it is possible to understand the way that gender is materially articulated in relation to the specific material qualities of the human body and human action. While a definition of gender as 'that which is materially expressed in the human body' may be narrow and in some ways exclusive, it lends itself to the construction of hypotheses, while retaining the potential to reveal new layers of non-artefactually based information.

Of course, not all gendered activities carried out by an individual or in relation to that individual by others during his or her lifetime have an effect on the skeleton. Traces or aspects of those that do may only refer to more severe or prolonged actions or exposures which were carried out repeatedly from a young age and which, given greater plasticity in youth, therefore exacerbate or induce morphological or degenerative change. Furthermore, the expression of gender in the body varies both qualitatively and quantitatively according to both the general level of lifestyle stress and the nature of the particular gendered activities in which individuals may be engaged on a regular basis, as well as on their predisposition to osseous changes. This may be difficult to gauge, although unique activities or lifestyles may have distinct skeletal consequences as morphologically different types of osseous change may also be aetiologically different (Sofaer Derevenski 2000c; Rothschild 1997). There is a need to build a database of the skeletal implications of known activities where these are available. In addition, a fine enough level of discrimination must be applied to the collection of data through the separate recording of morphologically and aetiologically distinct osseous changes.

Some particularly stressful activities which produce characteristic frequency distributions as a result of specific and localised biomechanical
changes may be easier to identify in the skeletal record than other more
general trends. It is also important to note that it is the pattern of skeletal
modifications, as well as their presence or absence, that is important in
the identification of gendered life-ways (Sofaer Derevenski 2000c).

Recognising the partiality of osteoarchaeology (and indeed of archaeological studies of material culture in general) does not, however, necessarily undermine it as an approach to studying gender in the past. Investigating gender in this manner, with all its variation and potential ambiguity in expression, means that gender becomes an exploratory concept
and a way of investigating patterns, rather than a way of allocating people to genders in a categorical fashion. Osteoarchaeological investigation
of gender highlights the variability of bodies. As such it sits easily with
many feminist-inspired pluralist understandings of gender (cf. Whelehan
1995). Furthermore, the specific identification of gender as visible in the
skeleton is useful since the means by which the skeleton becomes gendered through its life-ways is made explicit. A variety of different archaeologically accessible skeletal attributes become linked aspects of a single,
but multifaceted construction in as much as the material expression of
gender in the skeletal body can also be related to a range of other variables
that may potentially affect it. In particular, this understanding of gender
identifies it as being produced over the lifetime of individuals through the
gradual construction of the body and this means that the development of
gender is closely linked to age. Gender is a process that comes into being
over time as gender is both learnt and practised. Osseous changes take
time to develop and the impact of gender on the body may vary at different
points in the life course. It may be more pronounced when begun young,
while the expression of gender in the body may become exaggerated with
age, especially in terms of degenerative changes, as the expression of gender in the skeleton interacts with the inevitable age-related processes of
growth and degeneration.

The identification of the body as material culture can help to resolve
some of the tensions between method and theory in the archaeology
of gender as it removes some of the central and most problematic
dichotomies that give rise to those tensions. As it does not rely upon
a distinction between sexed bodies and gendered objects, it does away
with difficulties arising from the separation between bodies and objects
and their respective linkage with nature and culture that underlie many
current approaches to gender. In terms of the human skeleton, individuals both create, and are themselves created, as nature becomes culture,
and culture becomes nature. Oppositions which have dogged the study of

gender become redundant through their unification in the human body. The skeleton can be regarded as a site of 'articulation' (Haraway 1991) of sex and gender. The body as material culture acknowledges that archaeology relies on the identification of objects as meaningful in terms of the semiotic potential of material culture to investigate the past, but indicates that this potential also exists for the skeleton. Methodological difficulties inherent in the method of object association thus seem less pressing and the study of gender is returned to the person. Rather than assuming it to be a free-floating, conceptual or mental construct, with regard to the body, gender is material.

6   Age

no-one has ever grown out of biology or grown into society or culture.
Ingold 2001a: 235

The body is subject to a range of different narratives with regard to age and ageing (Featherstone and Hepworth 1998). On one hand, the investigation of age highlights links between the biological and the social (Featherstone and Hepworth 1998: 159) as physiological changes to the body that occur throughout the life course become key sites for social engagement and are incorporated into social life through processes of cultural negotiation. On the other hand, the perceived boundedness of the body has often meant that it is understood in terms of its limits, while its materiality, powerfully expressed though its inevitable decline and eventual death, is also taken to describe a limit to the social (Featherstone and Hepworth 1998). The lives of people are subject to biological limitations and the body is a limited biological resource (Elias 1985). It is the materiality of the body that lends it its finitude (Elias 1985; Harré 1991; Featherstone and Hepworth 1998).

As with sex and gender, there are a number of significant tensions in the ways that archaeologists currently use the body to identify age. These also arise from deeply engrained aspects of archaeological practice that reflect a divide between osteoarchaeology and interpretative archaeology, and they generate a series of theoretical and methodological problems. The investigation of age brings the relationship between osteoarchaeology and interpretative archaeology into sharp relief. This chapter examines current tensions between theory and method, and explores how the notion of the body as material culture offers a way of reconceptualising archaeological investigations of age.

Age and the skeletal body

The body is key to the investigation of age. As individuals grow, mature and senesce (Crews and Garruto 1994), changes to the physical body

117

become markers of time passed (James 2000), clearly visible in, for example, height or the development of secondary sex characteristics. The significance of changes to the body is frequently understood in terms of social identity as bodies and differences between bodies become signifiers of identity (James 1993). '[T]he trajectory of the body is given symbolic and moral value: bodily forms are paradigmatic of social transition' (Prendergast 1992: 1), or as James *et al.* state, 'The body [in childhood] is a crucial resource for making and breaking identity precisely because of its unstable materiality' (James *et al.* 1998: 156). Age is thus a temporal and material concept. These dual dimensions make the study of age particularly suited to archaeological investigation.

Investigations of age have, however, often focused on living, fleshed bodies. Studies have looked at understandings of the ways that adult bodies display signs of time passing, the first grey hairs and lines of age on the face being regarded as markers of mortality (Hockey and James 1993; Featherstone and Wernick 1995), or the intense and rapid 'whole body' change which occurs in childhood (James 2000). Nonetheless, for archaeology, the physical reality of the body within the archaeological record is potentially particularly powerful in terms of age and identity because of the sheer number of physiological changes to the skeleton, and the visibility and clarity with which they may be manifested. Growth and degenerative changes of the skeleton can be understood as metaphors for body changes observed in living fleshed bodies. Physiological changes of the body may be socially marked through life-cycle rituals and these may be materially expressed in objects associated with people at particular stages of life, such as infancy or menarche. The associations between artefacts and individuals may be used to actively create, manipulate and convey individual identity (Sørensen 1991, 1997).

With regard to the body, the study of age in archaeology is most frequently articulated through the dual study of the skeleton and the distribution of objects with individuals in given age categories. The tradition of associating objects with people reflects how archaeology differs from other disciplines with an interest in age, in that, in general, archaeological individuals cannot be tracked over their life course but instead are present at a single point in time. Cross-sectional studies are therefore possible but longitudinal ones are not. It also means that the study of age is easily split along party lines within archaeology. On one side lies a concern with the physical body expressed in terms of biology or physiology, which is the province of osteoarchaeology in terms of estimations of age from the skeleton. On the other side lies the social construction of age, often described in terms of the age category to which an individual belongs and which is the province of interpretative archaeology explored through the association of artefacts with groups of people of a given age range. Parallel issues to those concerned with gender thus emerge within the study of age in terms of the relationship between osteoarchaeology and interpretative archaeology, in terms of both how they go about defining age as a concept and as a category, and how age is methodologically accessed in the archaeological record.

The articulation of age in archaeology

While age has long been an important axis of archaeological investigation in mortuary contexts, it is only relatively recently that it has been explicitly theorised (e.g. Sofaer Derevenski 1994, 1997a and b, 2000a; Scott 1999; Gowland 2001; Lorentz 2003; Lillehammer 1989; Welinder 1998; Kamp 2001a and b; Joyce 2000a; Crawford 1991, 1999; Bird and Bird 2000). The same level of debate and politicisation has not yet emerged within archaeology regarding definitions of age as exist for sex and gender. Age is, however, a recurring theme in sociological, anthropological and historical studies of the body (e.g. Shilling 1993; Featherstone et al. 1991; Hockey and James 1993; Prout 2000). Influenced by these disciplines, the culturally variable character of age categories such as infant, child or adult have been recognised in archaeology and the potential complexity of age in terms of the relationship between biology and culture pointed out (Sofaer Derevenski 1994, 2000a; Scott 1999; Gowland 2001). While recognising the changing abilities and capabilities of the body with age (Featherstone and Hepworth 1998; James 2000), following on from feminist critiques, there has been a conscious move away from biological determinism in theoretical approaches to age, with a growing perception that social age is laid on to the biology of the body.

Ginn and Arber's (1995) three meanings of age have been seen as particularly relevant to archaeology as they take account of physical biological changes to the body that are visible in skeletal remains as well as the social dimensions of age identified in objects (Sofaer Derevenski 1994, 1997b; Gilchrist 1999). In this scheme, age is visualised as having chronological, physiological and social components (Ginn and Arber 1995). Chronological (or calendar) age is an essentially biological concept referring to age in years. Physiological age is a medical notion referring to the physiological ageing process, which although related to chronological age cannot be directly inferred from it. Social age is socio-culturally constructed and refers to age norms of appropriate attitudes and behaviours, in terms of self-perceptions and age ascribed by others, which is itself cross-cut by gender ideology.

Harré (1991) also argues that there are three interconnected strands
to the life course, these being the biological lifespan, the social lifespan
and the personal lifespan, each with its own beginning and end that need
not overlap with those of other strands. The biological life course begins
at conception and ends at death. Harré (1991: 35) argues that although
these two points are absolutes in the human time frame, they are external
to a sense of self and therefore stand outside the social and personal. The
biological life course is 'relative to the main acts of the drama of life as it
is lived, merely "noises off"' (Harré 1991: 35). Social identity may begin
before bodily identity takes shape, as in the parental definition of a child
to come, and may persist after death. The social lifespan is thus longer
than the biological. The personal lifespan, on the other hand, fits within
the time span of the physical body. Reflective of consciousness, it begins
in late infancy and often ends in old age in senility before the death of the
body. Conception and death lie outside the period of self-knowledge.

For Harré (1991), emphasis on development and meanings is
paramount. His division of age has received less attention within archaeological circles, and his focus on the development of the mental self might
be considered problematic when dealing with past people. Nonetheless,
despite the relegation of the biological body, his general model of the life
course might still be provocative in exploring the relationship between
the social and the individual. Social and cognitive developmental aspects
of age have hitherto been little explored in archaeology. As in other disciplines, where there is an emphasis on 'lived bodies', the process of becoming human as we enter the world or of becoming adult as we grow often
seems to be missing (cf. Birke 1999: 46; Dickens 2001), although the
ways that objects may be involved in cultural reproduction, learning and
the transmission of traditions have recently received some attention (e.g.
Sofaer Derevenski 1997a; Greenfield 2000; Kamp 2001a; Sillar 1994,
2000).

The kinds of divisions proposed by Ginn and Arber (1995) and Harré
(1991) both recognise the materiality of the body, and explicitly separate
the biological and the social. Such distinctions between different aspects
of age are not in themselves conceptually problematic, but in breaking
down the different components of age it becomes crucial to explore how
these different aspects might be related in specific settings. In archaeology, the implications of a conceptual division of age have not been frequently discussed. Theorisation of age is therefore unlike gender where
the relationship between sex and gender is hotly debated in terms of the
relationship between the physical characteristics of the body and social
understandings. It is clear, however, that age cannot be understood as
entirely culturally constructed since it is expressed through the physical

changes of the body. Nor can it be entirely biologically understood since it has social meaning and is a basic structure of society. In spite of this, discussions of age within archaeology implicitly tend to take one of these sides. A comparative exploration of notions of age and ageing drawn from human osteoarchaeology and interpretative archaeology that focuses on the ontological distinctions between 'child' and 'adult' illustrates this point.

Osteoarchaeological notions of 'child' and 'adult' are made through a key distinction between the physiologically immature skeleton and the mature skeleton. This distinction arises partly from the current limits of osteoarchaeological method in that somewhat different approaches are applied to the examination of each. For the skeletally immature, osteoarchaeological determinations of age are based on comparisons with observed relationships between skeletal or dental development and chronological age in populations with individuals of known chronological age. Estimates are most frequently drawn from the sequence of epiphyseal fusion (see Scheuer and Black 2000) (Fig. 6.1) or dental development (see Hillson 1996) (Fig. 6.2). Children are identified as a physiological age group in terms of stages in skeletal development and are categorised according to age in years, such that chronological age acts as a kind of shorthand or mutual reference point for biological change. Here growth is the important axis of investigation and forms the basis of definitions of age.

Crucially, in osteoarchaeology the category 'child' is understood in opposition to the contrasting category of 'adult'. Adults are those who are skeletally mature and so can be more easily and accurately sexed. Adults are implicitly regarded as complete. They are almost the biological 'real McCoy'; the children are 'sub'adults. Methods for ageing the skeletally mature are different from those used to age the immature skeleton. Although they may include assessment of the final stages of maturation that occur in the late second and third decades of life, and the continued ossification of hyaline cartilage, they are also based on morphological and degenerative changes to joints with limited or non-existent movement, such as the pubic symphyses, and changes to bone structure including involutional bone loss and osteon frequency (see Cox 2000b). Seriated tooth wear (e.g. Brothwell 1972) is also commonly used for ageing adult dentition. These methods do not give such fine resolution in terms of chronological age as those for subadults, but may frequently also be transformed into years or an age category (e.g. mature adult), giving a chronological dimension. True to its medical roots, in osteoarchaeology old age is often seen as a form of pathology (cf. Featherstone and Hepworth 1998), where the attributes of old age and the aged body become

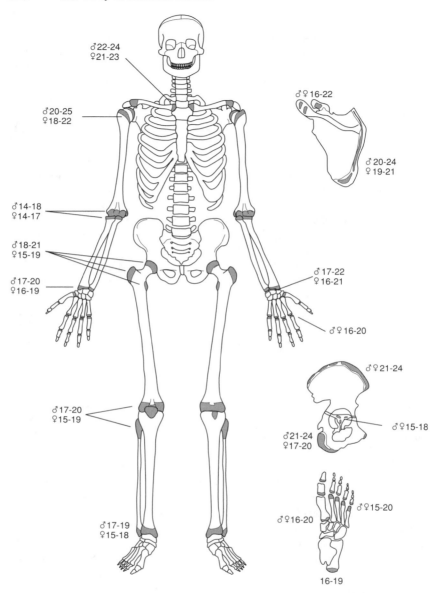

♂22-24
♀21-23

♂20-25
♀18-22

♂14-18
♀14-17

♂18-21
♀15-19

♂17-20
♀16-19

♂♀16-22

♂20-24
♀19-21

♂17-22
♀16-21

♂♀16-20

♂♀21-24

♂21-24
♀17-20

♂♀15-18

♂17-20
♀15-19

♂♀16-20

♂♀15-20

♂17-19
♀15-18

16-19

Figure 6.1 The times of epiphyseal union (data from Ferembach *et al.* 1980)

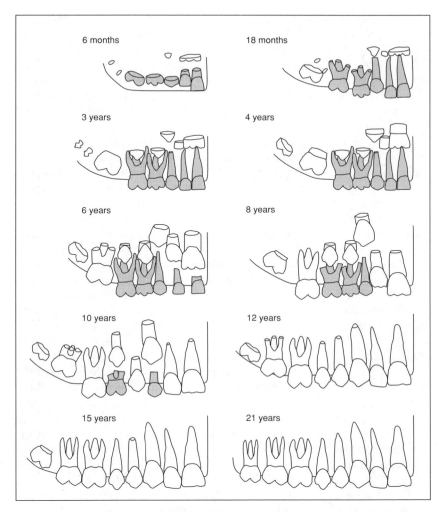

Figure 6.2 General sequence of human dental development. Average development stages of human dentition from 6 months to 21 years (based on Schour and Massler 1941; redrawn after Brothwell 1972)

indicators of each other's supposedly normal or pathological states (Katz 1996: 47). The young body is the 'ideal' or the standard, reflecting cultural priorities given to the young. Medical opinion, and in its wake public opinion at large, perceives a healthy body as remaining in a steady state – a body controllable and controlled. Bauman (1998: 223) points out that in the modern era, the healthy body is understood to be a strong enduring body, capable of prolonged exertion and with no excessive demands, easy to satisfy and keep in a 'workable' condition.

In interpretative archaeology, the physiological basis of ageing, and the chronological notion of age in years used in osteoarchaeology as a reference point for that physiological change, takes on a different meaning. In interpretative archaeology, the division between child and adult – in other words the division between the skeletally immature and skeletally mature, unsexed and sexed – become interpretative categories that are often imposed on to the analysis of material culture. Chronological categorisations of age in years which are used in osteoarchaeology as developmental reference points or, in the case of the skeletally mature, points against which to assess degrees of degenerative change, become benchmarks for accessing social life through the exploration of age-related patterns in the distribution of objects. Most importantly though, as with gender, in the search for social meaning, the emphasis shifts from the body to objects surrounding it. In material-culture-based interpretative archaeology, osteological determinations are regularly used as the basis for archaeological interpretation, but the physiological aspects of the body which form the foundation of osteoarchaeological assessments play no part in the process of interpretation. Notions of child and adult therefore acquire a status almost independent from the physiology of the body, as physiological age is transformed into chronological age, and from there to social age, in an almost linear manner. This process is reflected in the resources required for interpretative archaeology; whereas you need the body to be physically present in front of you to do osteoarchaeology, what you need for interpretative archaeology is a table of chronological ages in years and a list of artefacts in order to make associations between the two. Interpretative archaeology thus defines age in terms of categories of people associated with contextually specific objects. Here age is linked to biology but its cultural construction takes primacy. In this understanding of age, it is what is made of the body that counts in terms of its social significance. Nature is transformed into culture.

Age and archaeological practice

Though both osteoarchaeologists and material-culture archaeologists may be studying the same people, they tend to identify them in very different ways. The physical body is deemed to be the province of the osteoarchaeologist but archaeological science is left behind in the quest for past social life because archaeology has traditionally identified sociality as the province of the humanities. The sequence of conceptual transformations from physiological age, to chronological age, and from there to social age, represents the construction of disciplinary boundaries within the discipline along the lines of science and humanism. While each of these notions of age is conceptually distinct, this almost linear trans- formation from one concept into another is problematic because, while on one hand it assumes direct links between the biological and the social, on the other hand it separates elements of archaeological practice, and lacks any real theoretical framework through which to promote a cohesive archaeology. While the body is of critical importance to an understanding of age, in practice the divide between osteoarchaeology and interpretative archaeology has precluded a full incorporation of the fluid materiality of the body (particularly in terms of archaeologically visible physiological changes identifiable in human remains) into contextually specific under- standings of social identity. Once again, within archaeological practice the skeletal body is employed as a means of underpinning interpretations rather than as a source for generating them.

Tensions between method and theory in the archaeology of age: implications of archaeological practice

The physiology, chronology and sociology transformation has a number of implications that are expressed in terms of a series of tensions arising from archaeological practice. Although the osteoarchaeological location of age categories such as 'children' and 'adults' is firmly grounded in the identification of the physical body, as the transformation from physio- logical to social age takes place, archaeological understandings become ever more removed and abstracted from the body. This disjunction is problematic because, as interpretative archaeology loses touch with the physicality of the body, it also loses touch with its material reality. From a methodological point of view, dispensing with material reality by fail- ing to acknowledge the skeleton fundamentally challenges the basis of archaeology as a discipline since archaeology relies on making inferences from material remains of whatever kind. Removing the physicality of the body from view negates the potential ways in which social relations and the lives of people may shape, and are shaped by, their bodies (James 1993; Turner 1996; James *et al.* 1998). If the body becomes an abstraction rather than a person we have an archaeological paradox: a social archaeol- ogy that lacks the essence of social life. We have an archaeology that relies totally on the osteological physical body at one level of interpretation, but ignores it totally on the other. Through the primacy attached to biolog- ical identification, archaeology has created embodied people by default, yet they are vacuous, being devoid of social agency and identity (Sofaer

Derevenski 2000a). Osteoarchaeology and social archaeology lose the thread that binds them. In other words, those human remains that were someone's living body in the past.

A further tension arises from the difficulty that, although we might recognise on a theoretical level that culturally specific age categories are variable and culturally constructed through a network of social relationships, in archaeological practice the way that they are located primarily through the identification of the body, via osteological and dental estimates of age, is an approach that necessarily relies upon constant universals. The complexity of the relationship between biology and culture therefore seems to go largely unrecognised in the simplicity of practice. For example, the category 'child' is largely predicated upon the peculiarity of children's physiology (James 1993, 2000). As a result, bodily stereotypes of the 'normal' child, historically derived and ultimately contingent, are made to conform to that physiological classification of child (James 2000: 27). This linear transformation means that for the most part, bodies and bodily change have been interpreted solely from within a naturalistic frame, children's identities as children being understood as a 'natural' outcome of their bodily difference from adults, and vice versa (James 2000: 23; Burman 1994).

Such a methodological position leads to another archaeological paradox. For despite losing the materiality of the body as a point of contact, interpretative archaeology maintains distinctions between categories (e.g. child vs adult) which are the product of the limitations of current osteoarchaeological practice in terms of our ability (or inability) to accurately determine age and sex, but which are actually ontologically unsustainable for both osteoarchaeology and interpretative archaeology. From a social perspective, despite modern, western perceptions of children as dependent on adults – which lead archaeologists to construct interpretations that reduce children to passive, inert automatons – children are actors and constructors of their own lives who act not simply intuitively, but initiate action by choice (Wartofsky 1983). There is a wealth of ethnographic evidence from both traditional and modern societies documenting their participation in social and economic life (e.g. Cain 1977; Gullestad 1988; Morrow 1994; Rosenzweig and Evenson 1997; Magazine 2003). In this sense, it is difficult to attribute children and adults different ontological statuses (Qvortrup 1994). Even if one suggests that adults are more effective in elaborating the material world, this does not itself constitute ontological difference, but is merely a question of scale. From a developmental perspective, the age categories commonly described within osteoarchaeology are problematic as biologically accurate assessments of skeletal development form somewhat artificial divisions in terms of social and mental development. Furthermore, the skeleton is dynamic and changes of the body can occur throughout the life course from birth to death. The basis of the distinction between the skeletally mature and the immature is often seen as growth versus maturity, but maturity does not equal stasis. Change includes both growth and senescence, and although the body in relation to age is seen as natural (Prout 2000), the inevitable wear and tear to which it is subject may be influenced over time by life events and circumstances, albeit to different degrees. Bodies are never static.

Approaches to age in archaeology can be associated with a range of social, political and educational ideologies that developed as a trope in the nineteenth century with the development of mass schooling when children began to be explicitly grouped together by chronological age cohort. In the same period, the practices of child psychology, developmental linguistics and anthropometry offered templates for how children were expected to look at certain ages (Steedman 1995), and the charting and surveying of the child body began to define normal limits for bodies (Armstrong 1983). Growth became the key axis of investigation of the physical body and children became a physiological chronology, a history, as they made their way through the stages of growth (Steedman 1992: 37). This understanding reflects a notion of progress akin to that of evolution (another nineteenth-century idea), in which to grow up as an adult was to grow out of the body of a child (James 2000: 24; Morss 1990). Thus while changes to bodies over time, and the importance of differences between bodies to social life, can be seen as a basic structure of human societies, it is the reified and monitored body with its discrete classifications of the nineteenth century in the West (James 2000: 25), that have found themselves part of archaeological investigations of age.

Underlying much of the tension between method and theory in the investigation of age in archaeology is, therefore, a fundamental assumption that the investigation of age is about essential or intrinsic categories which can also be identified in the past. While the identification of social classifications is clearly of importance in as much as people operate in the world through the construction of categories, there is a tendency in both osteoarchaeology and interpretative archaeology to treat age in terms of fixed points in time that can be defined on a scale, a propensity that is exacerbated by dealing with dead bodies, where shifts or movements of individuals between categories cannot be followed over real time. The desire to turn biological categories into social ones by creating implicit and direct links between the two, causes problems by trying to turn a process (ageing), that has many potential points of contact, into a class (age). Although ageing is a dynamic concept that is about change in a person over time, studies of age in archaeology implicitly or explicitly become about ways of categorising people, be this, for example, in terms of the demography of a given site or the way that groups are socially perceived. Furthermore, while useful, studies of individual segments of the life course risk losing sight of the connections between age stages (Robb 2002). On the whole, age categories as they are commonly seen in archaeology do not emerge from close contextual exploration of data. Instead, both osteoarchaeology and interpretative archaeology have adopted a methodological distinction as the basis on which to construct interpretations of the past. The limitations of osteoarchaeology have become the limitations of interpretative archaeology in which social relations are read as epiphenomena of nature (James *et al.* 1998). Children and adults are both identified in a naturalised and reductionist manner as universal biological categories, rather than as social beings whose categorisation is a relative concept negotiated through context and the materiality of experience.

Recent work in archaeology has identified physiological changes occurring throughout the life course as signifiers of identity by exploring the associations between objects and particular kinds of bodies (e.g. Gowland 2001; Janik 2000; Mizoguchi 2000). This has not seen absolute age as important, but rather the ways that people are recognised in relation to their physiology. Robb (2002: 161) suggests that although we need to retain biological processes of growth, illness, ageing and death as universally recognisable and incorporated into social life, we need to do so without rigidly dictating the way in which they were understood. This line of enquiry has been extremely fruitful in considering how societies monitor changing bodies. It has, however, often tended to focus on growth as the key aspect of the skeleton around which categorisation revolves, with people of different growth stages associated with different objects. Thus, while it allows for a range of expression in what people made of the body, there is little room for cultural contingency in the expression of the body itself which is seen as universal. It therefore runs the risk of reiterating the linear transformation from biology to sociality, and does not entirely resolve the tensions between method and theory. The theoretical implications of distinguishing between age at a given point in time (i.e. age at death) and ageing (a process of change in life) have received little attention. Use of concepts of biography and the life course as heuristic devices through which to explore age provides potentially exciting avenues of investigation that seems to sidestep these problems by highlighting the ways that age may be crucial to the process of the creation of specific aged subjectivities (Gilchrist 2000; Meskell 2000b; Harlow and Lawrence 2002). It has highlighted the role of objects in constructing

individual biographies (Sofaer Derevenski 2000b), or the ways that particular aged and gendered bodies are produced in a culturally required
manner through the performance of a discrete series of ritual acts (Joyce
2000a). With rare exceptions (e.g. Robb 2002), such approaches have,
however, tended to place relatively little emphasis on skeletal remains.

Resolving the tensions: bodies and material practice

The question is then how it might be possible to identify age as constructed and contextually specific without falling back on potentially mis-
leading ethnocentric principles of interpretation, while taking account of
the specificities of the body. There are two potential approaches to this.
The first is to reduce the limitations of osteoarchaeology by improving
methods for sexing immature individuals and improving ageing methods
for mature individuals, thereby removing the methodological barrier that
separates children and adults in terms of the limits of sexing and ageing.
This is useful, and considerable energy has already been devoted to it
(e.g. Molleson *et al.* 1998; Schutkowski 1993; Mays and Faerman 2001;
Weaver 1980; Gowland and Chamberlain 2002), but it will still ultimately
need to be somehow related to social life. Archaeology will still have the
same problem of transforming physiological age into social age. The second approach is to think about theoretical frameworks for linking osteoarchaeology and interpretative archaeology in order to try and understand
the process of ageing in relation to material culture, rather than privileging either as the primary focus of analysis. This requires that we rethink
the relationship between bodies and objects, which in turn requires a shift
in emphasis regarding our understandings of bodies in relation to social
practices. Here the notion of the body as material culture may once again
be of use, and it is to this that I now wish to return.

Instability, contingency and age

In Chapter 4 I discussed how the materiality of the body is brought into
being over the life course through social practices. Social practices are
material as they literally shape the body through diet, exercise, health
risks, life-ways and disciplinary regimes (Prout 2000). They therefore
have particular implications for an investigation of age as they are implicated in the ways that bodies change over time. While inevitable age-
related visible changes to the body render it a crucial resource for making and breaking identities (James *et al.* 1998: 156), the instability of
the body and differences between bodies can be understood not simply in terms of categories of identities to which they belong, but also in

Table 6.1 *The average height of eighteenth-century British army recruits (data from Steegmann 1985)*

	Rural-born recruits	Urban-born recruits
Average height (cm)	168.6	167.5

terms of how bodies situated within particular categories are formed over time and the conditions under which they move from one category into another.

Social practices and material resources have a direct bearing on human physiological change and development with age. Poor nutrition and disease can disrupt and prolong growth (Bogin 1999, 2001), resulting in reduced size for chronological age or delayed skeletal and dental maturation, although the latter is less sensitive to disturbance (Humphrey 2000; Demirjian 1986). Thus eighteenth-century British military records show a significant difference between the average heights of urban- and rural-born recruits, reflecting contrasting lifestyles (Steegmann 1985) (Table 6.1). Choices regarding culturally specific child-rearing practices, including those related to weaning, may have lasting skeletal consequences (Stuart-Macadam and Dettwyler 1995; Dettwyler and Fishman 1992). The explosion of health, welfare and educational reforms of the nineteenth century led, by the twentieth century, to physiological changes in children's bodies in an increase in size and weight according to age as a direct result of state intervention to improve housing and sanitation for the children of the poor (Mayall 1996). Improvements in living conditions during the lives of individuals can lead to catch-up growth in skeletally immature individuals (Prader *et al.* 1963; Wall 1991; Bogin 1999).

In archaeological samples, diachronic comparisons, or comparisons of growth between groups, have been used to infer differences and similarities in stress levels between populations (e.g. Humphrey 2000; Mays 1995; Bogin and Keep 1998; Ribot and Roberts 1996). Many indicators of stress on the skeleton and dentition develop during childhood (Lewis 2000), although it has been argued that such lesions are only visible in the skeletons of individuals strong enough to survive a stress episode (Wood *et al.* 1992). Bone lesions may also remodel or disappear as individuals get older (Lewis 2000). Systemic degenerative changes that are rarely found subchondrally in individuals in the first three decades of life may be accelerated through activities that involve repeated mechanical loads placed upon the joints (Radin *et al.* 1972; Peyron 1986; Bridges 1991; Schmorl and Junghanns 1971; Krämer 1981). The expression of such changes may become highly exaggerated as the life course progresses. Following the degeneration of cartilage that is a histological and radiographic sign of osteoarthritis, the impingement of bone against bone can produce thickening of the subchondral plate by bone formation either before it has been penetrated or after, so that the bone becomes sclerotic. If wear occurs between the surfaces, they may become polished or eburnated (Ortner and Putschar 1985; Currey 1986; Rogers *et al.* 1997b). Since skeletal modifications provoked by life-ways or activities develop over time, they are therefore closely tied to understandings of the human life course.

This perspective has much in common with the concept of 'skeletal biographies' (Saul and Saul 1989; Robb 2002). Such an approach explores events and conditions in the composite lives of groups (rather than specific individuals) in terms of a cultural narrative (Robb 2002). The skeleton is thus 'read' in terms of the ways that events occurring at different stages in the life course both contribute to, and emerge from, culturally specific age categories, resulting in progressive and cumulative life stories. These life stories may be linked to status, gender or other aspects of identity, resulting in a series of simultaneous and constantly emerging narrative threads in any one group. They may involve deliberate modification of the body such as tooth removal (Robb 2002), as well as the chances of illness or trauma happening to people at different ages. While skeletal biographies cannot always describe the order of changes to the skeleton, the exact age at which they took place, or indeed how long before death they occurred (such as in the case of a healed pathology), it is possible to estimate the ongoing risk of injury or illness at each period of life (Robb 2002). For example, women of childbearing age run particular risks associated with this stage in their lives as childbirth has a higher risk of infections or death. Studies of this kind are able to generate models of probabilistic epigenesis (Robb 2002).

The notion that how bodies change is contingent upon social practices suggests that bodies are brought into being, not only through inevitable growth and degeneration, but also through action. The archaeological body is unstable both by virtue of inevitable physiological changes of ageing and through human agency. For example, in the nineteenth and twentieth centuries increases in children's height and weight and a decline in chronic sickness did not occur as a 'natural' follow-on from increased knowledge about nutrition or better housing. Nor was this simply a matter of seeing children differently. Rather, as Steedman (1990, 1992) and Urwin and Sharland (1992) have shown, it was the active participation of parents (and their children) in new theories of childrearing and parentcraft, their acceptance of a particular vision of the importance of child health, and their willingness to defer to, or to be the beneficiaries of, reformist social policies which combined to effect a change in childhood morbidity through physiological change in children's bodies (James 2000: 27; see also Gijswijt-Hofstra and Marland 2003). On the level of the individual the consequences of agency may also be expressed in bones and teeth. Recent studies of human migration and mobility have compared strontium, barium and lead isotope abundances or ratios in human tooth enamel as a signal of the place of birth, with values in human bone or modern or archaeological animal remains as a signal of the place of death (e.g. Price *et al.* 1994; Price *et al.* 1998; Ezzo *et al.* 1997; Price *et al.* 2000; Burton *et al.* 2003; Bentley *et al.* 2004). Since teeth do not remodel, differences between teeth and bones indicate movement of the individual from their place of origin and highlight the literal nature of the relationship between human action and the formation of the human body. A focus on the body and behaviour in terms of agency and causation challenges the mind–body dualism that is often associated with an archaeological notion of agency as abstract and mentalist (cf. Crossley 2001: 89; Farnell 2000), and promotes a view of the body as not divorced from the conscious, thinking and intentional mind (James 2000: 27; Knappett 2002).

Bodies change over time both on an individual level and in a broader historical sense. They do so in particular ways that are related to their specific life experiences and action, in addition to the intrinsic instability of the body that arises from inevitable physiological consequences of ageing. While the latter are often classed as biological, a focus on instability in relation to agency suggests that changes to the body need not be the function of biology alone. Such a perspective moves away from a linear and universal notion of body change over the life cycle where growth, maturity and senescence act as the key axis for the investigation of the skeleton, and where people of different physiological stages can be associated with different objects as a means of classification. Instead, this approach offers a more fragmented and contingent understanding of age and the body where ageing is not a unitary process as the plastic body is always open to reconfiguration (cf. Featherstone and Hepworth 1998: 152). Although age is necessarily a directional concept, it cannot be reduced to a notion of the life cycle that involves a steady progress through a series of pre-defined, purely biological stages since real life is more complicated (Featherstone and Hepworth 1998: 152).

It is also important to realise that, in addition to the multifaceted character of corporeal instability, bodies are variable and the material qualities of the skeleton change over the life course. Although the skeleton remains plastic throughout life, the degree of plasticity and its susceptibility to remodelling change with age. When young, it can be more easily modelled and altered, with greater osseous response to stressful activities and social practices (Knüsel 2000; Currey 2001). Thus cradleboarding in infancy may lead to occipital flattening (Schwartz 1995). Where categories of people are deliberately created through the body, the changing material qualities of the body can be deployed in social practices by working on the new body so that intentional modifications such as head-shaping take advantage of the increased plasticity of the infant skull (Lorentz 2003; Aufderheide and Rodriguez-Martin 1998; Torres-Rouff 2002). Indeed so plastic are some elements of the human body that the rapid turnover of bone during the active growth of childhood can also lead to the obliteration of subadult palaeopathology (Lewis 2000). Lewis (2000) points out that rates of fracture in archaeological samples of subadult skeletons are substantially lower than in adult samples. As it is unlikely that they did not suffer trauma in the past, it may be that they developed greenstick fractures where the bone did not break completely along the shaft and that these healed quickly and did not result in deformation (Roberts and Manchester 1995). Mechanically stressful actions to which the body may adapt in youth, when begun later in life are more likely to lead to fracture than remodelling. Human bones may become more brittle in older age with a decrease in bone density and changes in trabecular bone structure resulting in a greater likelihood of traumatic injury (Brickley and Howell 1999).

Taking the potential instability and contingency of the body into account, an investigation of age becomes about what happens to humans over their life course, rather than what particular point in time or age they are at. In other words, it becomes about the ways that people become cultural since bodies emerge through life-ways and modifications to the skeleton as well as mental developments. Shilling (1993) argues that the human body is biologically and socially 'unfinished' at birth and is only 'completed' through action in society (see Prout 2000: 4). Given the plasticity of the body, one might add that this completion takes many different potential forms and, given the possibility held out by the material qualities of the body for constant reworking, never reaches a final end point in the sense of having a particular given destination. Furthermore, because socialisation is not a fixed outcome of childhood in as much as people constantly have to make adjustments for others, learning to modify their behaviour in changing situations throughout their lives, the body is not completely fixed in childhood. There is potential for adult bodies to also change in ways that need not be understood in terms of an inevitable decline (Featherstone and Hepworth 1998: 151). This version of ageing displaces a persistent myth that some essence (sometimes called 'human nature') gets fixed in human beings at a very early age, or that people are stable within categories (Gullette 1988: xxi). Such a perspective places the body within a wider context of human development where development is understood as a lifelong process (Gullette 1988; Featherstone and Hepworth 1998), analogous to Goffman's (1968) 'career of the self' (Featherstone and Hepworth 1998). It places the emphasis on process, rather than on the identification of categories alone. Investigations of the skeleton become not simply about making and reporting a diagnosis, but about identifying the processes leading to the expression of osseous modifications or pathological conditions, in terms of the social practices that may have promoted them.

Human development and the learnt body

The historicity of bodies is vital to understanding the present state of skeletons (cf. Valsiner 2000). Getting to grips with process in relation to social practice, however, also requires an additional layer of understanding as it demands an appreciation that the historicity of bodies is not only a history of behaviour, but that behaviour itself can be studied only as a history of behaviour (Valsiner 2000: 58). Since the ways people act are learnt (Goffman 1972; Rogoff 1981), comprehending the histories of persons by identifying the processes leading to skeletal change over the life course involves not only the investigation of specific social practices, but awareness that social practices are learnt as people grow older and experience the world. Learning is itself a situated process. In addition to action and agency, physical changes to the body imply learnt behaviours repeated according to culturally described norms that are part of an active, dynamic organisation of past experience, rather than a passive, static framework for accommodating it (Ingold 1998: 41). Skeletal changes can be identified as material expressions of actions in as much as they are formed through repeated social practices, habitual actions or postures. Furthermore, people learn by doing and human customs are themselves forms of understanding and knowledge as the world is understood through the body; habit is 'knowledge in the hands which is forthcoming only when bodily effort is made' (Merleau-Ponty 1962: 144). Learning is not a purely mental phenomenon but is also a physical one grounded in active perceptual engagement with one's surroundings that involves co-ordinated movement of the learner's body in imitation of those of others (Ingold 2001a: 241). The acquisition of culturally specific skills thus comes to be literally embodied as part and parcel of the overall developmental process of the human organism (Ingold 1998). Learning is about the incorporation of knowledge into the body (Mauss 1979). It follows that as bodies age, people create their own materiality through learning in a social setting (Toren 1999, 2002). The ways in which they learn and act are related to the objects that surround them in their environment.

In Chapter 4 I argued that the materiality of the body is also a history of relations between people and objects. The cultural milieu in which people are situated has an important effect in relation to contextually specific development (Valsiner 2000; Vygotsky 1978; Greenfield 2000). Since objects are involved in social practices, they are involved in learning and thus in the production and reproduction of social traditions (Sofaer Derevenski 1997a, 2000a; Toren 1999; Greenfield 2000). As such, they are implicated in the developmental process. Learning about ideas requires learning about objects (Sofaer Derevenski 1997a) because ideas are constituted in material relations (Toren 1999: 5) and experiences are held through the material world (Sofaer Derevenski 2000a). Objects form a focus of shared understandings to which common references can be made, allowing our own perspectives to include an understanding of the perspectives of others (Toren 1999). For example, people become engendered, learning about gender through their relations with objects, as objects provide a framework for the organisation of gender knowledge and become associated with gendered behaviours (Sofaer Derevenski 1997a).

But becoming who we are is not simply a question of abstract concepts and actions but of the development of the body that cannot be separated from that of the mind. More specifically, as we saw in Chapter 4, the techniques of the body are related to the use of specific objects, or indeed their misuse or non-use. For example, individuals in societies that do not use furniture to sit on may adopt a squatting posture when resting or working on tasks close to the ground. In this position prolonged extreme dorsiflexion of the ankle may lead to the formation of squatting facets (anterior extensions to the joint surfaces on the talus and distal tibia) (Boulle 2001; Mays 1998; Trinkaus 1975) (Fig. 6.3). Comparisons between groups who habitually squat, such as Indians (Singh 1959), Australian Aboriginals (Wood 1920; Rao 1966), people from first- to second-century AD France (Boulle 2001) and medieval English peasants (Mays 1998), with those who use chairs, such as middle-class Georgian and Victorian Londoners (Molleson n.d. in Mays 1998) or modern Americans (Boulle 2001), show that squatting facets are relatively common in the former and relatively rare in the latter (Mays 1998; Boulle 2001) (Table 6.2). This approach allows us to explore the contingency of all bodies and to explore the relationship between the ontogeny of the

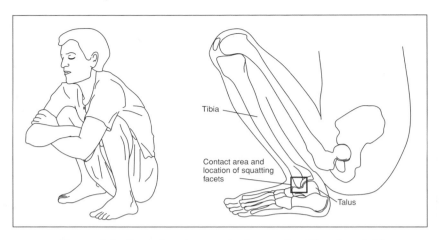

Figure 6.3   Squatting posture (redrawn after Huard and Montagne 1950 and Mays 1998)

individual and objects. Individuals placed into different social categories that may be materially described using objects, be that in terms of age, gender or class, will have different processes of ontogeny. Objects become not about the passive symbolic representation or categorisation of the body in terms of 'who got what in the past' but are *part of* its materiality in that they contribute to the development of particular categories of people. The association between artefacts and individuals may not only be used to actively create, manipulate and convey individual identity (Sørensen 1991, 1997) in terms of the ways that we recognise people in relation to their bodies, but actively *create* their bodies. This means that we can start to consider the implications of objects for the construction of the body as part of a developmental process that takes place in a cumulative manner throughout the life course.

What people learn is also related to their bodies in terms of their capabilities and the social categories to which they belong. Since bodies are vital in the construction and awareness of identity, the situation of individuals in social categories delimits behavioural choices (Blake 1999: 37). The changing bodies of children thus shape both what they are and what they can do, while inviting particular perceptions of what, as children, they should be and should do (James 2000: 26). Similarly, elderly, pregnant or impaired bodies present constraints as well as possibilities (Hockey and James 1993; Thomas 2002; Biggs 2002; Bailey 1999). Different kinds of bodies learn different things and act in different ways at different points in the life course, and this may also be fragmented according

Table 6.2 *The prevalence of squatting facets on the distal tibia and talus in cultural groups with different sitting habits. Indians and Australian Aboriginals habitually rest in a squatting position (Wood 1920; Singh 1959). Routine activities such as squatting to attend to a fire or other tasks low to the ground may have led to the production of squatting facets in the La Favorite and Wharram Percy samples (Boulle 2001; Mays 1998: 119). Chairs were rare in the English medieval countryside, although benches and low stools were known (Field 1965). The middle classes of Georgian and Victorian London would have used chairs, hence the rarity of squatting facets in this group (Mays 1998). Similarly, modern Americans sit on chairs or sofas and squatting is not part of their lifestyle (Boulle 2001). Data from Singh (1959), Wood (1920), Boulle (2001), Molleson (n.d.) in Mays (1998) and Mays (1998)*

	Australian Aboriginals	Indians	1st–2nd-century AD La Favorite, France	11th–16th-century medieval peasants, Wharram Percy, UK	18th–19th-century Georgian and Victorian middle classes, Spitalfields, UK	20th-century Hamann-Todd collection, US
Prevalence of Squatting Facets	80.5% (190[1])	77% (292[1])	45.2% (53[1])	55% (102[2])	2% (9[2])	0% (96[1])

([1]Total number of bones studied, [2]Total number of skeletons studied)

to categorisations such as class, ethnicity or gender. Bodies and bodily changes have implications in terms of limitations and potentials for apprehending the world as people grow (James 2000), setting the boundaries of experience and knowledge.

Actions are always set in the context of pre-existing knowledge, which can change only with increasing age. Changing bodies may view the same object in different ways at different points in the life course as the meanings attached to objects alter with experience. Objects need not therefore be *a priori* divided according to social categories such as child or adult, but a range of meanings may be experienced over time and may vary in strength (cf. Sørensen 1989). Contrasts between age groups may therefore lie in the *way* interaction takes place, in other words the meaning attached to the action, rather than being defined solely by the object itself (Sofaer Derevenski 1994). For example, young children learn the physical properties of objects through interaction with them (Piaget 1968). They may explore objects in terms of texture, taste, smell, vision or sound, whereas for an adult who has already acquired this knowledge and who has greater strength and manipulative skills, interaction with the same object may focus on its utilitarian or ritual significance. For a child learning about the world, a metal knife is smooth, cold and sharp. For an adult it is functional – it cuts things. One might consider the parameters of common archaeological objects, such as quern stones. For a young child these are cold, heavy and smooth. For an older child or an adult they are all these things, but are also used for grinding. This perspective suggests a more fluid understanding of relationships between objects and people than a straightforward association of artefacts with bodies allows as, while it does not discount the possibility of age-specific associations between people and objects, it acknowledges the way that individuals of all ages may be situated within the same cultural milieu. This has implications for the body as the differing ways that people relate to objects at different points in their lives may have potentially different skeletal consequences as they use objects in different ways and with changing intensity. Though of potential importance, such nuances, however, are currently difficult to identify on a skeletal level and require further investigation.

Age and hybrids

Understanding the body and age in terms of contextually specific development highlights the ways that the body, objects and society work on each other (Prout 2000: 5). 'What produces them [bodies] is not simply biological events, the phenomenology of bodily experience, and not merely structures of symbolic and discursive meaning – though all of these are important – but also the patterns of material organization and their modes of ordering' (Prout 2000: 15). The notion of the hybrid made up of changing associations and disassociations between human and non-human entities (Latour 1993) is therefore a particularly pertinent and useful way to investigate age as a means of understanding the cumulative formation of a complex and multilayered entity that comes into being over time.

The idea of the body as hybrid offers a framework for exploring the contingency of the body in terms of the networks in which bodies are situated, and the processes that may occur at different points in time for different groups of people. Since the material expression of action is related to differences between bodies, social practices, objects and the material qualities of the skeleton, each of which forms part of the network, different hybrids can be expected to emerge at different points in the life course for different social categories in different places and periods. Contrasts in the configuration of hybrids can be expected at least at four different levels to do with the age of the individual, their membership of other social categories such as gender or class, their location in space and their chronological setting.

Understanding bodies as hybrids has been used in sociology to analyse the changing bodies of dancers at the end of their careers (Wainwright and Turner 2004), cyberbodies and cyberpunk (Featherstone and Burrows 1995), the ways that seriously ill bodies are maintained through medical technologies and machines (Place 2000), and bodies in other medical settings (Van der Ploeg 2004). Analysis of bodies situated within networks focuses on translations. In other words, the movement back and forth between bodies and objects, the mediation between these different entities (Prout 2000) and the construction of links as well as boundaries (Strathern 1996). 'Examining bodies in this view thus becomes a matter of tracing through the means, the varied array of materials and practices involved in their construction and maintenance – and in some circumstances their unravelling and disintegration' (Prout 2000: 14–15).

Such an approach need not, however, be confined to recent or to living bodies. While acknowledging current practical difficulties involved in identifying the role of specific objects and their intensity of use from the human skeleton (Jurmain 1990: 92; Knüsel 2000), such a literal approach to the production of the archaeological body invites investigation of the potential effects and ramifications of interactions between persons and things in a range of ways, including those that traditionally involve detailed empirical study, scientific methods of hypothesis testing, as well as ethnographic and sociological observation. It promotes exploration of the means by which hybrids are created at a range of scales, from the use of specific objects to the implications of broader lifestyles and environments, rather than simply staying with the status quo and stating that they are difficult to identify.

To illustrate how archaeological bodies might be interrogated with regard to networks of materials situated within socially specific practices (cf. Jones 2002a), as an example, I return here to my study of individuals from the island of Ensay, Outer Hebrides (Sofaer Derevenski 1998, 2000c). In the previous chapter I suggested that differences in patterns of degenerative changes in the spines of men and women from Ensay could be related to contrasting gendered activities, particularly with regard to load-bearing using baskets known as creels which were primarily used by women. Skeletal modifications could be understood as gender, with the body as a form of material culture brought into being through practice. Understanding the body as a hybrid enables one step further in the analysis of these bodies, in as much as it becomes possible to consider the development of specific kinds of bodies in terms of a temporal process that takes place through a network of heterogeneous materials.

Many of the gendered skills and roles on Ensay were acquired during childhood, with children also integral to the division of labour. Tasks which may have had an impact on the skeleton were therefore undertaken throughout the life course from a very young age. Children were involved in minding cattle, herding, helping at seed time and harvest, procuring bait and baiting the lines. Large families were considered desirable as children made life easier for parents in their middle and old age (Macdonald 1978). Women in particular, however, learnt specific techniques of the body (Mauss 1979) as part of social conventions in the division of labour, that were intimately linked to the objects used as part of these social practices. The skeletal implications of carrying creels and grinding meal with hand querns were particularly severe. They resulted in accelerated degenerative changes including eburnation and remodelling of the apophyseal facets of the vertebrae, osteophytosis of the lumbar vertebral bodies (Sofaer Derevenski 1998, 2000c), and degenerative joint changes in the acromion (shoulder joint) (Miles 1996) that were visible in young individuals in the second decade of life and that got progressively worse with age (Fig. 6.4). Thus not only did the generally stressful lifestyle contribute to the formation of the body, but in this example the skeletal changes can be traced to learnt gendered practices involving the use of particular objects implicated in the physical creation of the body. These objects had a major role in literally shaping women's bodies over the course of their lives.

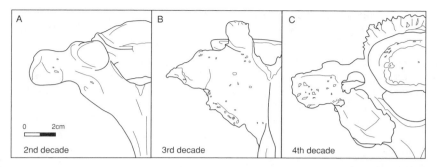

Figure 6.4   Progressive accelerated degenerative joint changes in the vertebrae of Ensay females in the second, third and fourth decades of life: a) Normal joint (superior aspect T1) b) Moderate joint remodelling (superior aspect T3) c) Extreme joint remodelling and osteophytosis (inferior aspect C7)

MacGregor (1952: 237) wrote, 'The first impression gained by the stranger to the Outer Hebrides . . . is that the womenfolk look careworn, sad, and prematurely old. A woman of forty in these parts often looks quite elderly. The menfolk, on the other hand, are better preserved, for they preserve themselves by leaving to the women all available work or worry.' What is important here is not the absolute age of the women involved, although estimates of chronological age play a part in tracking changes to the body over time, but the direction of the developments and changes to the body. The study of age becomes about analysing the character of the hybrid in terms of its formation over time. Changes in bodies with age are a question of social practices that can be analysed with regard to the networks of materials where people are agents rather than simply outcomes (cf. Prout 2000). Indeed we cannot understand the body without reference to those networks.

Such an approach is analytically challenging (Prout 2000: 12) as it requires that we examine the total milieu in which people live and the objects with which they interact, rather than simply referring to adaptations to the environment as explanations for osseous changes, or drawing isolated associations between people and objects in mortuary contexts. We cannot study age just in terms of biology or through traditional forms of material culture as there is no settled distinction between the natural and the social (cf. Prout 2000: 12). Clearly we may not be able to see all of the physical changes that occur in the body archaeologically, or to relate those that we can see to specific objects or events. There is also a need to accumulate baseline data on the skeletal implications of human activities, rather than to recount them on an anecdotal basis (Sofaer Derevenski 2000c). Nonetheless, understanding bodies as hybrids that develop over time also opens up a wide range of possibilities. In particular, archaeology's focus means that we are in a prime position to explore the role of the material. Social practices are material practices and are therefore potentially accessible through an examination of the skeletal body as well as artefacts. Archaeologically we might begin to identify such material practices implicated in the development of the body through an examination of actual or potential relationships between objects, patterns of material organisation and people. We may be able to access aspects of the networks within which they take part, and begin to unravel some of the translations. By explicitly linking the materiality of the body with objects, the notion of the hybrid questions the idea that human embodiment is simply concerned with issues of corporeality (Place 2000: 172).

Human ontogeny is material and it is impossible to separate the body from the material world. The contingency of the body is linked to objects, and because the body is material it becomes itself a topic for archaeological investigation. Once the material is highlighted, the ontological status of the body is not what matters – in other words it is not necessarily important whether a given body is that of a child or an adult – but what matters is trajectory of the developmental process and the expression of the materiality of the body for any given individual, be they living or dead. As Latour (2004: 206) puts it, the body is 'an interface that becomes more and more describable as it learns to be affected by more and more elements', where the more that is learnt, the more differences exist (Latour 2004: 213). From this point of view, what is important about the body from an archaeological perspective is not arguments over whether the body is biological or social, but how the body is materiality expressed in a contextually dependent and archaeologically accessible manner. The study of age is then not just about identifying social categories, but about exploring contextually dependent aspects of human development and how society both initiates and monitors that development in relation to those categories.

Such an approach requires that we reconceptualise our understanding of the body and age. It is understood that people may belong to social and physiologically described groups, but the main emphasis of archaeological investigation shifts towards understanding the processes and complexity of the formation of the body in terms of its contingency in the context of its total development, rather than the absolute categorisation of individuals. By framing the study of the body in these terms, a different aim, or end point, emerges that deals not only with categories (although these are without doubt important), but that situates these in an understanding of development and materiality. Viewed in this light, osteoarchaeology and interpretative archaeology are aiming at the same goal – to explore the contingency and instability of the materiality of the body through a notion of social practice. Rather than thinking of age in terms of a linear transformation that is methodologically and ontologically problematic, an appreciation of the contingency and instability of the development of the body as a hybrid, and of behaviour as learnt, provides a theoretical link between bodies and objects.

References

Acsádi, G. and Nemeskéri, J. (1970) *History of the Human Life Span and Mortality*, Budapest: Akadémiai Kiadò.

Albarella, U. (2001) Exploring the real nature of environmental archaeology. In: Albarella, U. (ed.) *Environmental Archaeology: Meaning and Purpose*, pp. 3–13. Dordrecht: Kluwer Academic Publishers.

Allison-Bunnell, S. W. (1998) Making nature 'real' again. In: Macdonald, S. (ed.) *The Politics of Display: Museums, Science, Culture*, pp. 77–97. London: Routledge.

Ambrose, S., Buikstra, J. and Harold, W. (2003) Status and gender differences in diet at Mound 72, Cahokia, revealed by isotopic analysis of bone. *Journal of Archaeological Science* 22(3): 217–26.

Andersen, J., Manchester, K. and Roberts, C. A. (1994) Septic bone changes in leprosy: a clinical, radiological and palaeopathological review. *International Journal of Osteoarchaeology* 4(1): 21–30.

Anderson, I. (1995) Bodies, disease and the problem of Foucault. *Social Analysis* 37: 67–81.

Anderson, T. (2003) A medieval bladder stone from Norwich, Norfolk. *International Journal of Osteoarchaeology* 13(3): 165–7.

Angel, J. L. (1981) History and development of paleopathology. *American Journal of Physical Anthropology* 56(4): 509–15.

Appadurai, A. (1986) Introduction: commodities and the politics of value. In: Appadurai, A. (ed.) *The Social Life of Things: Commodities in Cultural Perspective*, pp. 3–63. Cambridge: Cambridge University Press.

Arcadio, F., Moulay, A. and Chauvinc, P. (1973) *Gestes de la vie quotidienne*, Lyon: Masson et Cie, Editeurs.

Armelagos, G. J. (1998) Introduction: sex, gender and health status in prehistoric and contemporary populations. In: Grauer, A. L. and Stuart-Macadam, P. (eds.) *Sex and Gender in Paleopathological Perspective*, pp. 1–10. Cambridge: Cambridge University Press.

Armstrong, A. (1987) Foucault and the problem of human anatomy. In: Scambler, G. (ed.) *Sociological Theory and Medical Sociology*, pp. 59–76. London: Tavistock.

Armstrong, D. (1983) *Political Anatomy of the Body: Medical Knowledge in Britain in the Twentieth Century*, Cambridge: Cambridge University Press.

Arnold, B. (2002) 'Sein und Werden': gender as process in mortuary ritual. In: Milledge Nelson, S. and Rosen-Ayalon, M. (eds.) *In Pursuit of Gender:*

Worldwide Archaeological Approaches, pp. 239–56. Walnut Creek: AltaMira Press.

Astuti, R. (2001) Are we all natural dualists? A cognitive developmental approach. *Journal of the Royal Anthropological Institute* n.s. 7: 429–47.

Atkinson, P. (1995) *Medical Talk and Medical Work: The Liturgy of the Clinic*. London: Sage.

Aufderheide, A. C. and Rodriguez-Martin, C. (1998) *The Cambridge Encyclopedia of Human Paleopathology*, Cambridge: Cambridge University Press.

Baby, R. S. (1961) A Hopewell human bone whistle. *American Antiquity* 27(1): 108–10.

Bachand, H., Joyce, R. A. and Hendon, J. A. (2003) Bodies moving in space: ancient Mesoamerican sculpture and embodiment. *Cambridge Archaeological Journal* 13(2): 238–47.

Bailey, L. (1999) Refracted selves? A study of changes in self-identity in the transition to motherhood. *Sociology* 33(2): 335–52.

Baker, B. J. and Kealhofer, L. (eds.) (1996) *Bioarchaeology of Native American Adaptation in the Spanish Borderlands*, Gainesville: University Press of Florida.

Bakhtin, M. (1984) *Rabelais and His World*, Bloomington: Indiana University Press.

Banton, M. (1987) *Racial Theories*, Cambridge: Cambridge University Press.

Bapty, I. and Yates, T. (eds.) (1990) *Archaeology After Structuralism*, London: Routledge.

Barkan, E. (1988) Mobilizing scientists against Nazi racism 1933–1939. In: Stocking, G. W. Jr (ed.) *Bones, Bodies, Behavior: Essays on Biological Anthropology*, pp. 180–205. Madison, Wis.: University of Wisconsin Press.

Barkan, E. (1992) *The Retreat of Scientific Racism*, Cambridge: Cambridge University Press.

Barrett, J. (1988) The living, the dead and the ancestors: Neolithic and early Bronze Age mortuary practices. In: Barrett, J. C. and Kinnes, I. A. (eds.) *The Archaeology of Context in the Neolithic and Bronze Age: Recent Trends*, pp. 30–41. Sheffield: John Collis.

Barrett, J. (1994) *Fragments from Antiquity: An Archaeology of Social Life in Britain, 2900–1200 BC*, Oxford: Blackwell.

Barrett, J. (2000) A thesis on agency. In: Dobres, M. and Robb, J. (eds.) *Agency in Archaeology*, pp. 60–8. London: Routledge.

Barthes, R. (1985) *Système de la mode (The Fashion System)*, London: Cape.

Bass, W. M. (1983) The occurrence of Japanese trophy skulls in the United States. *Journal of Forensic Sciences* 28(3): 800–3.

Bass, W. M. (1995) *Human Osteology: A Laboratory and Field Manual*. Missouri Archaeological Society Special Publications, No. 2. Columbia, Mo.: Missouri Archaeological Society.

Battersby, C. (1993) Her body/her boundaries: gender and the metaphysics of containment. In: Benjamin, A. (ed.) *Journal of Philosophy and the Visual Arts: The Body*, pp. 31–9. London: Academic Group.

Baud, C. (1996) Paléopathologie du travail. In: *L'Identité des populations archéologiques. XVIe Rencontres internationales d'archéologie et d'histoire d'Antibes*, pp. 207–10. Sophia Antipolis: Editions APDCA.

Bauman, Z. (1973) *Culture as Praxis*, London: Routledge and Kegan Paul.

Bauman, Z. (1998) Postmodern adventures of life and death. In: Scambler, G. and Higgs, P. (eds.) *Modernity, Medicine and Health: Medical Sociology Towards 2000*, pp. 216–31. London: Routledge.

Becher, T. (1989) *Academic Tribes and Territories: Intellectual Enquiry and the Cultures of Disciplines*, Milton Keynes: Open University Press.

Becker, A. (1995) *Body, Self and Society: A View from Fiji*, Philadelphia: University of Pennsylvania Press.

Bedford, M. E., Russell, K. F., Lovejoy, C. O., Meindl, R. S., Simpson, S. W. and Stuart-Macadam, P. L. (1993) A test of multi-factorial aging methods using skeletons with known ages at death from the Grant Collection. *American Journal of Physical Anthropology* 91(3): 287–97.

Bender, B. (2002) Time and landscape. *Current Anthropology* 43: S103–S112.

Bender, B., Hamilton, S. and Tilley, C. (1997) Leskernick: stone worlds; alternative narratives; nested landscapes. *Proceedings of the Prehistoric Society* 63: 147–78.

Bennett, J. M. (1987) *Women in the Medieval English Countryside: Gender and Household in Brigstock Before the Plague*, Oxford: Oxford University Press.

Benthien, C. (2002) *Skin: On the Cultural Border between Self and the World*, trans. T. Dunlop, New York: Columbia University Press.

Bentley, A., Price, T. D. and Stephan, E. (2004) Determining the 'local' 87Sr/86Sr range for archaeological skeletons: a case study from Neolithic Europe. *Journal of Archaeological Science* 31(4): 365–75.

Benton, T. (1989) Marxism and natural limits: an ecological critique and reconstruction. *New Left Review* 178: 51–86.

Biggs, H. (2002) The ageing body. In: Evans, M. and Lee, E. (eds.) *Real Bodies: A Sociological Introduction*, pp. 167–84. Basingstoke: Palgrave.

Binford, L. R. (1962) Archaeology as anthropology. *American Antiquity* 28(2): 217–25.

Binford, L. R. (1964) A consideration of archaeological research design. *American Antiquity* 29(4): 425–41.

Binford, L. R. (1972) *An Archaeological Perspective*, New York: Seminar Press.

Binford, L. R. (1983a) *Working at Archaeology*, New York: Academic Press.

Binford, L. R. (1983b) *In Pursuit of the Past: Decoding the Archaeological Record*, London: Thames and Hudson.

Bird, D. W. and Bird, R. B. (2000) The ethnoarchaeology of juvenile foragers: shellfishing strategies among Meriam children. *Journal of Anthropological Archaeology* 19: 461–76.

Bird-David, N. (1993) Tribal metaphorization of human-nature relatedness: a comparative analysis. In: Milton, K. (ed.) *Environmentalism: The View from Anthropology*, pp. 112–25. London: Routledge.

Birke, L. (1986) *Women, Feminism and Biology: The Feminist Challenge*, New York: Methuen.

Birke, L. (1999) Bodies and biology. In: Price, J. and Shildrick, M. (eds.) *Feminist Theory and the Body*, pp. 42–9. Edinburgh: Edinburgh University Press.

Blackless, M., Charuvastra, A., Derryck, A., Fausto-Sterling, A., Lauzanne, K. and Lee, E. (2000) How sexually dimorphic are we? Review and synthesis. *American Journal of Human Biology* 12(2): 151–66.

Blackwood, E. (1984) Sexuality and gender in certain Native American tribes: the case of cross-gender females. *Signs* 10: 27–42.

Blake, C. F. (1994) Foot-binding in neo-Confucian China and the appropriation of female labour. *Signs* 19: 676–710.

Blake, E. (1999) Identity-mapping in the Sardinian Bronze Age. *European Journal of Archaeology* 2(1): 35–55.

Blakey, M., Leslie, T. E. and Reidy, J. P. (1994) Frequency and chronological distribution of dental enamel hypoplasia in enslaved African Americans: a test of the weaning hypothesis. *American Journal of Physical Anthropology* 95(4): 371–83.

Bloch, M. and Parry, J. (eds.) (1982) *Death and the Regeneration of Life*, Cambridge: Cambridge University Press.

Boas, F. (1911) *The Mind of Primitive Man*, New York: Macmillan.

Boas, F. (1912) Changes in bodily form of descendants of immigrants. *American Anthropologist* n.s. 14: 530–62.

Bogin, B. (1999) *Patterns of Human Growth*, 2nd edition. Cambridge: Cambridge University Press.

Bogin, B. (2001) *The Growth of Humanity*, New York: Wiley-Liss.

Bogin, B. and Keep, R. (1998) Eight thousand years of human growth in Latin America: economic and political history revealed by anthropometry. In: Komlos, J. and Baten, J. (eds.) *The Biological Standard of Living in Comparative Perspective*, pp. 268–93. Stuttgart: Franz Steiner Verlag.

Boivin, N. (2000) Life rhythms and floor sequences: excavating time in rural Rajasthan and Neolithic Çatalhöyük. *World Archaeology* 31(3): 367–88.

Boivin, N. (2004) Mind over matter? Collapsing the mind-matter dichotomy in material culture studies. In: DeMarrais, E., Gosden, C. and Renfrew, C. (eds.) *Rethinking Materiality: The Engagement of Mind with the Material World*, pp. 63–71. Cambridge: McDonald Institute for Archaeological Research.

Boldsen, J. L. (1995) The place of plasticity in the study of the secular trend for male stature: an analysis of Danish biological population history. In: Mascie-Taylor, C. G. N. and Bogin, B. (eds.) *Human Variability and Plasticity*, pp. 75–90. Cambridge: Cambridge University Press.

Boulle, E. (2001) Osteological features associated with ankle hyperdorsiflexion. *International Journal of Osteoarchaeology* 11(5): 345–9.

Bourbou, C. (2003) Health patterns of proto-Byzantine populations (6th–7th centuries AD) in south Greece: the cases of Eleutherna (Crete) and Messene (Peloponnese). *International Journal of Osteoarchaeology* 13(5): 303–13.

Bourdieu, P. (1969) Intellectual field and creative project. *Social Science Information* 8(2): 89–119.

Bourdieu, P. (1977) *Outline of a Theory of Practice*, Cambridge: Cambridge University Press.

Bourdieu, P. (1984) *Distinction: A Social Critique of the Judgement of Taste*, Cambridge, Mass.: Harvard University Press.

Bourdieu, P. (1990) *The Logic of Practice*, Cambridge: Polity Press.

Boylston, A. (2000) Evidence for weapon-related trauma in British archaeological samples. In: Cox, M. and Mays, S. (eds.) *Human Osteology in Archaeology and Forensic Science*, pp. 357–80. London: Greenwich Medical Media Ltd.

Brickley, M. and Howell, P. G. T. (1999) Measurement of changes in trabecular bone structure with age in an archaeological population. *Journal of Archaeological Science* 26(2): 151–7.

Brickley, M. and McKinley, J. (eds.) (2004) *Guidelines to the Standards for Recording Human Remains*, Southampton and Reading: BABAO and Institute of Field Archaeologists.

Bridges, P. S. (1983) Subsistence activity and biomechanical properties of long bones in two Amerindian populations. *American Journal of Physical Anthropology* 60(2): 177.

Bridges, P. S. (1985) Structural changes of the arms associated with the habitual grinding of corn. *American Journal of Physical Anthropology* 66(2): 149–50.

Bridges, P. S. (1989) Changes in activities with the shift to agriculture in the southeastern United States. *Current Anthropology* 30: 385–93.

Bridges, P. S. (1991) Degenerative joint disease in hunter-gatherers and agriculturalists from the southeastern United States. *American Journal of Physical Anthropology* 85(4): 379–91.

Brodie, N. (1994) *The Neolithic–Bronze Age Transition in Britain: A Critical Review of Some Archaeological and Craniological Concepts*, Oxford: BAR British Series 238. Tempus Reparatum.

Bronfen, E. and Goodwin, S. W. (1993) Introduction. In: Bronfen, E. and Goodwin, S. W. (eds.) *Death and Representation*, pp. 3–25. Baltimore: The Johns Hopkins Press.

Brothwell, D. (1972) *Digging Up Bones*, 2nd edition. London: Trustees of the British Museum.

Brothwell, D. (1999) Biosocial and bioarchaeological aspects of conflict and warfare. In: Carman, J. and Harding, A. (eds.) *Ancient Warfare*, pp. 25–38. Stroud: Sutton.

Brown, K. A. (1998) Gender and sex – what can ancient DNA tell us? *Ancient Biomolecules* 2: 3–15.

Brown, K. A. (2000) Ancient DNA applications in human osteoarchaeology: achievements, problems and potential. In: Cox, M. and Mays, S. (eds.) *Human Osteology in Archaeology and Forensic Science*, pp. 455–73. London: Greenwich Medical Media.

Brück, J. (1998) In the footsteps of the ancestors: a review of Tilley's 'A phenomenology of landscape: places, paths and monuments'. *Archaeological Review from Cambridge* 15(1): 23–36.

Brück, J. (1999) Ritual and rationality: some problems of interpretation in European archaeology. *Journal of European Archaeology* 2(3): 313–44.

Buckland, P. C., Amorosi, T., Barlow, L. K., Dugmore, A. J., Mayewski, P. A., McGovern, T. H., Ogilvie, A. E. J., Sadler, J. P. and Skidmore, P. (1996)

Bioarchaeological and climatological evidence for the fate of Norse farmers in Medieval Greenland. *Antiquity* 70: 88–96.

Buikstra, J. E. and Ubelaker, D. H. (eds.) (1994) *Standards for Data Collection from Human Skeletal Remains*, Fayetteville: Arkansas Archeological Survey.

Burman, E. (1994) *Deconstructing Developmental Psychology*, London: Routledge.

Burton, J. H., Price, T. D., Cahue, L. and Wright, L. E. (2003) The use of barium and strontium abundance in human skeletal tissues to determine their geographic origins. *International Journal of Osteoarchaeology* 13(1–2): 88–95.

Busby, C. (1997) Permeable and partible persons: a comparison of gender and body in south India and Melanesia. *Journal of the Royal Anthropological Institute* 3(2): 261–78.

Butler, J. (1990) *Gender Trouble: Feminism and the Subversion of Identity*, New York: Routledge.

Butler, J. (1993) *Bodies that Matter: On the Discursive Limits of 'Sex'*, New York: Routledge.

Buzhilova, A. (1999) Medieval examples of syphilis from European Russia. *International Journal of Osteoarchaeology* 9(5): 271–6.

Bynum, C. W. (1991) *Fragmentation and Redemption: Essays on Gender and the Human Body in Medieval Religion*, New York: Zone Books.

Caiger-Smith, A. (1995) *Pottery, People and Time: A Workshop in Action*, Shepton Beauchamp: Richard Dennis.

Cain, M. (1977) The economic activities of children in a village in Bangladesh. *Population and Development Review* 3: 210–27.

Cameron, A. D. (1986) *Go Listen to the Crofters: The Napier Commission and Crofting a Century Ago.* Stornoway: Acair.

Capasso, L., Kennedy, K. A. R. and Wilczak, C. (1998) *Atlas of Occupational Markers on Human Remains*, Teramo: Edigrafital SPA.

Carter, D. R., Orr, T. E., Fyrie, D. P. and Schurman, D. J. (1987) Influences of mechanical stress on prenatal and postnatal skeletal development. *Clinical Orthopaedics and Related Research* 219: 237–50.

Cassidy, C. M. (1984) Skeletal evidence for prehistoric subsistence adaptation in the Central Ohio River Valley. In: Cohen, M. and Armelagos, G. J. (eds.) *Paleopathology at the Origins of Agriculture*, pp. 307–46. Orlando: Academic Press.

Chalmers, A. F. (1982) *What is this Thing Called Science? An Assessment of the Nature and Status of Science and its Methods*, Milton Keynes: Open University Press.

Chamberlain, A. and Witkin, A. (2003) Early Neolithic diets: evidence from pathology and dental wear. In: Parker Pearson, M. (ed.) *Food, Culture and Identity in the Neolithic and Early Bronze Age*, pp. 53–8. Oxford: Archaeopress.

Chapman, J. (1999) *Fragmentation in Archaeology: People, Places and Broken Objects in the Prehistory of South Eastern Europe*, London: Routledge.

Chapman, J. (2000) Tension at funerals: social practices and the subversion of community structure in later Hungarian prehistory. In: Dobres, M. and Robb, J. (eds.) *Agency in Archaeology*, pp. 169–95. London: Routledge.

Chapman, R., Kinnes, I. and Randsborg, K. (eds.) (1981) *The Archaeology of Death*, Cambridge: Cambridge University Press.

Chavez, A. and Martinez, C. (1982) *Growing Up in a Developing Community*, Mexico City: Instituto Nacional de la Nutricion.

Ciranni, R. and Fornaciari, G. (2003) Luigi Boccherini and the Barocco cello: an 18th century striking case of occupational disease. *International Journal of Osteoarchaeology* 13(5): 294–302.

Claassen, C. (1992) Questioning gender: an introduction. In: Claassen, C. (ed.) *Exploring Gender through Archaeology: Selected Papers from the 1991 Boone Conference*, pp. 1–9. Madison: Prehistory Press.

Clark, N. (2000) Botanizing on the asphalt? The complex life of cosmopolitan bodies. *Body and Society* 6(3–4): 12–33.

Clark, S. R. L. (1988) Is Humanity a Natural Kind ? In: Ingold, T. (ed.) *What is an Animal?* pp. 17–34. London: Unwin & Hyman.

Clarke, D. (1973) Archaeology: the loss of innocence. *Antiquity* 47: 6–18.

Claussen, B. F. (1982) Chronic hypertrophy of the ulna in the professional rodeo cowboy. *Clinical Orthopaedica and Related Research* 164: 45–7.

Cohen, M. N. and Armelagos, G. J. (1984) *Paleopathology at the Origins of Agriculture*, Orlando: Academic Press.

Coleman, D. (1995) Human migration: effects on people, effects on populations. In: Mascie-Taylor, C. G. N. and Bogin, B. (eds.) *Human Variability and Plasticity*, pp. 115–45. Cambridge: Cambridge University Press.

Coles, G. (ed.) (1995) *The Teaching of Environmental Archaeology in Higher Education in the UK*, York: Working Papers of the Association for Environmental Archaeology.

Collier, J. F. and Yanagisako, S. (eds.) (1987) *Gender and Kinship: Essays Toward a Unified Analysis*. Stanford: Stanford University Press.

Colt Hoare, R. (1810–21) *The Ancient History of Wiltshire*, London: William Miller.

Coltrain, J. B., Hayes, M. G. and O'Rourke, D. H. (2003) Sealing, whaling and caribou: the skeletal isotope chemistry of eastern Arctic foragers. *Journal of Archaeological Science* 31(1): 39–57.

Conkey, M. (2001) Epilogue: thinking about gender with theory and methods. In: Klein, C. F. (ed.) *Gender in Pre-hispanic America: A Symposium at Dumbarton Oaks 12 and 13 October 1996*, pp. 341–62. Dumbarton Oaks, Washington, DC.

Conkey, M. W. and Gero, J. M. (1997) Programme to practice: gender and feminism in archaeology. *Annual Review of Anthropology* 26: 411–37.

Connerton, P. (1989) *How Societies Remember*, Cambridge: Cambridge University Press.

Cook, D. C. (1984) Subsistence and health in the lower Illinois Valley: osteological evidence. In: Cohen, M. and Armelagos, G. J. (eds.) *Paleopathology at the Origins of Agriculture*, pp. 237–70. Orlando: Academic Press.

Cooper, C., Javaid, M. K., Taylor, P., Walker-Bone, K., Dennison, E. and Arden, N. (2002) The fetal origins of osteoporotic fracture. *Calcified Tissue International* 70: 391–4.

Cooper, C., McAlindon, T., Coggon, D., Egger, P. and Dieppe, P. (1994) Occupational activity and osteoarthritis of the knee. *Annals of the Rheumatic Diseases* 53: 90–3.

Cornwall, A. and Lindisfarne, N. (eds.) (1994) *Dislocating Masculinity: Comparative Ethnographies*, London: Routledge.

Cowin, S. C. (2001) The false premise in Wolff's Law. In: Cowin, S. C. (ed.) *Bone Mechanics Handbook*, 2nd edition, pp. 30-1–30-15. Boca Raton: CRC Press.

Cox, G. and Sealy, J. (1997) Investigating identity and life histories: isotopic analysis and historical documentation of slave skeletons found on the Cape Town foreshore, South Africa. *International Journal of Historical Archaeology* 1: 207–24.

Cox, M. (1996) *Life and Death in Spitalfields 1700–1850*, York: Council for British Archaeology.

Cox, M. (2000a) Assessment of parturition. In: Cox, M. and Mays, S. (eds.) *Human Osteology in Archaeology and Forensic Science*, pp. 131–42. London: Greenwich Medical Media Ltd.

Cox, M. (2000b) Ageing adults from the skeleton. In: Cox, M. and Mays, S. (eds.) *Human Osteology in Archaeology and Forensic Science*, pp. 61–81. London: Greenwich Medical Media.

Cox, M. (ed.) (1998) *Grave Concerns: Death and Burial in England 1700–1850*, York: Council for British Archaeology.

Cox, M. and Scott, A. (1992) Evaluation of the obstetric significance of some pelvic characters in an 18th century British sample. *American Journal of Physical Anthropology* 89(4): 431–40.

Crawford, S. (1991) When do Anglo-Saxon children count? *Journal of Theoretical Archaeology* 2: 17–24.

Crawford, S. (1999) *Childhood in Anglo-Saxon England*, Stroud: Sutton Publishing.

Creed, B. and Hoorn, J. (eds.) (2001) *Body Trade: Captivity, Cannibalism and Colonialism in the Pacific*, Sydney: Pluto Press.

Crews, D. E. and Garruto, R. M. (eds.) (1994) *Biological Anthropology and Aging: Perspectives on Human Variation over the Life Span*, Oxford: Oxford University Press.

Crossley, N. (2001) *The Social Body: Habit, Identity and Desire*, London: Sage.

Csordas, T. J. (ed.) (1994) *Embodiment and Experience*, Cambridge University: Cambridge University Press.

Cucina, A. and Tiesler, V. (2003) Dental caries and antemortem tooth loss in the northern Peten area, Mexico: a biocultural perspective on social status differences among the Classic Maya. *American Journal of Physical Anthropology* 122(1): 1–10.

Currey, H. L. F. (ed.) (1986) *Mason and Currey's Clinical Rheumatology*, Edinburgh: Churchill Livingstone.

Currey, J. D. (2001) Ontogenetic changes in compact bone properties. In: Cowin, S. C. (ed.) *Bone Mechanics Handbook*, pp. 19-1–19-16. Boca Raton: CRC Press.

del Valle, T. (ed.) (1993) *Gendered Anthropology*, London: Routledge.

Demirjian, A. (1986) Dentition. In: Falkner, F. and Tanner, J. M. (eds.) *Human Growth, vol. II: Postnatal Growth and Neurobiology*, 2nd edition. pp. 269–98. New York: Plenum Press.

Demirjian, A. and Goldstein, H. (1976) New systems for dental maturity based on seven and four teeth. *Annals of Human Biology* 3: 411–21.

Dequeker, J., Goris, P. and Uytterhoeven, R. (1983) Osteoporosis and osteoarthritis (osteoarthrosis): anthropometric distinctions. *Journal of the American Medical Association* 249: 1448–51.

Descola, P. and Pálsson, G. (1996) Introduction. In: Descola, P. and Pálsson, G. (eds.) *Nature and Society: Anthropological Perspectives*, pp. 1–21. London: Routledge.

Dettwyler, K. A. and Fishman, C. (1992) Infant feeding practices and growth. *Annual Review of Anthropology* 21: 171–204.

Dickens, P. (1992) *Society and Nature: Towards a Green Social Theory*, Hemel Hempstead: Harvester Wheatsheaf.

Dickens, P. (2001) Linking the social and natural sciences: is capital modifying human biology in its own image? *Sociology* 35(1): 93–110.

Ditch, L. E. and Rose, J. C. (1972) A multivariate dental sexing technique. *American Journal of Physical Anthropology* 37(1): 61–4.

Dobres, M. and Robb, J. (2000) Agency in archaeology: paradigm or platitude? In: Dobres, M. and Robb, J. (eds.) *Agency in Archaeology*, pp. 3–17. London: Routledge.

Donaldson, C. L., Hulley, S. B., Vogel, J. M., Hatter, R. S., Buyers, J. H. and McMillar, D. E. (1970) Effect of prolonged bed rest on bone mineral. *Metabolism, Clinical & Experimental* 19: 1071–84.

Douglas, M. (1966) *Purity and Danger: An Analysis of the Concepts of Pollution and Taboo*, London: Routledge and Kegan Paul.

Douglas, M. (1973) *Rules and Meanings*, Harmondsworth: Penguin.

Dowson, T. (2000) Why queer archaeology? An introduction. *World Archaeology* 32(2): 161–5.

Duden, B. (1991) *The Woman Beneath the Skin: A Doctor's Patients in Eighteenth-Century Germany*, Cambridge, Mass., Harvard University Press.

Dunbar, R., Knight, C. and Power, C. (eds.) (1999) *The Evolution of Culture*, Edinburgh: Edinburgh University Press.

Duncan, N. (ed.) (1996) *Bodyspace: Destabilizing Geographies of Gender and Sexuality*, London: Routledge.

Dutour, O. (1986) Enthesopathies (lesions of muscular insertions) as indicators of the activities of Neolithic Saharan populations. *American Journal of Physical Anthropology* 71(2): 221–4.

Dutour, O. (1993) Les Marqueurs d'activités sur l'os humain fossile: une tracéologie paléoanthropologique? In: *Tracéologie et fonction: le geste retrouvé. Colloque international de Liège 50*, pp. 59–66. Liège, Editions ERAUL.

Elias, N. (1978) *The Civilizing Process*, New York: Urizen.

Elias, N. (1985) *The Loneliness of the Dying*, Oxford: Blackwell.

Eshed, V., Gopher, A., Galili, E. and Hershkovitz, I. (2004) Musculoskeletal stress markers in Natufian hunter-gatherers and Neolithic farmers in the

Levant: the upper limb. *American Journal of Physical Anthropology* 123(4): 303–15.

Evans, J. and O'Connor, T. (1999) *Environmental Archaeology: Principles and Methods*, Stroud: Sutton.

Ezzo, J. A., Johnson, C. M. and Price, T. D. (1997) Analytical perspectives on human migration: a case study from east-central Arizona. *Journal of Archaeological Science* 24(5): 447–66.

Farnell, B. (2000) Getting out of the habitus: an alternative model of dynamically embodied social action. *Journal of the Royal Anthropological Institute* (n.s.) 6: 397–418.

Fausto-Sterling, A. (1995) Gender, race, and nation: the comparative anatomy of 'Hottentot' women in Europe, 1815–1817. In: Terry, J. and Urla, J. (eds.) *Deviant Bodies: Critical Perspectives on Difference in Science and Popular Culture*, pp. 19–48. Bloomington: Indiana University Press.

Featherstone, M. (1982) The body in consumer culture. *Theory, Culture and Society* 1(2): 18–33.

Featherstone, M. and Burrows, R. (eds.) (1995) *Cyberspace: Cyberbodies, Cyberpunk: Cultures of Technological Embodiment*, London: Sage.

Featherstone, M. and Hepworth, M. (1998) Ageing, the life course and the sociology of embodiment. In: Higgs, P. and Scambler, G. (eds.) *Modernity, Medicine and Health: Issues Confronting Medical Sociology Towards 2000*, pp. 147–75. London: Routledge.

Featherstone, M. and Wernick, A. (eds.) (1995) *Images of Ageing: Cultural Representations of Later Life*, London: Routledge.

Featherstone, M., Hepworth, M. and Turner, B. S. (1991) *The Body: Social Process and Cultural Theory*, London: Sage.

Ferembach, D., Schwidetzdy, I. and Stroukal, M. (1980) Recommendations for age and sex diagnoses of skeletons. *Journal of Human Evolution* 9: 517–49.

Field, R. K. (1965) Worcestershire peasant buildings, household goods and farming equipment in the later Middle Ages. *Mediaeval Archaeology* 9: 105–45.

Fisher, G. and DiPaolo Loren, D. (2003) Embodying identity in archaeology. *Cambridge Archaeological Journal* 13(2): 225–30.

Foucault, M. (1973) *The Birth of the Clinic: An Archaeology of Medical Perception*, London: Tavistock.

Foucault, M. (1977) *Discipline and Punish: The Birth of the Prison*, London: Allen Lane.

Foucault, M. (1978) *The History of Sexuality, vol. I: An Introduction*, London: Penguin.

Fowler, C. (2002) Body parts: personhood and materiality in the earlier Manx Neolithic. In: Hamilakis, Y., Pluciennik, M. and Tarlow, S. (eds.) *Thinking Through the Body: Archaeologies of Corporeality*, pp. 47–69. New York: Kluwer Academic / Plenum Publishers.

Fox Keller, E. (2000) *The Century of the Gene*, Cambridge, Mass., Harvard University Press.

Fox Keller, E. and Longino, H. E. (eds.) (1996) *Feminism and Science*, Oxford: Oxford University Press.

Frank, A. W. (1990) Bringing bodies back in: a decade review. *Theory, Culture and Society* 7: 131–62.

Franklin, A. (2002) *Nature and Social Theory*, London: Sage.

Fudge, E., Gilbert, R. and Wiseman, S. (eds.) (1999) *At the Borders of the Human: Beasts, Bodies and Natural Philosophy in the Early Modern Period*, London: Macmillan.

Fuller, B. T., Richards, M. P. and Mays, S. A. (2003) Stable carbon and nitrogen isotope variations in tooth dentine serial sections from Wharram Percy. *Journal of Archaeological Science* 30(12): 1673–84.

Gans, E. (1985) *The End of Culture: Toward a Generative Anthropology*, Berkeley: University of California Press.

Garruto, R. M. (1995) Biological adaptability, plasticity and disease: patterns in modernizing societies. In: Mascie-Taylor, C. G. N. and Bogin, B. (eds.) *Human Variability and Plasticity*, pp. 190–212. Cambridge: Cambridge University Press.

Gatens, M. (1996) *Imaginary Bodies*, London: Routledge.

Gell, A. (1998) *Art and Agency: Towards a New Anthropological Theory*, Oxford: Clarendon Press.

Gero, J. (1996) Archaeological practice and gendered encounters with field data. In: Wright, R. (ed.) *Gender and Archaeology*, pp. 251–80. Philadelphia: University of Pennsylvania Press.

Gero, J. M. (2000) Troubled travels in agency and feminism. In: Dobres, M. and Robb, J. (eds.) *Agency in Archaeology*, pp. 34–9. London: Routledge.

Gibbs, L. (1987) Identifying gender representation in the archaeological record: a contextual study. In: Hodder, I. (ed.) *The Archaeology of Contextual Meanings*, pp. 79–89. Cambridge: Cambridge University Press.

Giddens, A. (1991) *Modernity and Self Identity*, Cambridge: Polity Press.

Gijswijt-Hofstra, M. and Marland, H. (2003) *Cultures of Child Health in Britain and the Netherlands in the Twentieth Century*, Amsterdam: Rodopi.

Gilchrist, R. (1999) *Gender and Archaeology: Contesting the Past*, London: Routledge.

Gilchrist, R. (2000) Archaeological biographies: realizing human lifecycles, -courses and -histories. *World Archaeology* 31(3): 325–8.

Giles, E. (1970) Discriminant function sexing of the human skeleton. In: Stewart, T. D. (ed.) *Personal Identification in Mass Disasters*, pp. 99–107. Washington: Smithsonian Institution.

Gilman, S. (1991) *The Jew's Body*, London: Routledge.

Ginn, J. and Arber, S. (1995) 'Only connect': gender relations and ageing. In: Arber, S. and Ginn, J. (eds.) *Connecting Gender and Ageing: A Sociological Approach*, pp. 1–14. Buckingham: Open University Press.

Godfrey, K., Walker-Bone, K., Robinson, S., Taylor, P., Shore, S., Wheeler, T. and Cooper, C. (2001) Neonatal bone mass: influence of parental birthweight, maternal smoking, body composition and activity during pregnancy. *Journal of Bone and Mineral Research* 16: 1694–703.

Goffman, E. (1959) *The Presentation of Self in Everyday Life*, Harmondsworth: Penguin.

Goffman, E. (1968) *Asylums: Essays on the Social Situation of Mental Patients and Other Inmates*, Harmondsworth: Penguin.

Goffman, E. (1972) *Interaction Ritual: Essays on Face-to-Face Behaviour*, London: Allen Lane.

Goldschmidt, W. (1993) On the relationship between biology and anthropology. *Man* n.s. 28: 341–59.

Goodman, A. H. and Rose, J. C. (1990) Assessment of systemic physiological perturbations from dental enamel hypoplasias and associated histological structures. *Yearbook of Physical Anthropology* 33: 59–110.

Goodman, A. H. and Rose, J. C. (1991) Dental enamel hypoplasias as indicators of nutritional status. In: Kelley, M. A. and Larsen, C. S. (eds.) *Advances in Dental Anthropology*, pp. 279–93. New York: Wiley-Liss.

Goodman, A. H., Lallo, J., Armelagos, G. J. and Rose, J. C. (1984) Health change at Dickinson Mounds, Illinois (AD 950–1300). In: Cohen, M. and Armelagos, G. J. (eds.) *Paleopathology at the Origins of Agriculture*, pp. 271–306. Orlando: Academic Press.

Goodship, A. E. and Cunningham, J. L. (2001) Pathophysiology of functional adaptation of bone in remodeling and repair in vivo. In: Cowin, S. C. (ed.) *Bone Mechanics Handbook*, 2nd edition, pp. 26-1–26-31. Boca Raton: CRC Press.

Gosden, C. (1999) *Anthropology and Archaeology: A Changing Relationship*, London: Routledge.

Gould, C. (2002) *Charles LeDray*, Philadelphia: University of Pennsylvania, Institute of Contemporary Arts.

Gowland, R. (2001) Playing dead: implications of mortuary evidence for the social construction of childhood in Roman Britain. In: Davies, G., Gardner, A. and Lockyear, K. (eds.) *TRAC 2000: Proceedings of the Tenth Annual Theoretical Roman Archaeology Conference*, pp. 152–68. Oxford: Oxbow.

Gowland, R. (2004) Ageing the past: examining age identity from funerary evidence. Unpublished paper presented at the European Association of Archaeologists Xth Annual Meeting. Lyon.

Gowland, R. L. and Chamberlain, A. T. (2002) A Bayesian approach to ageing perinatal skeletal material from archaeological sites: implications for the evidence for infanticide in Roman Britain. *Journal of Archaeological Science* 29(6): 677–85.

Grauer, A. L. (ed.) (1995) *Bodies of Evidence: Reconstructing History through Skeletal Analysis*, New York: Wiley-Liss.

Grauer, A. L. and McNamara, E. (1995) A piece of Chicago's past: exploring subadult mortality in the Dunning Poorhouse cemetery. In: Grauer, A. L. (ed.) *Bodies of Evidence: Reconstructing History through Skeletal Analysis*, pp. 91–103. New York: Wiley-Liss.

Grauer, A. L. and Stuart-Macadam, P. (eds.) (1998) *Sex and Gender in Paleopathological Perspective*, Cambridge: Cambridge University Press.

Greenfield, P. (2000) Children, material culture and weaving: historical change and developmental change. In: Sofaer Derevenski, J. (ed.) *Children and Material Culture*, pp. 72–86. London: Routledge.

Grosz, E. (1994) *Volatile Bodies: Toward a Corporeal Feminism*, Bloomington: Indiana University Press.

Gullestad, M. (1988) Agents of modernity: children's care for children in urban Norway. *Social Analysis* 23: 38–52.

Gullette, M. M. (1988) *Safe at Last in the Middle Years: The Invention of the Midlife Progress Novel: Saul Bellow, Margaret Drabble, Anne Tyler, and John Updike*, Berkeley: University of California Press.

Gustafson, G. and Koch, G. (1974) Age estimation up to 16 years of age based on dental development. *Ondontologisk Revy* 25: 295–306.

Hallam, E., Hockey, J. and Howarth, G. (1999) *Beyond the Body: Death and Social Identity*, London: Routledge.

Ham, J. and Senior, M. (1997) Introduction. In: Ham, J. and Senior, M. (eds.) *Animal Acts: Configuring the Human in Western History*, pp. 1–7. London: Routledge.

Hamilakis, Y. (2002) The past as oral history: towards an archaeology of the senses. In: Hamilakis, Y., Pluciennik, M. and Tarlow, S. (eds.) *Thinking Through the Body: Archaeologies of Corporeality*, pp. 121–36. New York: Kluwer Academic / Plenum Publishers.

Hamilakis, Y., Pluciennik, M. and Tarlow, S. (eds.) (2002a) *Thinking Through the Body. Archaeologies of Corporeality*, New York: Kluwer Academic / Plenum Publishers.

Hamilakis, Y., Pluciennik, M. and Tarlow, S. (2002b) Introduction: thinking through the body. In: Hamilakis, Y., Pluciennik, M. and Tarlow, S. (eds.) *Thinking Through the Body: Archaeologies of Corporeality*, pp. 1–21. New York: Kluwer Academic / Plenum Publishers.

Handsman, R. (1988) Algonkian women resist colonialism. *Artifacts* 16(3–4): 29–31.

Hanna, R. E. and Washburn, L. (1953) The determination of the sex of skeletons as illustrated by the Eskimo pelvis. *Human Biology* 132: 21–7.

Haraway, D. J. (1976) *Crystals, Fabrics and Fields: Metaphors of Organicism in Twentieth-Century Developmental Biology*, Cambridge: Cambridge University Press.

Haraway, D. J. (1988) Remodelling the human way of life. Sherwood Washburn and the new physical anthropology, 1950–1980. In: Stocking, G. W. Jr (ed.) *Bones, Bodies, Behavior: Essays on Biological Anthropology*, pp. 206–59. Madison, Wis.: University of Wisconsin Press.

Haraway, D. J. (1989) *Primate Visions: Gender, Race and Nature in the World of Modern Science*, New York: Routledge.

Haraway, D. J. (1991) *Simians, Cyborgs, and Women: The Reinvention of Nature*, London: Free Association Books.

Harding, S. (1986) *The Science Question in Feminism*, Ithaca, N.Y.: Cornell University Press.

Harding, S. (1991) *Whose Science? Whose Knowledge? Thinking from Women's Lives*. New York: Cornell University Press.

Harlow, M. and Lawrence, R. (2002) *Growing Up and Growing Old in Ancient Rome: A Life Course Approach*, London: Routledge.

Harré, R. (1991) *Physical Being: A Theory for a Corporeal Psychology*, Oxford: Blackwell.

Hastorf, C. (1991) Gender, space and food in prehistory. In: Gero, J. M. and Conkey, M. W. (eds.) *Engendering Archaeology: Women and Prehistory*, pp. 132–59. Oxford: Blackwell.

Hawkey, D. E. (1998) Disability, compassion, and the skeletal record: using musculoskeletal stress markers (MSM) to construct an osteobiography from early New Mexico. *International Journal of Osteoarchaeology* 8(5): 326–40.

Hawkey, D. E. and Merbs, C. F. (1995) Activity-induced musculoskeletal markers (MSM) and subsistence strategy changes among ancient Hudson Bay Eskimos. *International Journal of Osteoarchaeology* 5(4): 324–38.

Hawkey, D. E. and Street, S. R. (1992) Activity-induced stress markers in prehistoric remains from the eastern Aleutian Islands. *American Journal of Physical Anthropology (Supplement)* 14: 89.

Heidegger, M. (1972) Building dwelling thinking. In: Krell, D. (ed.) *M. Heidegger: Basic Writings*, London: Routledge.

Herdt, G. (ed.) (1994) *Third Sex, Third Gender: Beyond Sexual Dimorphism in Culture and History*, Cambridge, Mass.: MIT Press.

Herring, D. A., Saunders, S. R. and Katzenberg, M. A. (1998) Investigating the weaning process in past populations. *American Journal of Physical Anthropology* 105(4): 425–39.

Hess, B. B. and Ferree, M. M. (eds.) (1987) *Analysing Gender: A Handbook of Social Science Research*, Newbury Park: Sage.

Hester, T. R. (1969) Human bone artifacts from Texas. *American Antiquity* 34(3): 326–8.

Hill, E. (1998) Gender informed archaeology: the priority of definition, the use of analogy, and the mutivariate approach. *Journal of Archaeological Method and Theory* 5(1): 99–128.

Hillson, S. (1996) *Dental Anthropology*, Cambridge: Cambridge University Press.

Hinde, R. A. (1991) A biologist looks at anthropology. *Man* n.s. 26: 583–608.

Hockey, J. and James, A. (1993) *Growing Up and Growing Old: Ageing and Dependency in the Life Course*, London: Sage.

Hodder, I. (1982) *Symbols in Action*, Cambridge: Cambridge University Press.

Hodder, I. (1984) Archaeology in 1984. *Antiquity* 58: 25–32.

Hodder, I. (1991) Interpretative archaeology and its role. *American Antiquity* 56(1): 7–18.

Hodder, I. (1999) *The Archaeological Process: An Introduction*, Oxford: Blackwell Publishers.

Hodder, I., Shanks, M., Alexandri, A., Buchli, V., Carman, J., Last, J. and Lucas, G. (eds.) (1995) *Interpreting Archaeology: Finding Meaning in the Past*, London: Routledge.

Hodson, F. R. (1990) *Hallstatt, the Ramsauer Graves: Quantification and Analysis*, Bonn: R. Habelt.

Hollimon, S. E. (1992) Health consequences of sexual division of labour among prehistoric Native Americans: the Chumash of California and the Arikara of the North Plains. In: Claassen, C. (ed.) *Exploring Gender through Archaeology:*

158   References

Selected Papers from the 1991 Boone Conference, pp. 81–8. Madison: Prehistory Press.

Hollimon, S. E. (2000a) Archaeology of the 'Aqi: gender and sexuality in prehistoric Chumash society. In: Schmidt, R. and Voss, B. (eds.) *Archaeologies of Sexuality*, pp. 179–96. London: Routledge.

Hollimon, S. E. (2000b) Sex, health, and gender roles among the Arikara of the northern plains. In: Rautman, A. E. (ed.) *Reading the Body: Representations and Remains in the Archaeological Record*, pp. 25–37. Philadelphia: University of Pennsylvania Press.

Hoppa, R. D. and FitzGerald, C. M. (1999) From head to toe: integrating studies from bones and teeth in biological anthropology. In: Hoppa, R. D. and FitzGerald, C. M. (eds.) *Human Growth in the Past: Studies from Bones and Teeth*, pp. 1–31. Cambridge: Cambridge University Press.

Hoppa, R. D. and Vaupel, J. W. (eds.) (2002) *Paleodemography: Age Distributions from Skeletal Samples*, Cambridge: Cambridge University Press.

Hoskins, J. (1998) *Biographical Objects: How Things Tell the Stories of People's Lives*, London: Routledge.

Houston, S. D. and McAnany, P. A. (2003) Bodies and blood: critiquing social construction in Maya archaeology. *Journal of Anthropological Archaeology* 22(1): 26–41.

Howells, W. W. (1973) *Cranial Variation in Man: A Study by Multivariate Analysis of Patterns of Difference among Recent Human Populations*, Papers of the Peabody Museum No. 67. Cambridge, Mass.: Harvard University Press.

Howells, W. W. (1989) *Skull Shapes and the Map: Craniometric Analyses in the Dispersion of Modern Homo*, Papers of the Peabody Museum No. 79. Cambridge, Mass.: Harvard University Press.

Huard, P. and Montagne, M. (1950) Le Squelette humain et l'attitude accroupie. *Bulletin de la Société des Etudes Indochinoises* 25: 401–26.

Hudson, J. (ed.) (1993) *From Bones to Behavior: Ethnoarchaeological and Experimental Contributions to the Interpretation of Faunal Remains*, Center for Archaeological Investigations, Carbondale, Illinois: Southern Illinois University.

Hulse, F. S. (1981) Habits, habitats and heredity: a brief history of studies in human plasticity. *American Journal of Physical Anthropology* 56(4): 495–501.

Humphrey, L. (2000) Growth studies of past populations: an overview and an example. In: Cox, M. and Mays, S. (eds.) *Human Osteology in Archaeology and Forensic Science*, pp. 23–8. London: Greenwich Medical Media.

Ingold, T. (1986) *Evolution and Social Life*, Cambridge: Cambridge University Press.

Ingold, T. (1988) The animal in the study of humanity. In: Ingold, T. (ed.) *What is an Animal?*, pp. 84–99. London: Unwin Hyman.

Ingold, T. (1990) An anthropologist looks at biology. *Man* n. s. 25: 208–29.

Ingold, T. (1991) Becoming persons: consciousness and sociality in human evolution. *Cultural Dynamics* 4(3):355–78.

Ingold, T. (1992) Culture and the perception of the environment. In: Croll, E. and Parkin, D. (eds.) *Bush Base, Forest Farm: Culture and Development*, pp. 39–56. London: Routledge.

Ingold, T. (1993a) The temporality of the landscape. *World Archaeology* 23(2): 203–13.

Ingold, T. (1993b) Technology, language, intelligence: a reconsideration of basic concepts. In: Gibson, K. R. and Ingold, T. (eds.) *Tools, Language and Cognition in Human Evolution*, pp. 449–72. Cambridge: Cambridge University Press.

Ingold, T. (1996) Situating Action VI: a comment on the distinction between the material and the social. *Ecological Psychology* 8: 183–7.

Ingold, T. (1998) From complementarity to obviation: on dissolving the boundaries between social and biological anthropology, archaeology and psychology. *Zeitschrift für Ethnologie* 123: 21–52.

Ingold, T. (2001a) Evolving skills. In: Rose, H. and Rose, S. (eds.) *Alas Poor Darwin: Arguments Against Evolutionary Psychology*, pp. 225–46. London: Vintage.

Ingold, T. (2001b) From the transmission of representations to the education of attention. In: Whitehouse, H. (ed.) *The Debated Mind: Evolutionary Psychology Versus Ethnography*, pp. 113–53. Oxford: Berg.

James, A. (1993) *Childhood Identities: Self and Social Relationships in the Experience of the Child*, Edinburgh: Edinburgh University Press.

James, A. (2000) Embodied being(s): understanding the self and the body in childhood. In: Prout, A. (ed.) *The Body, Childhood and Society*, pp. 19–37. London: Macmillan Press Ltd.

James, A., Jenks, C. and Prout, A. (1998) *Theorizing Childhood*, Cambridge: Polity Press.

Janik, L. (2000) The construction of the individual among north European fisher-gatherer-hunters in the Early and Mid-Holocene. In: Sofaer Derevenski, J. (ed.) *Children and Material Culture*, pp. 117–30. London: Routledge.

Jee, W. S. S. (2001) Integrated bone tissue physiology: anatomy and physiology. In: Cowin, S. C. (ed.) *Bone Mechanics Handbook*, pp. 1-1–1-68. Boca Raton: CRC Press.

Jenks, C. (1998) *Core Social Dichotomies*, London: Sage.

Johnson, F. E. and Mann, A. (1997) United States of America. In: Spencer, F. (ed.) *History of Physical Anthropology: An Encyclopedia*, pp. 1069–81. New York: Garland Publishing.

Johnson, M. (1989) Conceptions of agency in archaeological interpretation. *Journal of Anthropological Archaeology* 8: 189–211.

Johnson, M. (1999) *Archaeological Theory: An Introduction*, Oxford: Blackwell.

Jones, A. (2002a) *Archaeological Theory and Scientific Practice*, Cambridge: Cambridge University Press.

Jones, A. (2002b) A biography of colour: colour, material histories and personhood in the Early Bronze Age of Britain and Ireland. In: Jones, A. and MacGregor, G. (eds.) *Colouring the Past: The Significance of Colour in Archaeological Research*, pp. 159–74. Oxford: Berg.

Jones, H. H., Priest, J. D., Hayes, W. C., Tichenor, C. C. and Nagel, D. A. (1977) Humeral hypertrophy in response to exercise. *Journal of Bone and Joint Surgery* 59A: 204–8.

Joyce, R. A. (2000a) Girling the girl and boying the boy: the production of adult-hood in ancient Mesoamerica. *World Archaeology* 31(3): 473–83.

Joyce, R. A. (2000b) *Gender and Power in Prehispanic Mesoamerica*, Austin: University of Texas Press.

Joyce, R. A. (2002a) *The Languages of Archaeology: Dialogue, Narrative and Writing*, Oxford: Blackwell.

Joyce, R. A. (2002b) Beauty, sexuality, body ornamentation and gender in ancient Meso-America. In: Milledge Nelson, S. and Rosen-Ayalon, M. (eds.) *In Pursuit of Gender: Worldwide Archaeological Approaches*, pp. 81–91. Walnut Creek, Cal.: AltaMira Press.

Joyce, R. A. (2003) Making something of herself: embodiment in life and death at Playa de los Muertos, Honduras. *Cambridge Archaeological Journal* 13(2): 248–61.

Judd, M. A. and Roberts, C. A. (1999) Fracture trauma in a medieval British farming village. *American Journal of Physical Anthropology* 109(2): 229–43.

Jurmain, R. (1977) Stress and the etiology of osteoarthritis. *American Journal of Physical Anthropology* 46(2): 353–66.

Jurmain, R. (1990) Paleoepidemiology of a central California prehistoric pop-ulation from CA-ALA-329: II. Degenerative disease. *American Journal of Physical Anthropology* 83(3): 83–94.

Kaestle, F. A. and Horsburgh, A. (2002) Ancient DNA in anthropology: methods, applications, and ethics. *American Journal of Physical Anthropology* 119(S35): 92–130.

Kamp, K. (2001a) Prehistoric children working and playing: a southwestern case study in learning ceramics. *Journal of Anthropological Research* 57: 427–50.

Kamp, K. (2001b) Where have all the children gone?: The archaeology of child-hood. *Journal of Archaeological Method and Theory* 8(1): 1–34.

Katz, S. (1996) *Disciplining Old Age: The Formation of Gerontological Knowledge*, Charlottesville: University Press of Virginia.

Katzenberg, M. A. (2000) Stable isotope analysis: a tool for studying past diet, demography and life history. In: Katzenberg, M. A. and Saunders, S. R. (eds.) *Biological Anthropology of the Human Skeleton*, pp. 305–27. New York: Wiley-Liss.

Keating, D. and Miller, F. (1999) Individual pathways in competence and coping: from regulatory systems to habits of mind. In: Keating, D. and Hertzman, C. (eds.) *Developmental Health and the Wealth of Nations*, pp. 220–34. New York: Guilford.

Kelley, J. and Angel, J. L. (1987) Life stresses of slavery. *American Journal of Physical Anthropology* 74(2): 199–211.

Kelley, M. A. (1989) Infectious disease. In: Iscan, M. Y. and Kennedy, K. A. R. (eds.) *Reconstruction of Life from the Skeleton*, pp. 191–9. New York: Alan R. Liss.

Kennedy, K. A. R. (1989) Skeletal markers of occupational stress. In: Iscan, M. Y. and Kennedy, K. A. R. (eds.) *Reconstruction of Life from the Skeleton*, pp. 129–60. New York: Alan R. Liss.

Kennedy, K. A. R. (1998) Markers of occupational stress: conspectus and prog-nosis of research. *International Journal of Osteoarchaeology* 8(5): 305–10.

Kirkham, P. and Attfield, J. (1996) Introduction. In: Kirkham, P. (ed.) *The Gendered Object*, pp. 1–11. Manchester: Manchester University Press.

Kligman, G. (1988) *The Wedding of the Dead: Ritual, Poetics, and Popular Culture in Transylvania*, Berkeley: University of California Press.

Knapp, B. (2000) Archaeology, science-based archaeology, and the Mediterranean Bronze Age metals trade. *European Journal of Archaeology* 3(1): 31–56.

Knapp, B. (2002) Disciplinary fault lines: science and social archaeology. *Mediterranean Archaeology and Archaeometry* 2(2): 37–44.

Knapp, B. and Meskell, L. (1997) Bodies of evidence on prehistoric Cyprus. *Cambridge Archaeological Journal* 7(2): 183–204.

Knappett, C. (2002) Photographs, skeumorphs and marionettes: some thoughts on mind, agency and object. *Journal of Material Culture* 7(1): 97–117.

Knappett, C. (2005) *Thinking Through Material Culture: An Interdisciplinary Perspective*, Philadelphia: University of Pennsylvania Press.

Knorr-Certina, K. (1999) *Epistemic Cultures: How the Sciences Make Knowledge*, Cambridge, Mass.: Harvard University Press.

Knüsel, C. (2000) Bone adaptation and its relationship to physical activity in the past. In: Cox, M. and Mays, S. (eds.) *Human Osteology in Archaeology and Forensic Science*, pp. 381–402. London: Greenwich Medical Media.

Knüsel, C. J., Göggel, S. and Lucy, D. (1997) Comparative degenerative joint disease of the vertebral column in the medieval monastic cemetery of the Gilbertine priory of St Andrew, Fishergate, York, England. *American Journal of Physical Anthropology* 103(4): 481–95.

Kopytoff, I. (1986) The cultural biography of things: commoditization as a process. In: Appadurai, A. (ed.) *The Social Life of Things: Commodities in Cultural Perspective*, pp. 64–91. Cambridge: Cambridge University Press.

Kossinna, G. (1911) *Die Herkunft der Germanen*, Leipzig: Kabitzsch.

Krämer, J. (1981) *Intervertebral Disk Diseases: Causes, Diagnosis, Treatment and Prophylaxis*, Chicago: Year Book Medical Publishers, Inc.

Krogman, W. M. (1946) The skeleton in forensic medicine. *Transactions of Institute of Medicine Chicago* 16: 154–67.

Krogman, W. M. (1962) *The Human Skeleton in Forensic Medicine*, Springfield, Illinois: Charles C. Thomas.

Kuhn, T. (1962) *The Structure of Scientific Revolutions*, Chicago: University of Chicago Press.

Kuhn, T. (1977) *The Essential Tension: Selected Studies in Scientific Tradition and Change*, Chicago: Chicago University Press.

Kustár, A. (1999) Facial reconstruction of an artificially distorted skull of the 4th to the 5th century from the site of Mözs. *International Journal of Osteoarchaeology* 9(5): 325–32.

Lai, P. and Lovell, N. C. (1992) Skeletal markers of occupational stress in the fur trade: a case study from a Hudson's Bay Company fur trade post. *International Journal of Osteoarchaeology* 2(3): 221–34.

Lalueza-Fox, C., Gilbert, M. T. P., Martínez-Fuentes, A. J., Calafell, F. and Bertranpetit, F. (2003) Mitochondrial DNA from pre-Columbian Ciboneys from Cuba and the prehistoric colonization of the Caribbean. *American Journal of Physical Anthropology* 121(2): 97–108.

Lanyon, L. E. (1987) Functional strain in bone tissue as an objective, and controlling stimulus for adaptive bone remodelling. *Journal of Biomechanics* 20: 1083–93.

Lanyon, L. E., Goodship, A. E., Pye, C. J. and MacFie, J. H. (1982) Mechanically adaptive bone remodelling. *Journal of Biomechanics* 15, 141–52.

Laqueur, T. (1990) *Making Sex: Body and Gender from the Greeks to Freud*, Cambridge, Mass.: Harvard University Press.

Larsen, C. S. (1995) Biological changes in human populations with agriculture. *Annual Review of Anthropology* 24: 185–213.

Larsen, C. S. (1997) *Bioarchaeology Interpreting Behaviour from the Human Skeleton*, Cambridge: Cambridge University Press.

Larsen, C. S. and Milner, G. R. (eds.) (1994) *In the Wake of Contact: Biological Responses to Conquest*, New York: Wiley-Liss.

Larsen, C. S., Ruff, C. B. and Kelly, R. L. (1995) Structural analysis of the Stillwater postcranial human remains: behavioural implications of articular joint pathology and long bone diaphyseal morphology. In: Larsen, C. S. and Kelly, R. L. (eds.) *Bioarchaeology of the Stillwater Marsh: Prehistoric Human Adaptation in the Western Great Basin*, pp. 107–33.

Larsen, C. S., Ruff, C. B., Schoeninger, M. J. and Hutchinson, D. L. (1992) Population decline and extinction in La Florida. In: Verano, J. W. and Ubelaker, D. H. (eds.) *Disease and Demography in the Americas*, pp. 25–39. Washington: Smithsonian Institution Press.

Lasker, G. (1969) Human biological adaptability. *Science* 166: 1480–6.

Latour, B. (1987) *Science in Action: How to Follow Scientists and Engineers through Society*, Milton Keynes: Open University Press.

Latour, B. (1993) *We Have Never Been Modern*, Cambridge, Mass.: Harvard University Press.

Latour, B. (2004) How to talk about the body? The normative dimension of science studies. *Body and Society* 10(2–3): 205–29.

Latour, B. and Woolgar, S. (1979) *Laboratory Life: The Construction of Scientific Knowledge*, London: Sage.

Lerner, R. M. (1984) *On the Nature of Human Plasticity*, Cambridge: Cambridge University Press.

Leroi, A. M. (2004) *Mutants: On the Form, Varieties and Errors of the Human Body*. London: HarperCollins.

Leroi-Gourhan, A. (1943) *L'Homme et la matière*. Paris: Editions Albin Michel (repr. 1971).

Leroi-Gourhan, A. (1945) *Milieu et technique*. Paris: Editions Albin Michel (repr. 1973).

Leroi-Gourhan, A. (1968) *The Art of Prehistoric Man in Western Europe*, London: Thames and Hudson.

Levy, L. F. (1968) Porter's neck. *British Medical Journal* 2: 16–19.

Lewis, M. (2000) Non-adult palaeopathology: current status and future potential. In: Cox, M. and Mays, S. (eds.) *Human Osteology in Archaeology and Forensic Science*, pp. 39–57. London: Greenwich Medical Media.

Lewis, M. (2002) Impact of industrialization: comparative study of child health in four sites from medieval and postmedieval England (AD 850–1859). *American Journal of Physical Anthropology* 119(3): 211–23.

Lillehammer, G. (1989) A child is born: the child's world in an archaeological perspective. *Norwegian Archaeological Review* 22(2): 89–105.

Lindholm-Romantschuk, Y. (1998) *Scholarly Book Reviewing in the Social Sciences and Humanities: The Flow of Ideas Within and Among Disciplines*, Westport, Conn.: Greenwood Press.

Lock, M. (2001) The alienation of body tissue and the biopolitics of immortalized cell lines. *Body and Society* 7(2–3): 63–91.

Longino, H. E. (1990) *Science as Social Knowledge: Values and Objectivity in Scientific Enquiry*, Princeton, N.J.: Princeton University Press.

Lorber, J. (1994) *Paradoxes of Gender*, New Haven: Yale University Press.

Lorentz, K. O. (2003) Minding the body: the growing body in Cyprus from the aceramic Neolithic to the Late Bronze Age. Unpublished PhD thesis. Department of Archaeology, University of Cambridge.

Lovejoy, C. O., McCollum, M. A., Reno, P. L. and Rosenman, B. A. (2003) Developmental biology and human evolution. *Annual Review of Anthropology* 32: 85–109.

Lovell, N. C. (1994) Spinal arthritis and physical stress at Bronze Age Harappa. *American Journal of Physical Anthropology* 93(2): 149–64.

Lovell, N. C. and Dublenko, A. (1999) Further aspects of fur trade life depicted in the skeleton. *International Journal of Osteoarchaeology* 9(4): 248–59.

Lovell, N. C. and Lai, P. (1994) Lifestyle and health of voyageurs in the Canadian fur trade. In: Herring, A. and Chan, L. (eds.) *Strength and Diversity: A Reader in Physical Anthropology*, pp. 327–43. Toronto: Canadian Scholars' Press.

Lucas, G. (2001) *Critical Approaches to Field Archaeology: Contemporary and Historical Archaeological Practice*, London: Routledge.

Lucchinetti, E. (2001) Composite models of bone properties. In: Cowin, S. C. (ed.) *Bone Mechanics Handbook*, 2nd edition, pp. 12-1–12-19. Boca Raton: CRC Press.

Lucy, S. (2000) *The Anglo-Saxon Way of Death*, Thrupp, Stroud: Sutton Publishing.

Lukacs, J. R. (1992) Dental palaeopathology and agricultural intensification in south Asia: new evidence from Bronze Age Harappa. *American Journal of Physical Anthropology* 87(2): 133–50.

Lukacs, J. R. and Walimbe, S. R. (1998) Physiological stress in prehistoric India: new data on localized hypoplasia of primary canines linked to climate and subsistence change. *Journal of Archaeological Science* 25(6): 571–85.

McCall, J. (1999) *Dancing Histories: Heuristic Ethnography with the Ohafia Igbo*, Ann Arbor: University of Michigan Press.

Macdonald, D. (1978) *Lewis: A History of the Island*, Edinburgh: G. Wright.

Macdonald, S. (1998) Exhibitions of power and powers of exhibition: an introduction to the politics of display. In: Macdonald, S. (ed.) *The Politics of Display: Museums, Science, Culture*, pp. 1–24, London: Routledge.

MacGregor, A. A. (1952) *The Western Isles*, London: Robert Hale Ltd.

McKeag, D. B. (1992) The relationship of osteoarthritis and exercise. *Clinics in Sports Medicine* 11: 471–87.

McKern, T. and Stewart, T. D. (1957) *Skeletal Changes in Young American Males*, Natick., Mass. Technical Report. Headquarters Quartermaster Research and Development Command.

Mclean, M. (1982) A chronological and geographical sequence of Maori flute scales. *Man* n.s. 17(1): 123–57.

McMurray, R. G. (1995) Effects of physical activity on bone. In: Anderson, J. J. B. and Garner, S. C. (eds.) *Calcium and Phosphorous in Health and Disease*, pp. 301–17. Boca Raton: CRC Press.

Macnaghten, P. and Urry, J. (1998) *Contested Natures*, London: Sage.

McNay, L. (2000) *Gender and Agency: Reconfiguring the Subject in Feminist and Social Theory*, Cambridge: Polity Press.

Magazine, R. (2003) Action, personhood and the gift economy among so-called street children in Mexico City. *Social Anthropology – Cambridge* 11(3): 303–18.

Malafouris, L. (2004) The cognitive basis of material engagement: where brain, body and culture conflate. In: DeMarrais, E., Gosden, C. and Renfrew, C. (eds.) *Rethinking Materiality: The Engagement of Mind with the Material World*, pp. 53–62.Cambridge: McDonald Institute for Archaeological Research.

Malgosa, A., Alesan, A., Safont, S., Ballbé, M. and Ayala, M. (2004) A dystocic childbirth in the Spanish Bronze Age. *International Journal of Osteoarchaeology* 14(2): 98–103.

Manchester, K. (1992) The palaeopathology of urban infections. In: Bassett, S. (ed.) *Death in Towns: Urban Responses to the Dying and the Dead 100–1600*, pp. 8–14. London: Leicester University Press.

Maresh, M. M. (1955) Linear growth of long bones of extremities from infancy through adolescence. *American Journal of Diseases of Childhood* 89: 725–42.

Maresh, M. M. (1970) Measurements from roentgenograms. In: McCammon, R. W. (ed.) *Human Growth and Development*, pp. 157–99. Springfield: Charles C. Thomas.

Marks, J. (1995) *Human Biodiversity: Genes, Race and History*, New York: Walter de Gruyter.

Martin, M. (1703) *A Description of the Western Islands of Scotland*, London.

Martin, R. B. and Burr, D. B. (1989) *Structure, Function and Adaptation of Compact Bone*, New York: Raven.

Mascie-Taylor, N. (ed.) (1990) *Biosocial Aspects of Social Class*, Oxford: Oxford University Press.

Mauss, M. (1979) Body techniques. In: Mauss, M. *Sociology and Psychology: Essays by Marcel Mauss, Part IV*, trans. B. Brewster, pp. 97–123. London: Routledge & Kegan Paul.

Mayall, B. (1996) *Children, Health and the Social Order*, Milton Keynes: Open University Press.

Mays, S. (1993) Infanticide in Roman Britain. *Antiquity* 67: 883–8.

Mays, S. (1995) The relationship between Harris lines and other aspects of skeletal development in adults and juveniles. *Journal of Archaeological Science* 22(4): 511–20.

Mays, S. (1996) Age-dependent cortical bone loss in a medieval population. *International Journal of Osteoarchaeology* 6(2): 144–54.

Mays, S. (1997) A perspective on human osteoarchaeology in Britain. *International Journal of Osteoarchaeology* 7(6): 600–4.

Mays, S. (1998) *The Archaeology of Human Bones*, London: Routledge.

Mays, S. (1999) A biomechanical study of activity patterns in a medieval human skeletal assemblage. *International Journal of Osteoarchaeology* 9(1): 68–73.

Mays, S. and Cox, M. (2000) Sex determination in skeletal remains. In: Cox, M. and Mays, S. (eds.) *Human Osteology in Archaeology and Forensic Science*, pp. 117–30. London: Greenwich Medical Media.

Mays, S. and Faerman, M. (2001) Sex identification in some putative infanticide victims from Roman Britain using ancient DNA. *Journal of Archaeological Science* 28(5): 555–9.

Mays, S., Rogers, J. and Watt, I. (2001) A possible case of hyperparathyroidism in a burial of 15–17th century AD date from Wharram Percy, England. *International Journal of Osteoarchaeology* 11(5): 329–35.

Meindl, R. S., Lovejoy, C. O., Mensforth, R. P. and Carlos, L. D. (1985) Accuracy and direction of error in the sexing of the skeleton. *American Journal of Physical Anthropology* 68(1): 79–85.

Merbs, C. F. (1983) *Patterns of Activity-Induced Pathology in a Canadian Inuit Population*, Ottowa: Archaeological Survey of Canada. National Museum of Man Mercury Series 119.

Merleau-Ponty, M. (1962) *Phenomenology of Perception*, London: Routledge.

Merton, R. (1973) *The Sociology of Science*, Chicago: Chicago University Press.

Meskell, L. (1994) Dying young: the experience of death at Deir el Medina. *Archaeological Review from Cambridge* 13(2): 35–45.

Meskell, L. (1996) The somatisation of archaeology: institutions, discourses, corporeality. *Norwegian Archaeological Review* 29(1): 1–16.

Meskell, L. (1998a) The irresistible body and the seduction of archaeology. In: Monsterrat, D. (ed.) *Changing Bodies, Changing Meanings: Studies of the Body in Antiquity*, pp. 139–61. London: Routledge.

Meskell, L. (1998b) An archaeology of social relations in an Egyptian village. *Journal of Archaeological Method and Theory* 5(3): 209–43.

Meskell, L. (2000a) Writing the body in archaeology. In: Rautman, A. E. (ed.) *Reading the Body: Representations and Remains in the Archaeological Record*, pp. 13–21. Philadelphia: University of Pennsylvania Press.

Meskell, L. (2000b) Cycles of life and death: narrative homology and archaeological realities. *World Archaeology* 31(3): 423–41.

Meskell, L. (2001) Archaeologies of identity. In: Hodder, I. (ed.) *Archaeological Theory Today*, pp. 187–213. Cambridge: Polity Press.

Meskell, L. (2002a) *Private Life in New Kingdom Egypt*, Princeton, N.J.: Princeton University Press.

Meskell, L. (2002b) The intersections of identity and politics in archaeology. *Annual Review of Anthropology* 31: 279–301.

Meskell, L. and Joyce, R. A. (2003) *Embodied Lives: Figuring Ancient Maya and Egyptian Experience*, London: Routledge.

Miles, A. E. W. (1963) The dentition in the assessment of individual age in skeletal material. In: Brothwell, D. (ed.) *Dental Anthropology*, pp. 191–209. London: Pergamon Press.

Miles, A. E. W. (1989) *An Early Christian Chapel and Burial Ground on the Isle of Ensay, Outer Hebrides, Scotland with a Study of the Skeletal Remains*, Oxford: BAR, British Series 212.

Miles, A. E. W. (1996) Humeral impingement on the acromion in a Scottish island population of c.1600 AD. *International Journal of Osteoarchaeology* 6(3): 259–88.

Milton, K. (1993) Introduction: environmentalism and anthropology. In: Milton, K. (ed.) *Environmentalism: The View from Anthropology*, pp. 1–17. London: Routledge.

Mitchell, P. D. (2003) Pre-Columbian treponemal disease from 14th century AD Safed, Israel, and implications for the medieval eastern Mediterranean. *American Journal of Physical Anthropology* 121(2): 117–24.

Mizoguchi, K. (1992) A historiography of a linear barrow cemetery: a structurationist's point of view. *Archaeological Review from Cambridge* 11(1): 39–49.

Mizoguchi, K. (2000) The child as a node of past, present and future. In: Sofaer Derevenski, J. (ed.) *Children and Material Culture*, pp. 141–50. London: Routledge.

Molleson, T. (1989) Seed preparation in the Mesolithic: the osteological evidence. *Antiquity* 63: 356–62.

Molleson, T. (1992) Mortality patterns in the Romano-British cemetery at Poundbury Camp, Dorchester. In: Bassett, S. (ed.) *Death in Towns: Urban Responses to the Dying and the Dead, 100–1600*, pp. 43–55. London: Leicester University Press

Molleson, T. (1994) The eloquent bones of Abu Hureyra. *Scientific American* 271: 70–5.

Molleson, T. and Cox, M. (1993) *The Spitalfields Project: Volume II – The Anthropology: The Middling Sort*, London: Council for British Archaeology Report 86.

Molleson, T., Cruse, K. and Mays, S. (1998) Some sexually dimorphic features of the human juvenile skull and their value in sex determination in immature juvenile remains. *Journal of Archaeological Science* 25(8): 719–28.

Molnar, S. (1971) Human tooth wear, tooth function and cultural variability. *American Journal of Physical Anthropology* 34(2): 175–90.

Montserrat, D. (1998) Introduction. In: Montserrat, D. (ed.) *Changing Bodies, Changing Meanings: Studies on the Human Body in Antiquity*, pp. 1–9. London: Routledge.

Moore, H. (1986) *Space, Text and Gender: An Anthropological Study of the Marakwet of Kenya*, Cambridge: Cambridge University Press.

Moore, H. (1988) *Feminism and Anthropology*, Cambridge: Polity Press.

Moore, H. (1994) *A Passion for Difference: Essays in Anthropology and Gender*, Cambridge: Polity Press.

Moorrees, C. F. A., Fanning, E. A. and Hunt, E. E. (1963a) Age variation of formation stages for ten permanent teeth. *Journal of Dental Research* 42: 1490–502.

Moorrees, C. F. A., Fanning, E. A. and Hunt, E. E. (1963b) Age variation of formation and reabsorption of three deciduous teeth in children. *American Journal of Physical Anthropology* 21(2): 205–13.

Morgan, D. and Scott, S. (1993) Bodies in a social landscape. In: Scott, S. and Morgan, D. (eds.) *Body Matters*, pp. 1–21. London: The Falmer Press.

Morris, A. G. (1992) *The Skeletons of Contact: A Study of Protohistoric Burials from the Lower Orange River Valley, South Africa*, Johannesburg: Witwatersrand University Press.

Morris, R. C. (1995) All made up: performance theory and the new anthropology of sex and gender. *Annual Review of Anthropology* 24: 567–92.

Morrow, V. (1994) Responsible children? Aspects of children's work and employment outside school in contemporary UK. In: Mayall, B. (ed.) *Children's Childhoods: Observed and Experienced*, pp. 128–43. London: Falmer.

Morss, J. (1990) *The Biologising of Childhood: Developmental Psychology and the Darwinian Myth*, London: Lawrence Erlbaum.

Morton, J. (1995) The organic remains: remarks on the constitution and development of people. *Social Analysis* 37: 101–18.

Murray, J. E. and Herndon, R. W. (2002) Markets for children in early America: a political economy of pauper apprenticeship. *Journal of Economic History* 62(2): 356–82.

Murray, W. H. (1966) *The Hebrides*, London: Cox & Wyman.

Museum of London Archaeology Service (1994) *Archaeological Site Manual*, 3rd edition. London: Museum of London.

Needham, S. (1998) Modelling the flow of metal in the Bronze Age. In: Mordant, C., Pernot, M. and Rychner, V. (eds.) *L'Atelier du Bronzier en Europe du XXe au Viiie siècle avant notre ère, III: Production, circulation et consommation du Bronze*, pp. 285–307. Paris: Comité des Travaux Historiques et Scientifiques.

Nielsen-Marsh, C., Gernaey, A., Turner-Walker, G., Hedges, R., Pike, A. and Collins, M. (2000) The chemical degradation of bone. In: Cox, M. and Mays, S. (eds.) *Human Osteology in Archaeology and Forensic Science*, pp. 439–54. London: Greenwich Medical Media.

Nordbladh, J. and Yates, T. (1990) This perfect body, this virgin text: between sex and gender in archaeology. In: Bapty, I. and Yates, T. (eds.) *Archaeology after Structuralism*, pp. 222–37. London: Routledge.

Olwig, K. R. (1993) Sexual cosmology: nation and landscape at the conceptual interstices of nature and culture; or what does landscape really mean? In: Bender, B. (ed.) *Landscape, Politics and Perspectives*, pp. 307–43. Oxford: Berg.

O'Neill, J. (1985) *Five Bodies: The Human Shape of Modern Society*, Ithaca: Cornell University Press.

O'Rourke, D. H., Hayes, M. G. and Carlyle, S. W. (2000) Ancient DNA studies in physical anthropology. *Annual Review of Anthropology* 29: 217–42.

Ortner, D. and Putschar, W. (1985) *Identification of Pathological Conditions in Human Skeletal Remains*, Washington: Smithsonian University Press.

Ortner, S. and Whitehead, H. (1981) *Sexual Meanings: The Cultural Construction of Gender and Sexuality*, Cambridge: Cambridge University Press.

O'Shea, J. M. (1984) *Mortuary Variability: An Archaeological Investigation*, Orlando: Academic Press.

Ots, T. (1994) The silenced body – the expressive Leib: on the dialectic of mind and life in Chinese cathartic healing. In: Csordas, T. J. (ed.) *Embodiment and Experience: The Existential Grounds of Culture and Self*, pp. 116–36. Cambridge: Cambridge University Press.

Ovid (1997) *Tales from Ovid: Twenty-four Passages from the 'Metamorphoses' Ovid*, trans. Ted Hughes. London: Faber and Faber.

Oxley, J. (1820) *Journals of Two Expeditions into the Interior of New South Wales in the Years 1817–18*, London: John Murray.

Pader, E. J. (1982) *Symbolism, Social Relations and the Interpretation of Mortuary Remains*, Oxford: BAR Supplementary Series 130.

Pálfi, G. (1992) Traces des activités sur les squelettes des anciens Hongrois. *Bulletin et Mémoires de la Société d'Anthropologie de Paris* 4(3–4): 209–31.

Pálfi, G. and Dutour, O. (1996) Les Marqueurs d'activité sur le squelette humain: aspects théoriques et application à des séries ostéoarchéologiques européennes. In: *L'Identité des populations archéologiques. XVIe Rencontres international d'archéologie et d'histoire d'Antibes*, pp. 245–69. Sophia Antipolis: Editions APDCA.

Pálsson, G. and Harðardóttir, K. E. (2002) For whom the cell tolls: debates about biomedicine. *Current Anthropology* 43(2): 271–301.

Parfitt, A. M. (1983) The physiologic and clinical significance of bone histomorphometric data. In: Recker, R. R. (ed.) *Bone Histomorphometry: Techniques and Interpretation*, pp. 143–224. Boca Raton: CRC Press.

Parker Pearson, M. (1982) Mortuary practices, society and ideology: an ethnoarchaeological study. In: Hodder, I. (ed.) *Symbolic and Structural Archaeology*, pp. 99–113. Cambridge: Cambridge University Press.

Parker Pearson, M. (1999a) *The Archaeology of Death and Burial*, Thrupp, Stroud: Sutton Publishing.

Parker Pearson, M. (1999b) Fearing and celebrating the dead in southern Madagascar. In: Downes, J. and Pollard, A. (eds.) *The Loved Body's Corruption: Archaeological Contributions to the Study of Human Mortality*, pp. 9–18. Glasgow: Cruithne Press.

Pate, F. D. (1994) Bone chemistry and paleodiet. *Journal of Archaeological Method and Theory* 1: 161–209.

Pearson, G. A. (1996) Of sex and gender. *Science* 274: 328–9.

Peterson, J. (2000) Labor patterns in the southern Levant in the Early Bronze Age. In: Rautman, A. E. (ed.) *Reading the Body: Representations and Remains in the Archaeological Record*, pp. 38–54. Philadelphia: University of Pennsylvania Press.

Peterson, J. (2002) *Sexual Revolutions: Gender and Labor at the Dawn of Agriculture*, Walnut Creek: AltaMira Press.

Peyron, J. G. (1986) Osteoarthritis: the epidemiologic viewpoint. *Clinical Orthopaedics* 213: 13–19.

Piaget, J. (1968) *On the Development of Memory and Identity*, Worcester, Mass.: Clark University Press.

Pickering, R. B. (1979) Hunter-gatherer / agriculturalist arthritic patterns: a preliminary investigation. *Henry Ford Hospital Medical Journal* 27: 50–3.

Pinker, S. (1999) *How the Mind Works*, London: Penguin.

Place, B. (2000) Constructing the bodies of ill children in the intensive care unit. In: Prout, A. (ed.) *The Body, Childhood and Society*, pp. 172–94. London: Macmillan Press.

Polanyi, M. (1958) *Personal Knowledge*, London: Routledge.

Porter, R. (2001) *Bodies Politic: Disease, Death and Doctors in Britain, 1650–1900*, Ithaca: Cornell University Press.

Powell, M. L., Bridges, P. S. and Mires, M. W. (eds.) (1991) *What Mean these Bones? Studies in Southeastern Bioarchaeology*, Tuscaloosa: University of Alabama Press.

Prader, A., Tanner, J. M. and Von Harnack, G. A. (1963) Catch-up growth following illness or starvation. *Journal of Paediatrics* 62: 646–59.

Prag, J. and Neave, R. (1997) *Making Faces: Using Forensic and Archaeological Evidence*, London: Trustees of the British Museum.

Prendergast, S. (1992) *'This is the Time to Grow Up': Girls' Experiences of Menstruation in School*, Cambridge: Health Promotion Trust.

Price, T. D., Grupe, G. and Schröter, P. (1998) Migration in the Bell Beaker period of central Europe. *Antiquity* 72: 405–11.

Price, T. D., Johnson, C. M., Ezzo, J. A., Ericson, J. A. and Burton, J. H. (1994) Residential mobility in the prehistoric southwest United States: a preliminary study using strontium isotope analysis. *Journal of Archaeological Science* 21(3): 315–30.

Price, T. D., Manzanilla, L. and Middleton, W. D. (2000) Immigration and the ancient city of Teotihuacan in Mexico: a study using strontium isotope ratios in human bone and teeth. *Journal of Archaeological Science* 27(10): 903–13.

Privat, K. L., O'Connell, T. C. and Richards, M. (2002) Stable isotope analysis of human and faunal remains from the Anglo-Saxon cemetery at Berinsfield, Oxfordshire: dietary and social implications. *Journal of Archaeological Science* 29(7): 779–90.

Proctor, R. (1988) From Anthropologie to Rassenkunde: concepts of race in German physical anthropology. In: G. W. Stocking, Jr (ed.) *Bones, Bodies and Behavior: Essays on Biological Anthropology*, pp. 139–79. Madison, Wis.: University of Wisconsin Press.

Prout, A. (2000) Childhood bodies: construction, agency and hybridity. In: Prout, A. (ed.) *The Body, Childhood and Society*, pp. 1–18. London: Macmillan Press.

Qvortrup, J. (1994) Childhood matters: an introduction. In: Qvortrup, J., Bardy, M., Sgritta, G. and Wintersberger, H. (eds.) *Childhood Matters: Social Theory, Practice and Politics*, pp. 1–23. Aldershot: Avebury.

Radin, E. L. (1982) Mechanical factors in the causation of osteoarthritis. *Rheumatology* 7: 46–52.

Radin, E. L., Paul, I. L. and Rose, R. M. (1972) Mechanical factors in osteoarthritis. *Lancet* 1: 519–22.

Radosevich, S. E. (1993) The six deadly sins of trace element analysis: a case of wishful thinking in science. In: Sandford, M. K. (ed.) *Investigations of Ancient Human Tissue*, pp. 269–332. Reading: Gordon and Breach.

Rao, P. D. P. (1966) Squatting facets on the talus and tibia in Australian Aborigines. *Archaeology and Physical Anthropology in Oceania* 1: 51–6.

Rautman, A. E. (ed.) (2000) *Reading the Body: Representations and Remains in the Archaeological Record*, Philadelphia: University of Pennsylvania Press.

Renfrew, C. (2001) Symbol before concept: material engagement and the early development of society. In: Hodder, I. (ed.) *Archaeological Theory Today*, pp. 122–40. Cambridge: Polity Press.

Renfrew, C. (2004) Towards a theory of material engagement. In: DeMarrais, E., Gosden, C. and Renfrew, C. (eds.) *Rethinking Materiality: The Engagement of Mind with the Material World*, pp. 23–31. Cambridge: McDonald Institute for Archaeological Research.

Ribot, I. and Roberts, C. (1996) A study of non-specific stress indicators and skeletal growth in two mediaeval subadult populations. *Journal of Archaeological Science* 23(1): 67–79.

Richards C. (1993) Monumental choreography. In: Tilley, C. (ed.) *Interpretative Archaeology*, pp. 143–78. Oxford: Berg.

Richards, M. P., Hedges, R. E. M., Molleson, T. I. and Vogel, J. C. (1998) Stable isotope analysis reveals variations in human diet at the Poundbury Camp cemetery site. *Journal of Archaeological Science* 25(12): 1247–52.

Richardson, R. (1987) *Death, Dissection and the Destitute*, London: Routledge.

Rival, L. (1993) The growth of family trees: understanding Huaorani perceptions of the forest. *Man* 28(4): 635–52.

Rixecker, S. S. (2000) Exposing queer biotechnology via queer archaeology: the quest to (re)construct the human body from the inside out. *World Archaeology* 32(2): 263–74.

Robb, J. (1994) Skeletal signs of activity in the Italian Metal Ages: methodological and interpretative notes. *Human Evolution* 9: 215–29.

Robb, J. (1997) Intentional tooth removal in Neolithic Italian women. *Antiquity* 71: 659–69.

Robb, J. (1998a) Violence and gender in early Italy. In: Frayer, D. W. and Martin, D. (eds.) *Violence and Warfare in the Past*, pp. 111–44. London: Routledge.

Robb, J. (1998b) The interpretation of skeletal muscle sites: a statistical approach. *International Journal of Osteoarchaeology* 8(5): 363–77.

Robb, J. (2002) Time and biography: osteobiography of the Italian Neolithic lifespan. In: Hamilakis, Y., Pluciennik, M. and Tarlow, S. (eds.) *Thinking Through the Body: Archaeologies of Corporeality*, pp. 153–71. New York: Kluwer Academic / Plenum Publishers.

Robb, J., Bigazzi, R., Lazzarini, L., Scarsini, C. and Sonego, F. (2001) Social 'status' and biological 'status': a comparison of grave goods and skeletal indicators from Pontecagnano. *American Journal of Physical Anthropology* 115(3): 213–22.

Roberts, C. (2000a) Did they take sugar? The use of skeletal evidence in the study of disability in past populations. In: Hubert, J. (ed.) *Madness, Disability and Social Exclusion: The Archaeology and Anthropology of 'Difference'*, pp. 46–59. London: Routledge.

Roberts, C. (2000b) Trauma in biocultural perspective: past, present and future work in Britain. In: Cox, M. and Mays, S. (eds.) *Human Osteology in Archaeology and Forensic Science*, pp. 337–56. London: Greenwich Medical Media.

Roberts, C. and Buikstra, J. E. (2003) *The Bioarchaeology of Tuberculosis: A Global View on a Re-emerging Disease*, Gainesville: University Presses of Florida.

Roberts, C. and Cox, M. (2003) *Health and Disease in Britain: From Prehistory to the Present Day*, Stroud: Sutton Publishing.

Roberts, C. and Manchester, K. (1995) *The Archaeology of Disease*, Stroud: Sutton.

Roberts, D. F. (1995) The pervasiveness of plasticity. In: Mascie-Taylor, N. and Bogin, B. (eds.) *Human Variability and Plasticity*, pp. 1–17. Cambridge: Cambridge University Press.

Robertson, A. F. (1996) The development of meaning: ontogeny and culture. *Journal of the Royal Anthropological Institute* n.s. 2: 591–610.

Rogers, J. and Waldron, T. (1995) *A Field Guide to Joint Disease in Archaeology*, Chichester: Wiley.

Rogers, J., Shepstone, L. and Dieppe, P. (1997a) Bone formers: osteophyte and enthesophyte formation are positively associated. *Annals of the Rheumatic Diseases* 56: 85–90.

Rogers, J., Waldron, T., Dieppe, P. and Watt, I. (1997b) Arthropathies in palaeopathology: the basis of classification according to most probable cause. *Journal of Archaeological Science* 14(2): 179–93.

Rogoff, B. (1981) Adults and peers as agents of socialization. *Ethos* 9: 18–36.

Roscoe, W. (1998) *Changing Ones: Third and Fourth Genders in Native North America*, New York: St Martin's Press.

Rose, H. and Rose, S. (eds.) (2001) *Alas Poor Darwin: Arguments Against Evolutionary Psychology*, London: Vintage.

Rosenzweig, M. R. and Evenson, R. (1997) Fertility, schooling, and the economic contribution of children in rural India: an econometric analysis. *International Library of Critical Writings in Economics* 86(2): 113–27.

Rothschild, B. M. (1997) Porosity: a curiosity without diagnostic significance. *American Journal of Physical Anthropology* 104(4): 529–33.

Roux, V. (ed.) (2000) *Cornaline de l'Inde: des pratiques techniques de Cambay aux techno-systèmes de l'Indus*, Paris: MSH.

Roux, V. and Corbetta, D. (1990) *Le Tour du potier: spécialisation artisanale et compétences techniques*, Paris: CNRS.

Rubin, C. T., McLeod, K. J. and Bain, S. D. (1990) Functional strains and cortical bone adaptation: epigenetic assurance of skeletal integrity. *Journal of Biomechanics* 23: 43–54.

Ruff, C. B. and Runestad, J. A. (1992) Primate limb bone structural adaptations. *Annual Review of Anthropology* 21: 407–33.

Ruff, C. B., Larsen, C. S. and Hayes, W. C. (1984) Structural changes in the femur with the transition to agriculture on the Georgia coast. *American Journal of Physical Anthropology* 64(2): 125–36.

Sandford, M. K. and Weaver, D. S. (2000) Trace element research in anthropology: new perspective and challenges. In: Katzenberg, M. A. and Saunders, S. R. (eds.) *Biological Anthropology of the Human Skeleton*, pp. 329–50. New York: Wiley-Liss.

Saul, F. P. and Saul, J. M. (1989) Osteobiography: a Maya example. In: Iscan, M. Y. and Kennedy, A. R. (eds.) *Reconstruction of Life from the Skeleton*, pp. 287–301. New York: Alan Liss.

Saunders, S. R. and Hoppa, R. D. (1993) Growth deficit in survivors and non-survivors: biological mortality bias in subadult skeletal samples. *Yearbook of Physical Anthropology* 36: 127–51.

Schell, L. M. (1995) Human biological adaptability with special emphasis on plasticity: history, development and problems for future research. In: Mascie-Taylor, C. G. N. and Bogin, B. (eds.) *Human Variability and Plasticity*, pp. 213–37. Cambridge: Cambridge University Press.

Schell, L. M. and Denham, M. (2003) Environmental pollution in urban environments and human biology. *Annual Review of Anthropology* 32: 111–34.

Scheper-Hughes, N. (2001) Bodies for sale – whole or in parts. *Body and Society* 7(2–3): 1–8.

Scher, A. T. (1978) Injuries to the cervical spine sustained while carrying loads on the head. *Paraplegia* 16: 94–101.

Scheuer, L. (1998) Age at death and cause of death of the people buried in St Brides's Church, Fleet Street London. In: Cox, M. (ed.) *Grave Concerns: Death and Burial in England 1700–1850*, pp. 100–11. York: Council for British Archaeology.

Scheuer, L. and Black, S. (2000) *Developmental Juvenile Osteology*, London: Academic Press.

Scheuer, L. and Bowman, J. E. (1995) Correlation of documentary and skeletal evidence in the St Brides crypt population. In: Saunders, S. R. and Herring, A. (eds.) *Grave Reflections: Portraying the Past Through Cemetery Studies*, pp. 49–70. Toronto: Canadian Scholars' Press.

Schillaci, M. A. and Stojanowski, C. M. (2002) Postmarital residence and biological variation at Pueblo Bonito. *American Journal of Physical Anthropology* 120(1): 1–15.

Schmidt, C. W. (2001) Dental microwear evidence for a dietary shift between two nonmaize-reliant prehistoric human populations from Indiana. *American Journal of Physical Anthropology* 114(2): 139–45.

Schmidt, R. A. and Voss, B. L. (eds.) (2000) *Archaeologies of Sexuality*, London: Routledge.

Schmorl, G. and Junghanns, H. (1971) *The Human Spine in Health and Disease*, 2nd edition. New York: Grune and Stratton.

Schoeninger, M. J. and Moore, K. (1992) Bone stable isotope studies in archaeology. *Journal of World Prehistory* 6: 247–96.

Schour, I. and Massler, M. (1941) The development of the human dentition. *Journal of the American Dental Association* 28: 1153–60.

Schulting, R. and Richards, M. (2001) Dating women and becoming farmers: new palaeodietary and AMS evidence from the Breton Mesolithic cemeteries of Téviec and Hoëdic. *Journal of Archaeological Science* 20(3): 314–44.

Schurr, M. R. (1998) Using stable nitrogen-isotopes to study weaning behavior in past populations. *World Archaeology* 30(2): 327–42.

Schutkowski, H. (1993) Sex determination of infant and juvenile skeletons: 1. Morphognostic features. *American Journal of Physical Anthropology* 90(2): 199–205.

Schutkowski, H., Herrmann, B., Wiedemann, F., Bocherens, H. and Grupe, G. (1999) Diet, status and decomposition at Weingarten: trace element and isotope analyses on early mediaeval skeletal material. *Journal of Archaeological Science* 26(6): 675–85.

Schwartz, J. (1995) *Skeleton Keys*, Oxford: Oxford University Press.

Schwarzenbach, S. 1998. On owning the body. In: Elias, J., Bullough, V., Elias, V. and Brewer, G. (eds.) *Prostitution: On Whores, Hustlers and Johns*, pp. 345–52. Amherst, N.Y.: Prometheus.

Scott, E. (1999) *The Archaeology of Infancy and Infant Death*, Oxford: BAR International Series 819. Archaeopress.

Sealy, J., Armstrong, R. and Schrire, C. (1995) Beyond lifetime averages: tracing life histories through isotopic analysis of different calcified tissues from archaeological human skeletons. *Antiquity* 69: 290–300.

Shanks, M. and Tilley, C. (1982) Ideology, symbolic power and ritual communication: a reinterpretation of Neolithic mortuary practices. In: Hodder, I. (ed.) *Symbolic and Structural Archaeology*, pp. 129–54. Cambridge: Cambridge University Press.

Shanks, M. and Tilley, C. (1987) *Social Theory and Archaeology*, Cambridge: Polity Press.

Shaver, P. and Hendrick, C. (eds.) (1987) *Sex and Gender*, Newbury Park: Sage.

Shay, T. (1985) Differentiated treatment of deviancy at death as revealed in the anthropological and archaeological material. *Journal of Anthropological Archaeology* 4: 221–41.

Shennan, S. (2002) *Genes, Memes and Human History: Darwinian Archaeology and Cultural Evolution*, London: Thames and Hudson.

Shilling, C. (1993) *The Body and Social Theory*, London: Sage.

Sillar, B. (1994) Playing with god: cultural perceptions of children, play and miniatures in the Andes. *Archaeological Review from Cambridge* 13(2): 47–63.

Sillar, B. (2000) *Shaping Culture: Making Pots and Constructing Households: An Ethnoarchaeological Study of Pottery Production, Trade and Use in the Andes*, BAR International Series 883. Oxford: John and Erica Hedges.

Sinclair, Sir S. J. (ed.) (1794) *The Statistical Account of Scotland*. Edinburgh.

Singh, I. (1959) Squatting facets on the talus and tibia in Indians. *Journal of Anatomy* 93: 540–50.

Smith, B. H. (1984) Patterns of molar wear in hunter-gatherers and agriculturalists. *American Journal of Physical Anthropology* 63(1): 39–56.

Smith, P. and Kahila, G. (1992) Identification of infanticide in archaeological sites: a case study from the Late Roman-Early Byzantine periods at Ashkelon, Israel. *Journal of Archaeological Science* 19(6): 667–75.

Sofaer Derevenski, J. (1994) Where are the children? Accessing children in the past. *Archaeological Review from Cambridge* 13(2): 7–20.

Sofaer Derevenski, J. (1997a) Engendering children, engendering archaeology. In: Moore, J. and Scott, E. (eds.) *Invisible People and Processes*, pp. 192–202. London: Leicester University Press.

Sofaer Derevenski, J. (1997b) Linking gender and age as social variables. *Ethnographisch-Archäologischen Zeitschrift* 38(3–4): 485–93.

Sofaer Derevenski, J. (1998) Gender archaeology as contextual archaeology: a critical examination of the tensions between method and theory in the archaeology of gender. Unpublished PhD thesis, University of Cambridge.

Sofaer Derevenski, J. (2000a) Material culture shock: confronting expectations in the material culture of children. In: Sofaer Derevenski, J. (ed.) *Children and Material Culture*, pp. 3–16. London: Routledge.

Sofaer Derevenski, J. (2000b) Rings of life: the role of early metalwork in mediating the gendered life course. *World Archaeology* 31(3): 389–406.

Sofaer Derevenski, J. (2000c) Sex differences in activity-related osseous change in the spine and the gendered division of labor at Ensay and Wharram Percy, UK. *American Journal of Physical Anthropology* 111(3): 333–54.

Sofaer Derevenski, J. (2001) Is human osteoarchaeology environmental archaeology? In: Albarella, U. (ed.) *Environmental Archaeology: Meaning and Purpose*, pp. 113–33. Dordrecht: Kluwer Academic Publishers.

Sofaer Derevenski, J. (2002) Engendering context: context as gendered practice in the Early Bronze Age of the Upper Thames Valley, UK. *European Journal of Archaeology* 5(2): 191–211.

Sofaer Derevenski, J. and Sørensen, M. L. S. (2005) Technological change as social change: the introduction of metal in Europe. In: Bartelheim, M. and Heyd, V. (eds.) *Continuity – Discontinuity: Transition Periods in European Prehistory*, Forschungen zur Archäometrie und Altertumswissenschaft, Rahden (Westf.): Marie Leidorf.

Solís, F., Alonso, R. V. and Gallegos, A. (2002) 318. Femur with inscriptions. In: *Aztecs*, p. 338. London: Royal Academy of Arts.

Sørensen, M. L. S. (1989) Period VI reconsidered: continuity and change at the transition from Bronze to Iron Age in Scandinavia. In: Sørensen, M. L. S. and Thomas, R. (eds.) *The Bronze Age – Iron Age Transition in Europe: Aspects of Continuity and Change*, pp. 457–92. Oxford: BAR British Series 483.

Sørensen, M. L. S. (1991) The construction of gender through appearance. In: Walde, D. and Willows, D. E. (eds.) *The Archaeology of Gender: Proceedings of the 22nd Annual Chacmool Conference*, pp. 121–9. Calgary: Archaeological Association of the University of Calgary.

Sørensen, M. L. S. (1997) Reading dress: the construction of social categories and identities in Bronze Age Europe. *Journal of European Archaeology* 5(1): 93–114.

Sørensen, M. L. S. (2000) *Gender Archaeology*, Cambridge: Polity Press.

Sørensen, M. L. S. (2004) The archaeology of gender. In: Bintliff, J. (ed.) *A Companion to Archaeology*, pp. 75–91. Oxford: Blackwell.

Spencer, F. (1981) The rise of academic physical anthropology in the United States 1880–1980. *American Journal of Physical Anthropology* 56(4): 353–64.

Spencer, F. (1997) United Kingdom. In: Spencer, F. (ed.) *History of Physical Anthropology. An Encyclopedia*, pp. 1054–69. New York: Garland Publishing.

Sperduti, A. (1997) Life condition of a Roman Imperial Age population: occupational stress markers and working activities in Lucus Feroniae. *Human Evolution* 12: 253–67.

Sperry, R. W. (1982) Some effects of disconnecting the cerebral hemispheres. *Science* 217: 1223–6.

Spindler, K. (1994) *The Man in the Ice*, London: Weidenfeld & Nicholson.

Steedman, C. (1990) *Childhood, Culture and Class in Britain: Margaret McMillan 1860–1931*, London: Virago.

Steedman, C. (1992) Bodies, figures and physiology: Margaret McMillan and the late nineteenth century remaking of working class childhood. In: Cooter, R. (ed.) *In the Name of the Child: Health and Welfare, 1880–1940*, pp. 19–43. London: Routledge.

Steedman, C. (1995) *Strange Dislocations: Childhood and the Idea of Human Interiority 1780–1930*, Cambridge, Mass.: Harvard University Press.

Steegmann, A. T. (1985) 18th century British stature: growth cessation, selective recruiting, secular trends, nutrition at birth, cold and occupation. *Human Biology* 57: 77–95.

Steele, J. (2000) Skeletal indicators of handedness. In: Cox, M. and Mays, S. (eds.) *Human Osteology in Archaeology and Forensic Science*, pp. 307–23. London: Greenwich Medical Media.

Steele, J., Adams, J. and Sluckin, T. (1998) Modelling Paleoindian dispersals. *World Archaeology* 30(2): 286–305.

Steen, S. L. and Lane, R. W. (1998) Evaluation of habitual activities among two Alaskan Eskimo populations based on musculoskeletal stress markers. *International Journal of Osteoarchaeology* 8(5): 341–53.

Stirland, A. (1991) Diagnosis of occupationally related palaeopathology: can it be done? In: Ortner, D. and Aufderheide, A. C. (eds.) *Human Paleopathology: Current Syntheses and Future Options*, pp. 40–7. Washington DC: Smithsonian Institution Press.

Stirland, A. (1993) Asymmetry and activity-related change in the male humerus. *International Journal of Osteoarchaeology* 3(2): 105–13.

Stirland, A. (1998) Musculoskeletal evidence for activity: problems of evaluation. *International Journal of Osteoarchaeology* 8(5): 354–62.

Stirland, A. (2000) *Raising the Dead: The Skeleton Crew of Henry VIII's Great Ship, the Mary Rose*, Chichester: John Wiley.

Stock, J. T. and Pfeiffer, S. K. (2004) Long bone robusticity and subsistence behaviour among Later Stone Age foragers of the forest and fynbos biomes of South Africa. *Journal of Archaeological Science* 31(7): 999–1013.

Stocking, G. W. Jr (1968) *Race, Culture and Evolution: Essays in the History of Anthropology*, New York: Free Press.

Stone, A. C. (2000) Ancient DNA from skeletal remains. In: Katzenberg, M. A. and Saunders, S. R. (eds.) *Biological Anthropology of the Human Skeleton*, pp. 351–71. New York: Wiley-Liss.

Storer, N. (1972) *The Social System of Science*, New York: Holt, Rinehart and Winston.

Strathern, M. (1980) No nature, no culture: the Hagen case. In: MacCormack, C. and Strathern, M. (eds.) *Nature, Culture and Gender*, pp. 174–219. Cambridge: Cambridge University Press.

Strathern, M. (1988) *The Gender of the Gift: Problems with Women and Problems with Society in Melanesia*, Berkeley: University of California Press.

Strathern, M. (1992) *After Nature: English Kinship in the Late Twentieth Century*, Cambridge: Cambridge University Press.

Strathern, M. (1996) Cutting the network. *Journal of the Royal Anthropological Institute* n.s. 2: 517–35.

Stuart-Macadam, P. (1988) Iron deficiency anemia: exploring the difference. In: Grauer, A. L. and Stuart-Macadam, P. (eds.) *Sex and Gender in Paleopathological Perspective*, pp. 45–63. Cambridge: Cambridge University Press.

Stuart-Macadam, P. (1989) Nutritional deficiency disease: a survey of scurvy, rickets, and iron deficiency anaemia. In: Iscan, M. Y. and Kennedy, K. A. R. (eds.) *Reconstruction of Life from the Skeleton*, pp. 211–22. New York: Alan Liss.

Stuart-Macadam, P. and Dettwyler, K. A. (eds.) (1995) *Breastfeeding: Biocultural Perspectives*, New York: Aldine de Gruyter.

Sullivan, A. (2004) Reconstructing relationships among mortality, status, and gender at the medieval Gilbertine Priory of St Andrew, Fishergate, York. *American Journal of Physical Anthropology* 124(4): 330–45.

Tarlow, S. (1999) *Bereavement and Commemoration: An Archaeology of Mortality*, Oxford: Blackwell.

Thomas, C. (2002) The 'disabled' body. In: Evans, M. and Lee, E. (eds.) *Real Bodies: A Sociological Introduction*, pp. 64–78. Basingstoke: Palgrave.

Thomas, J. (1990) Monuments from the inside: the case of the Irish megalithic tombs. *World Archaeology* 22(2): 168–78.

Thomas, J. (1991) Reading the body: Beaker funerary practice in Britain. In: Garwood, P., Jennings, D., Skeates, R. and Toms, J. (eds.) *Sacred and Profane: Proceedings of a Conference on Archaeology, Ritual and Religion, Oxford 1989*, pp. 33–42. Oxford: Oxbow Books.

Thomas, J. (1993a) The hermeneutics of megalithic space. In: Tilley, C. (ed.) *Interpretative Archaeology*, pp. 73–97. Oxford: Berg.

Thomas, J. (1993b) The politics of vision and the archaeologies of landscape. In: Bender, B. (ed.) *Landscape: Politics and Perspectives*, pp. 19–48. Oxford: Berg.

Thomas, J. (2002) Archaeology's humanism and the materiality of the body. In: Hamilakis, Y., Pluciennik, M. and Tarlow, S. (eds.) *Thinking Through the Body: Archaeologies of Corporeality*, pp. 29–45. New York: Kluwer Academic / Plenum Publishers.

Tiesler, V. (1999) Head shaping and decoration among the ancient Maya: archaeological and cultural aspects. Paper presented at 64th Meeting of the Society of American Archaeology, Chicago.

Tilley, C. (1991) *Material Culture and Text: The Art of Ambiguity*, London: Routledge.

Tilley, C. (1993) Art, architecture, landscape [Neolithic Sweden]. In: Bender, B. (ed.) *Landscape: Politics and Perspectives*, pp. 49–84. Oxford: Berg.

Tilley, C. (1994) *A Phenomenology of Landscape: Places, Paths and Monuments*, Oxford: Berg.

Tilley, C. (1999a) *Metaphor and Material Culture*, Oxford: Blackwell.

Tilley, C. (1999b) Why material things matter: some theses on material forms, mind and body. In: Gustafsson, A. and Karlsson, H. (eds.) *Glyfer och Arkeologiska Rum – en Vänbok till Jarl Nordbladh*, pp. 315–39. Gothenburg: Gothenburg University.

Toren, C. (1993) Making history: the significance of childhood cognition for a comparative anthropology of mind. *Man* n.s. 28: 461–78.

Toren, C. (1994) On childhood cognition and social institutions. *Man* 29: 979–81.

Toren, C. (1999) *Mind, Materiality and History: Explorations in Fijian Ethnography*, London: Routledge.

Toren, C. (2001) The child in mind: In: Whitehouse, H. (ed.) *The Debated Mind: Evolutionary Psychology versus Ethnography*, pp. 155–79. Oxford: Berg.

Toren, C. (2002) Anthropology as the whole science of what it means to be human. In: Fox, R. and King, B. (eds.) *Anthropology Beyond Culture*, pp. 105–24. Oxford: Berg.

Torres-Rouff, C. (2002) Cranial vault modification and ethnicity in Middle Horizon San Pedro de Atacama, Chile. *Current Anthropology* 43(1): 163–71.

Trigger, B. G. (1989) *A History of Archaeological Thought*, Cambridge: Cambridge University Press.

Tringham, R. (1991) Households with faces: the challenge of gender in prehistoric architectural remains. In: Gero, J. M. and Conkey, M. W. (eds.) *Engendering Archaeology: Women and Prehistory*, pp. 93–131. Oxford: Blackwell.

Trinkaus, E. (1975) Squatting among the Neanderthals: a problem in the behavioural interpretation of skeletal morphology. *Journal of Archaeological Science* 2(4): 327–51.

Trotter, M. (1964) Accessory sacroiliac articulations in East African skeletons. *American Journal of Physical Anthropology* 22(2): 137–42.

Turnbull, P. (2001) 'Rare work amongst the professors': the capture of indigenous skulls within phrenological knowledge in early colonial Australia. In: Creed, B. and Hoorn, J. (eds.) *Body Trade*, pp. 3–23. New York: Routledge.

Turner, B. S. (1984) *The Body and Society: Explorations in Social Theory*, Oxford: Blackwell.

Turner, B. S. (1991) Recent developments in the theory of the body. In: Featherstone, M., Hepworth, M. and Turner, B. S. (eds.) *The Body: Social Processes and Cultural Theory*, pp. 1–35. London: Sage.

Turner, B. S. (1996) *The Body and Society*, 2nd edition. London: Sage.

Turner, B. S. (2003) Foreword: the phenomenology of lived experience. In: Meskell, L. M. and Joyce, R. A. (eds.) *Embodied Lives: Figuring Ancient Maya and Egyptian Experience*, pp. xiii–xx. London: Routledge.

Turner, G. and Anderson, T. (2003) Marked occupational dental abrasion from medieval Kent. *International Journal of Osteoarchaeology* 13(3): 168–72.

Twine, R. (2002) Physiognomy, phrenology and the temporality of the body. *Body and Society* 8(1): 67–88.

Ubelaker, D. H. (1979) Skeletal evidence for kneeling in prehistoric Ecuador. *American Journal of Physical Anthropology* 51(4): 679–86.

Ubelaker, D. H. (1989) *Human Skeletal Remains: Excavation, Analysis, Interpretation*, 2nd edition. Washington DC: Taraxacum Press.

Uhthoff, H. K. and Jaworski, Z. F. G. (1978) Bone loss in response to long term immobilization. *Journal of Bone and Joint Surgery* 60-B: 420–9.

Urwin, K. and Sharland, E. (1992) From bodies to minds in childcare literature: advice to parents in inter-war Britain. In: Cooter, R. (ed.) *In the Name of the Child: Health and Welfare 1880–1940*, pp. 174–99. London: Routledge.

Valsiner, J. (2000) *Culture and Human Development*, London: Sage.

Van der Ploeg, I. (2004) 'Only angels can do without skin': on reproductive technology's hybrids and the politics of body boundaries. *Body and Society* 10(2): 153–81.

Virilio, P. (1994) *Die Eroberung des Körpers: vom Übermenschen zum überreizten Menschen*, Munich: Hanser.

Voss, B. L. (2000) Feminisms, queer theories, and the archaeological study of past sexualities. *World Archaeology* 32(2): 180–92.

Voss, B. L. and Schmidt, R. A. (2000) Archaeologies of sexuality. In: Schmidt, R. A. and Voss, B. L. (eds.) *Archaeologies of Sexuality*, pp. 1–34. London: Routledge.

Vygotsky, L. S. (1978) *Mind in Society: The Development of Higher Psychological Processes*, Cambridge, Mass.: Harvard University Press.

Wade, P. (1993) 'Race', nature and culture. *Man* n.s. 28: 17–34.

Wainwright, S. P. and Turner, B. S. (2004) Narratives of embodiment: body, aging, and career in Royal Ballet dancers. In: Thomas, H. and Ahmed, J. (eds.) *Cultural Bodies: Ethnography and Theory*, pp. 98–120. Oxford: Blackwell.

Waldron, T. (2000) Hidden or overlooked? Where are the disadvantaged in the skeletal record? In: Hubert, J. (ed.) *Madness, Disability and Social Exclusion: The Archaeology and Anthropology of Difference*, pp. 29–45. London: Routledge.

Walker, P. L. (1995) Problems of preservation and sexism in sexing: some lessons from historical collections for palaeodemographers. In: Saunders, S. R. and Herring, A. (eds.) *Grave Reflections: Portraying the Past through Cemetery Studies*, pp. 31–47. Toronto: Canadian Scholars' Press.

Walker, P. L. (2001) A bioarchaeological perspective on the history of violence. *Annual Review of Anthropology* 30: 573–96.

Walker, P. L. and Cook, D. C. (1998) Gender and sex: vive la difference. *American Journal of Physical Anthropology* 106(2): 255–9.

Wall, C. E. (1991) Evidence of weaning stress and catch-up growth in the long bones of a central Californian Amerindian sample. *Annals of Human Biology* 18: 9–22.

Walvin, J. (2001) *Black Ivory: Slavery in the British Empire*, Oxford: Blackwell.

Wartofsky, M. (1983) The child's construction of the world and the world's construction of the child: from historical epistemology to historical psychology.

In: Kessel, F. S. and Siegel, A. W. (eds.) *The Child and Other Cultural Inventions. Houston Symposium 4*, pp. 188–215. New York: Praeger.

Weaver, D. S. (1980) Sex differences in the ilia of a known sex and age sample of fetal and infant skeletons. *American Journal of Physical Anthropology* 52(2): 191–5.

Weaver, D. S. (1998) Osteoporosis in the bioarchaeology of women. In: Grauer, A. L. and Stuart-Macadam, P. (eds.) *Sex and Gender in Paleopathological Perspective*, pp. 27–44. Cambridge: Cambridge University Press.

Weeratunge, N. (2000) Nature, harmony and the Kaliyugaya: global / local discourses on the human–environment relationship. *Current Anthropology* 41(2): 249–68.

Weiss, E. (2003) Effects of rowing on humeral strength. *American Journal of Physical Anthropology* 121(4): 293–302.

Weiss, K. (1998) Coming to terms with human variation. *Annual Review of Anthropology* 27: 273–300.

Welinder, S. (1998) The cultural construction of childhood in Scandinavia 3500 BC–1350 AD. *Current Swedish Archaeology* 6: 185–204.

Wetterstrom, W. (1992) Climate, diet and population at a prehistoric pueblo in New Mexico. In: Balaam, N. and Rackham, J. (eds.) *Issues in Environmental Archaeology*, pp. 35–61. London: Institute of Archaeology.

Whelehan, I. (1995) *Modern Feminist Thought: From the Second Wave to 'Post-Feminism'*, Edinburgh: Edinburgh University Press.

White, C. D., Healy, P. F. and Schwarcz, H. P. (1993) Intensive agriculture, social status, and Maya diet at Pacbitun, Belize. *Journal of Anthropological Research* 49(375): 347.

Whitehouse, R. (2002) Gender in the south Italian Neolithic: a combinatory approach. In: Milledge Nelson, S. and Rosen-Ayalon, M. (eds.) *In Pursuit of Gender: Worldwide Archaeological Approaches*, pp. 15–42. Walnut Creek: AltaMira Press.

Whitley, R. (1984) *The Intellectual and Social Organization of the Sciences*, Oxford: Clarendon Press.

Williams, R. (1983) *Keywords*, London: Fontana Paperbacks.

Williamson, M. A., Johnston, C. A., Symes, S. A. and Schultz, J. J. (2003) Interpersonal violence between 18th-century Native Americans and Europeans in Ohio. *American Journal of Physical Anthropology* 122(2): 113–22.

Wolff, J. (1892) *Das Gesetz der Transformation der Knochen*, Berlin: Hirschwald.

Wood, J. W., Milner, G. R., Harpending, H. C. and Weiss, K. M. (1992) The osteological paradox: problems of inferring prehistoric health from skeletal samples. *Current Anthropology* 33(4): 343–70.

Wood, W. Q. (1920) The tibia of the Australian aborigine. *Journal of Anatomy* 54: 232–57.

Woolgar, S. (1988) *Science: The Very Idea*, London: Routledge.

Worthman, C. M. (1995) Hormones, sex and gender. *Annual Review of Anthropology* 24: 593–616.

Wright, L. E. (1990) Stresses of conquest: a study of Wilson bands and enamel hypoplasias in the Maya of Lamanai. *American Journal of Human Biology* 2(1): 25–35.

Wylie, A. (1992) The interplay of evidential constraints and political interests: recent archaeological research on gender. *American Antiquity* 57(1): 15–35.

Wylie, A. (2000) Questions of evidence, legitimacy, and the (dis)unity of science. *American Antiquity* 65(2): 227–37.

Yarrow, T. (2003) Artefactual persons: the relational capacities of persons and things in the practice of excavation. *Norwegian Archaeological Review* 36(1): 65–73.

Yates, T. (1993) Frameworks for an archaeology of the body. In: Tilley, C. (ed.) *Interpretative Archaeology*, pp. 31–72. Oxford: Berg.

Zakrzewski, S. (2003) Variation in ancient Egyptian stature and body proportions. *American Journal of Physical Anthropology* 121(3): 219–29.

Index

Abu Hureyra, Syria, activity-induced
        stress, 83, 105
acclimatisation, 71
actions
    ergonomic study of, 80
    objects and, 80, *81*, 138
adaptation, 6, 38, 71–6
adults
    as an age category, 121
    cultural variability in, 124, 126
    in interpretative archaeology, 124
    osteologically determined, 121–4,
        125
    paradox of age categories, 126–7
age
    ageing and, 59, 128
    artefacts associated with bodies in
        age-related patterns, 118, 124, 128,
        129
    chronological, 119
    definition, 118, 119
    hybrids and, 138–43
    methods for determining, 17, 20,
        119–24
        dental development, 36, 70, 74, *123*
        osteological, 2, 24, 36, 37, 121–4,
            129
    physiological, 117–19, 129
    as a process, 134
    social, 119, 129
    tensions between method and theory,
        117, 125–9
    resolution of, 129
    theories of, 120
age categories
    cultural variability in, 124, 126
    as essential or intrinsic, 127
    in interpretative archaeology, 124
    osteologically determined, 121–4, 125
    paradox of, 126–7
ageing, 59
    age and, 59, 128

agents/agency, 18, 43, 48, 79
    social identity and, 125
ancestors, 43
Ancient History of Wiltshire (Hoare), 13
anthropology
    biological (physical), 5
    forensic, 46
Arber, S., 119
archaeologists, as synthesisers of data, 17
archaeology
    bioarchaeology, 6, 23–4, 25–7
    Boasian fourfold perspective, xiv, 5–6
    British approach, 6–7
    of death, 16
    of gender, xiii, 97–101
    knowledge production within, 10
    New Archaeology, 14–18, 38
    See also interpretative archaeology;
        osteoarchaeology
archers, 72
artefacts
    associated with bodies, 2, 50, 143
        age-related patterns, 118, 124, 128,
            129
        gender-related patterns, 90, 101
    copper arm rings, 67
    creating identity, 47, 118, 136–8
    Ingold on, 87
    regional studies, 14
    See also objects
Astuti, R., 60
atheoretical approaches, 32–4
*Atlas of Occupational Markers on Human
        Remains* (Capasso, Kennedy and
        Wilczak), 73
Aztecs, gender construction in children, 66

ballet dancers, ageing studies, 59
Barrett, J., 20
Barthes, R., 19
Battersby, C., 44
Bauman, Z., 124

Becker, A., 49
Benthien, C., 47
bilateral asymmetry, 105
binary oppositions in the study of
    archaeological bodies, 31–2
  atheoretical : theoretical, 32–4
  dead : living, 40–1
    accessing the living from the dead,
      68–9
    continuity between, 41–5, 52, 58, 62,
      68
    as objects : subjects, 69, 103
  inside : outside, 45–8
    reconfiguring boundaries, 48–51
  male : female, 91–6
  nature : culture, 32, 51–5, 69, 104, 120
  resolution of oppositions, 60, 84–5, 86,
    105–16, 129
  See also paradoxes
Binford, L. R., 14–15
bioarchaeology, 6, 23–4, 25–7
biographies, 131, 134–8
  role of objects in constructing, 128
biological anthropology, 5
biological determinism, 105
biologism, 4, 26–7
biology, 69
  conflation with genetics, 27, 53, 56
  relationship with culture, 2
Birke, L., 23, 55, 56, 58, 59, 60, 69, 120
birth
  isotope ratios indicating place of, 132
Boas, F., xiv, 5–6
bodies
  as archaeological resources, 3, 20, 23,
    24–5, 50
  associated with artefacts, 2, 50, 143
    age-related patterns, 118, 124, 128,
      129
    gender-related patterns, 90, 101
  boundaries of
    individual, 47, 48–9
    interpretative, 3
    reconfiguring, 48–51
  as constructed, 54
  as culturally constructed, 1–2, 17, 59,
    60–1, 129–34
    paradox of, 23, 26
  deformed, 73
  experiential understanding of, 21–3, 47,
    76, 88
  as heuristic tools, 18
  historicity of, 78, 131, 134–8
  as hybrids, 84, 138–43
  as material culture, xv, 86–8, 113

materiality of, 62–3, 64–70, 71, 76–9,
    117, 142
  composition of, 70–6
  methodological implications,
    85–6
  as non-binary, 61
  as objects, 62, 63–4, 68, 69, 85
  paradox of rejection of the body, 15
  paradox of the nexus between nature
    and culture, 6, 9, 52, 55–60,
    125
  scientific approach to, xiii, 1–3, 17,
    34–8
  symbolic representation of, 19
  as technomorphic, 50–1
  See also binary oppositions in the study
    of archaeological bodies;
    osteoarchaeology; skeletal
    modifications
body: mind
  as inseparable, 85, 132
  split, 42–3, 52, 58, 66, 104
Boivin, N., 65, 67
bone, 70
  degenerative joint changes, 45, 72–3,
    121, 141
    acromion, 140
    metatarsal-phalangeal, 105
    spine, 83, 108, 110–12
    ulnarcarpal and radioulnar, 106
  properties of, 75
  remodelling, 71–2, 110
  sex in non-adults, 91
  use of, 64
boundaries, disciplinary
  interpretative, 3
  reconfiguring, 48–51
  specialisation and, 8–10
boundaries of bodies, 47, 48–51
  interpretative, 3
  reconfiguring, 48–51
Bridges, P. S., 105
Bronfen, E., 44–5
burials. See mortuary practices
Butler, J., 65, 66, 94–5, 98

Capasso, L., Kennedy, K. A. R. and
    Wilczak, C., *Atlas of Occupational
    Markers on Human Remains*, 73
carrying methods, *82*
  skeletal implications of, 80–3, *107*,
    106–10, *111*, *112*
Cartesian dualism, 42–3, 52, 58, 66,
    104
  challenges to, 85, 132